THE RUSSIAN CENTURY

THE RUSSIAN CENTURY

A PHOTOGRAPHIC HISTORY
OF RUSSIA'S 100 YEARS

TEXT BY BRIAN MOYNAHAN

FOREWORD BY YEVGENY YEVTUSHENKO

PHOTOGRAPHS RESEARCHED
BY ANNABEL MERULLO AND
SARAH JACKSON

BARNES
&NOBLE
BOOKS
NEW YORK

FOR THE JACKSONS OF HURTWOOD – B.M.

FOR FARIT GUBAYEV, VLADIMIR SIOMIN AND IGOR MOUKHIN – A. M. & S. J.

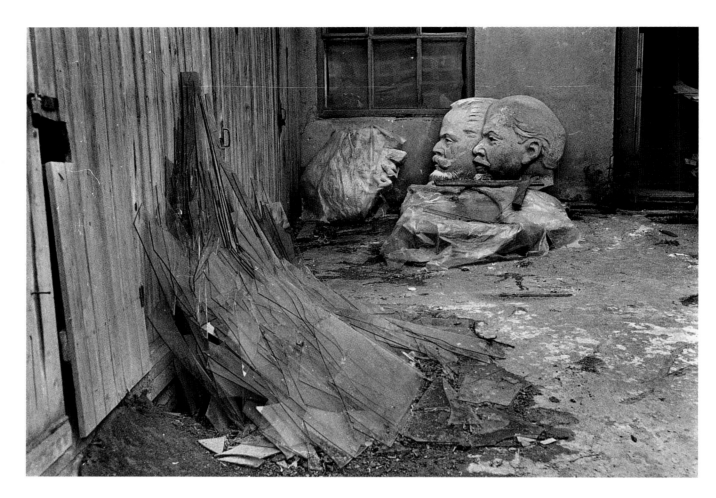

Half title page *A Dzhigit woman puts her horse through its paces in Kirghizstan, 1936.*
If she catches the man of her choice, and touches him with her whip, custom dictates that he
marry her. [PHOTO: M. ALPERT] Title page *The Hermitage in Leningrad, 1930. The foot belongs to one of the ten*
gigantic atlantes, male figures supporting a porch, at present threatened by subsidence. [PHOTO: B. IGNATOVICH]
Title verso page *After the fall: heads of Marx and Lenin torn down after the failure of the*
Communist coup in August 1991. [PHOTO: G. BODROV]

Copyright © 1994 Endeavour Group UK

This edition published by Barnes & Noble, Inc.
by arrangement with Endeavour Group UK

1999 Barnes & Noble Books

M 10 9 8 7 6 5 4 3 2 1

ISBN 0-7607-1869-5

THIS BOOK WAS CREATED, DESIGNED AND PRODUCED BY
THE ENDEAVOUR GROUP UK, 12a COLVILLE MEWS, LONDON W11 2DA.

PROJECT MANAGER: Annabel Merullo
EDITOR: Roger Hudson
ASSOCIATE EDITOR: Peter Smith
DESIGNER: Paul Welti
TYPESET BY Peter Howard
ORIGINATION BY IMAGO
PRINTED BY Nuovo Istituto Italiano d'Arti
Grafiche SpA, Bergamo, Italy

CONTENTS

PICTURE EDITORS' NOTE

The photographs reproduced in this book are the result of extensive original research in the archives, museums and private collections of the former Soviet Union. Additional material was provided by many contemporary photographers. The original idea for the book came from an historic album of Russian photographs at the Hulton Deutsch Collection in London and was expanded to its present scope by Harold Evans of Random House, Inc. We are most grateful to Harold for his support and guidance. We are also indebted to the knowledgeable archivists and skilled photographers in the former Soviet Union who entrusted us with such a rich treasure trove of images. Without them the book would simply not have been possible.

We have treated the photographs in the book as historical documents and it has been our policy not to alter the images in any way. Consequently no attempt has been made to retouch or remove any marks or blemishes on the prints – such as tears, negative numbers or marks caused by cracks on glass negatives. Many photographs were printed up from these original glass negatives and we are grateful to Agfa-Gevaert Ltd who generously supplied quality paper and chemicals for this purpose.

The photographers' names, when known, are credited in the captions. The sources of the photographs are listed in the acknowledgements on page 317.

FOREWORD
by Yevgeny Yevtushenko

THERE IS A STORY OF HOW THE GREAT RUSSIAN POET Alexander Blok came to his country estate during the Revolution that he himself had apocalyptically prophesied, and saw only ruins and ashes. Suddenly something flashed amidst the ruins. It was shattered pieces of a mirror that had fallen out of its burned walnut frame. He took the largest piece and walked about with it among the ashes the entire day, as though hoping that concealed in its depths was at least a tiny remainder of history. Red guards with a growth of stubble, as if they came straight from his poem 'The Twelve', ordered the great poet to stop and hold the mirror for them while they shaved. The apostles of the Revolution, machine-gun belts criss-crossed on their chests, were displeased that the soot-blackened mirror obscured their faces full of revolutionary intransigence. Cursing, they wiped the mirror with their tattooed arms and the hems of their striped jerseys. And the poet continued on in the role of 'saver of the mirror'.

What is this visual history of Russia in the twentieth century that you are now holding in your hands? It is a mirror smashed by wars and revolutions whose fragments suddenly have grown together again and contain in their depths all that was once reflected in them. In this mirror you will see piles of deer, slaughtered by the Tsarist aristocracy, not suspecting that they themselves would soon lie in similar piles, slaughtered by their serfs of yesterday. In this mirror you will see Russia: now with the weak-willed, lifeless face of Nicholas II; now with the cunning-crazy eyes of Rasputin; now with the wig of Lenin in disguise; now with the pipe of Stalin, through which passed as smoke more human lives than through the smoke-stacks of Auschwitz and the rest; now with the anxious eyes of Shostakovich that flash out distress signals; now with the swarthy cheek-bones of Pasternak, which gave him the look of an Arabian race horse; now with the wily peasant shrewdness of Khrushchev; now with the irresistibly charming smile of Gagarin; now with Brezhnev's chest heaving like meat-jelly hung with an ikon wall of medals; now with the desperate but well-calculated daring of Solzhenitsyn, learnt in the camps; now with the magnetic lamp-like eyes of Gorbachev, soon, however, to lose their magnetism; now with Yeltsin's chin, cut out of Ural stone, that for some reason appears, in boxer's terminology, to be made of glass; now with the eyes of sweaty Zhirinovsky, like those of a black grouse rolling in response to political mating calls, not so much terrifying as repulsive, although he or someone of his kind might be terrifying. And whether you like it or not, all of these faces are the face of Russia

– a land of giant writers, scientists of genius, magnificent grandmothers, of the first cosmonauts, but also of cannibalism during famines, and now even a Mafia of racketeers and pimps.

If there is something shocking in this book, remember the good Russian proverb: 'The mirror is not to blame if your mug is crooked'. But History is that rare woman who doesn't like to look at herself in the mirror. History, when she finds herself in front of one, wipes and wipes its surface as though in this way she might change her face to something better. After the collapse of Communist ideology, a frightening vacuum was created in the spiritual life of Russia. Communism had removed all value from the textbooks of Russian history and new ones, apparently, will not soon be written. This book at the present moment is the best visual textbook of Russian history not only for students, but even for professional politicians and business people.

Among the many hundreds of faces in this book is the face of Alexis, the young heir to the throne with his good-natured, mustached sailor-'uncle' companion. Beside him is the bicycle specially built to protect him from falling – this boy who suffered from hemophilia, the failure of blood to coagulate. But we readers know what the boy in the photograph did not know. We know, when there was no longer a Rasputin to stop the continuous hemorrhaging with his Siberian sorcery, that the boy was to be savagely murdered together with his father, mother, and sisters. We know that this sailor-'uncle' only seems kindly, and that he will soon betray his ward and join with those who torment the Tsar's family. But did his betrayal save himself? Many of those who shot the Tsar's family were themselves shot. The gushing blood did not coagulate – it kept on flowing and was transformed into civil war, and then into the horrors of the Terror, bearing out what the French had already learnt: 'revolution is the mother who devours her own children'.

The inability to stop the flow of blood turned out to be a sickness not only of the last Tsarevich, but of all Russia in the twentieth century. When did this Russian sickness begin? During the two hundred years of the Tartar-Mongol yoke, when the Russian princes, instead of uniting, endlessly fought one another – this national tradition, this habit of Russians shedding Russian blood, began then. The poet Maksimilian Voloshin (1877-1932) wrote in 1925: 'Peter the Great was the first Bolshevik ... more a sculptor than a butcher, but carving in flesh and not in stone.' And the blood did not coagulate, but flowed on and on. The last photograph of Lenin in this book is staggering. His eyes are filled with horror, perhaps from the realisation that all the ideals of the Revolution will be washed in blood. Russia was the last country in Europe to abolish serfdom but, a few decades later, a Communist feudalism was formed under the pseudonym of 'socialism'. The old Russian empire was concealed similarly under the pseudonym 'USSR'. In place of the slain Tsarevich Alexis, socialism became the heir to the throne, but inherited hemophilia along with it: the blood of civil war, the blood of collectivisation, and industrialisation, and now even the blood of democratisation, in ethnic wars between Azerbaijanis and Armenians, Georgians and Abkhazians, Russians and Moldavians. There is danger of conflict between Ukraine and Russia, even danger of civil war between Russians. We have already stood on the edge of that abyss, first during the unsuccessful putsch in August 1991, and then during the opposition's desperate attempt to seize the television center by force, and the shelling of the Parliament by government tanks in October 1993.

Why do we have such an inept, ill-bred, undemocratic democracy? And could it be otherwise without traditions of tolerance? Culturally, Russia was always a great nation, except in its political life and intolerance is the primary index of this condition. Once before intolerance prevented revolution from mutating into evolution, and right now it is doing the same thing. This intolerance does not stem from loyalty to one party or another, but is rather a habit of mind. It is the only thing in Russia that unites both the ultra-communists and the ultra-anticommunists. Once we had forced collectivisation, now forced capitalisation. As long as there is intolerance we will not cure ourselves of national hemophilia. Along with a Statue of Liberty we need to erect a Statue of Responsibility.

The time has come to acknowledge the imperfection of freedom. By transforming freedom into an idol and praying to it like heathens, we subject ourselves to dangerous self-deception. Incautious attempts to accelerate history lead to people receiving freedom who turn out not to have been prepared for it, and freedom for people who are not ready for freedom is dangerous, both for them and for all humanity. Alexander Herzen wrote: 'You cannot liberate people more than they are liberated within.' Nonetheless, with all the chaos of irresponsible freedom, what has been achieved is magnificent.

The threat of a third world war as the result of nuclear conflict between the USA and the USSR has disappeared. The Berlin Wall has been smashed into souvenirs. No matter how Gorbachev is maligned, without him it might not have happened for a long time. Ideological censorship has been removed, though commercial censorship quickly made its appearance. Political barriers to travel abroad have been removed, though economic barriers quickly arose. Private enterprise is permitted, although it is passing through a period of untamed capitalism. Private ownership of land has been introduced, though it is still not understood how it will be sold and who will be able to buy it. A multi-party system is not a panacea for all woes, but it is nevertheless better than dictatorship of the Party. And this would not have happened for a long time if Yeltsin had not climbed up on a tank on an August morning in 1991.

The irreconcilable opponents, Gorbachev and Yeltsin, have much in common. They both came up out of poverty to achieve power; both are former Party feudal lords. In consequence, our democracy is feudal. To give time for new kinds of political leaders to be born in Russia, ones not chained to feudalism by habit from birth, we will have to wander long in the wilderness, and resist the temptation of hoping for some sort of home-grown Moses, to lead us to the Promised Land. We received freedom as a desert and we must learn how to plant trees in it. Our freedom has still not learned how to conduct itself with dignity and for the time being it behaves not only foolishly but like someone half-starved. Yet there is no desire to exchange it for the former golden cage with prison rations.

The amount of nostalgia for the former Soviet Union is exaggerated, and it doesn't necessarily mean chauvinism, boastfully promising 'to wash the dusty boots of our soldiers in the Indian Ocean'. After passing through the first months of euphoria many former Soviet republics are beginning to understand that their proud independence may turn into impoverished isolation. If the transformation of the Baltic republics into foreign countries was natural, for the majority in other republics of the former USSR the introduction of customs controls, visa systems, the multiplicity of new currencies, seems uncivilised and humiliating. Separatists, in their stupid nationalistic bombast, forget that their countries are deficient in electricity, natural gas, and lumber, and that now they must pay for them in dollars. Complete independence for the former republics is impractical for their relationships are inseparable, historically and geographically intertwined. Two possibilities can be seen: an ever-deepening Balkanisation with ethnic conflict and even war, or a de-Balkanisation, a gradual and nonviolent resurrection of union under a new name on democratic foundations without the imperial dictates from the center.

This is the strategy of the patchwork quilt – the convalescence of a once-great country, scrap by scrap, and the gradual growing together of one patch with another. In none of the many new nationalisms, including Russian nationalism, is there a happy future. Russia will once again be great if it does not hysterically try to inspire itself with ideas of its own greatness. Greatness is not inspired, but achieved, and then not by alien hands, but by one's own. Russia can play an enormous and unifying role in the destiny of many peoples, if it will reject forced annexation, which always ends infamously, and if it can attract others to it by the magnetic example of spiritual and material prosperity.

I do not want some poet of the future, like Alexander Blok, to wander through the ruins of his own cremated motherland with a piece of a mirror, in which are reflected only corpses and ashes. I would like us to look into the mirror of History and to see there only our faces and the faces of our children before whom we would not be ashamed.

Translated by Albert C. Todd

Patchwork Quilt

Scrap
*   by scrap*
Granny put the quilt together for us,
and to this day I remember the kindness
with which the quilt was endowed.
Patches glowed red,
*   like warm cozy corners,*
and shone golden,
*   like the eyes of bears,*
exhaled blue,
*   as do cornflowers in a field,*
and darkened black,
*   like the tatters of the night.*
I came to Siberia not as the meteorite,
and was myself, in Zima's chimney corners,
sheltered from blizzards by a rainbow of patchwork,
and was myself, like a small patchwork,
*   all in tiny flowers.*
Scrap
*   by scrap*
we somehow gathered Russia together,
sewing into her might scraps of melancholy
and into her strength
*   scraps of impotence.*
False ideals ripped us asunder,
and without mercy,
senselessly mocking our homeland
*   like a quilt,*
we tear our ideals into shreds.
And above the again ravished land
as if once more before there were tsars, once more at a crossroads
nothing but ashes of unending holocaust –
miserable scraps of banners and destinies.
Salvation will not come down from Moscow –
It will rise up along the Vologdas, the Irkutsks.
Salvation will be slow
*   made of scraps,*
but the scraps will grow onto each other.

Farewell, Empire!
*   Greetings, Russia!*
Rule Russia –
*   but only over yourself.*
Amidst our quarrels, shelter the children
by a future, like Granny's quilt, made of patchwork.
To the gentle singing of the stove pipe
I so want
*   to press myself into Granny's patchwork,*
so that she can sew Russia together anew
scrap
*   by scrap …*

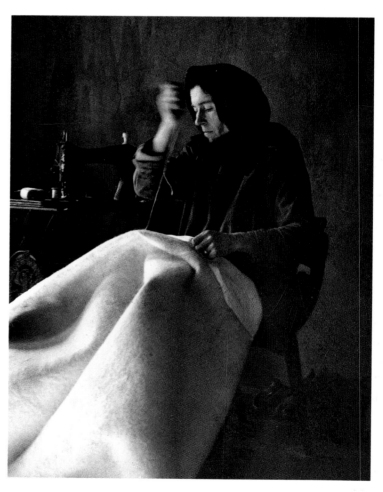

by Yevgeny Yevtushenko
Translated by Albert C. Todd

INTRODUCTION

HISTORY HAS FLUNG ITSELF AT RUSSIA THIS CENTURY, riding it bareback and at the gallop. The country has changed capitals and names; it has swelled west of Warsaw and retreated east of Minsk; it has been seen as a vision of the future, but now seems a place that is collapsing into the ruins of its past. Its people have been killed by the million, in execution cellars, in Arctic work camps, on the world's greatest battlefields. It has produced cosmonauts; and the cannibals who flourished in starvation years. It put paid to old concepts – religious faith, private property, the rule of law – that are only now fitfully reappearing.

Russia was transformed by the 1917 revolution into the 20th century's first modernist state; totalitarian, brutish, its people coerced by purges, secret policemen and concentration camps, its ideology passed off as scientific, but really theocratic in its party – and leader – worship. It became a template for eastern Europe, China, Cuba, Vietnam. It predated and outlived Nazi Germany, whose upbringing it profoundly influenced; scratch a Brownshirt, and you will find a Red.

The change was made with breakneck speed. Moneyed life in Russia – the formal balls, sleigh rides, picnics and feasts whose pre-war pleasures are pictured here – was snuffed out within a few months of the Bolsheviks controlling a region. The *burzhui*, the Russian bourgeoisie, suffered a class catastrophe. In its place fresh castes were spawned. The *nomenklatura*, the 'new class' of Communism, enjoyed Party privilege: special limousine lanes on city streets, Party stores and canteens with spreads of salmon, cream cakes and imported brandy, Party *dachas* (country houses) and health resorts amid the geraniums of the Black Sea coast. Later another invention, the *zampolits* – political officers – ensured that the crews of nuclear submarines off Miami, with their mission to keep the world safe for the creed, remained loyal to the Party with their thrice-daily lectures.

What happened before 1917 was brutalism, the Party insisted; what came after, just. It was a lie, of course. 'My Tsarist interrogators didn't even dare address me rudely!' a dissident cried as he was returned half-dead to his cell after a torture session by interrogators working to Party orders. The largest number of prisoners recorded under the Tsars was 189,949 in 1912; by 1938, the number was at least thirty, and probably forty times higher.

A Soviet is a committee; in place of Russia, a name stretching back eleven centuries to ancient Rus, the country became the Committee Union. Until 1988, all maps for public use were distorted at the orders of the KGB. 'Almost everything' was changed, the head of the Cartography Administration admitted, 'roads and rivers moved, streets tilted.' Even the weather was a secret too important to divulge to any but Party eyes; no weather reports were published in newspapers until the late 1970s. It is a struggle now to return to normality: easy enough to restore old names, Russia, St Petersburg; more difficult to revive a forgotten soul. How to bring back the banker, trader and shopkeeper, when for so long these had respectively been hyena, speculator and profiteer? 'They stole our past,' a former Moscow dentist told me on a bleak November night in 1991. 'It was dangerous to ask who we once were.' Avidly reading once banned books, he made his discovery. 'You know, we were a fiery people who had pleasures,' he said. 'We loved gipsy music and gambling.' Thus enlightened, he took himself to Atlantic City. He brought back blackjack tables and roulette wheels, and opened the first ruble casino to operate in Moscow since the revolution. 'I do this for Christ,' he said. 'So that Russia can again be what God made it.'

By 1918, the Romanovs were dead in a cellar and Lenin was, as the painter Marc Chagall put it, 'turning Russia upside down, the way I hang my paintings'. After Lenin, Stalin, the 'Kremlin mountaineer with a cockroach whistler's leer', as Osip Mandelstam described him in brilliant verse that cost him his life; liquidator of millions, a man of black humor who almost certainly had the too-popular Party boss Sergei Kirov murdered, and then commemorated his name by giving it to a leading ballet, a cruiser class, countless lakes and five towns. Stalin was transformed in Western eyes in 1941 from mass murderer to Uncle Joe, the pipe-puffing patriot whose troops snapped the spine of the invading German army in the greatest land battles in history.

Repression continued after 1945. Only one in eight Russian soldiers survived German captivity; those who did, because they had been exposed to foreign ideas, passed 'like shoals of herring' from Nazi to Red camps. There was no respite for the people. Work norms were set higher after the war. Rations were often less than before; US aid ended, and Soviets no longer ate Spam and rode Studebakers. Stalin now shaped the Cold War, whose outlines can still be made out by passing satellites: the aerospace plants in California and the Urals, the tank complexes in Detroit and Omsk, the missile silos in Wyoming and western Siberia, the rocket ranges from Vandenberg to Kwajalein and from Tyuratam to Kamchatka. It was continued by Nikita Khrushchev, Hollywood sensation, spy catcher and sputnik builder, political tightrope artist who was near to calamitous fall

in Cuba, the 'maize freak' who plowed the virgin lands. Then, as if history had unnerved itself and was shouting 'enough', came the long sleep under Leonid Brezhnev, Yuri Andropov and Konstantin Chernenko, the living-dead. The sweet awakening by Mikhail Gorbachev soon gave way to new storms, and under Boris Yeltsin Russia is being hung upside down once more.

In the end, the Russians could not compete with the *glavny vrag*, the main enemy, America. The collapse has been swift and pitiless. The East European satellites have spun out of orbit, the peripheries have come unglued. In the ruined European cities of 1945, the man with a supply of penicillin was king. In modern Moscow, it is the man with hard currency. A taxi driver makes more on an airport trip than a university professor makes in three months; a *valutnya*, a currency girl, more in a half-hour trick than a navy captain in a year. In a society where State terror flourished, people were necessarily law-abiding. Moscow streets were among the safest on earth. Now the born-again stockbrokers and speculators must be driven by hard-eyed bodyguards along hostile avenues in armored limousines, because the State has become too weak to protect them. The poor are preyed on at will.

The remarkable images in this book are culled from Russian sources. Many were previously in sealed archives and are published here for the first time; tracing them has been a painstaking and delicate business. Together, they bear vivid witness to the century's madcap progress.

1
THE LAND OF THE ROMANOVS

Church and countryside *were at the heart of Old Russia. They come together in this picture of a nun fetching water at Ponetayevsky Convent, in 1904, when four fifths of the people still lived in villages. This scene remains sentimental bedrock, a glimpse of intimacy amid the vast indifference of the Russian plain.*
[PHOTO: M. DMITRIEV]

THE RUSSIAN EMPIRE AT THE TURN OF THE CENTURY WAS A colossus. The United States could be dropped into it and leave room to spare for China and India. Body and soul, it was the possession and creation of a dynasty. The first Romanov Tsar, Michael, had been crowned three centuries before in the Moscow Kremlin when Russia was a narrow and barren compression between Europe and Asia, Swedes held the Baltic coast and the Poles had recently sacked Moscow. Although Russian fur traders had penetrated east of the Urals into Siberia, the Tartar heirs of the Mongols clung to the lands east of the Crimea and the Caspian.

Nicholas Romanov now ruled south to the shores of the Black and Caspian seas. The southern confines of his empire ran along the Turkish, Persian, Afghan, Mongolian and Chinese borders until they reached the foggy waters of the Sea of Japan. Poland, the Baltic States and Finland were Romanov possessions. Treaties forced on weakened China had transferred the north shore of the Amur and the Maritime Province east of the Ussuri river to the Tsar. More than a hundred nationalities owed allegiance to him. Of the 125 million souls recorded in the census of 1897, only fifty-five million were Great Russians. Nicholas II himself was less than one hundredth part Russian by blood; generations of Romanovs had made dynastic marriages with princesses from the West. The Empress Alexandra was part English, part German; her blood, from her grandmother Queen Victoria, carried the defective gene that made her son Alexis a hemophiliac. Nicholas was a shy man, wistful and melancholic. His German cousin, the Kaiser, thought him best suited to 'be a country gentleman growing turnips', but his powers over his subjects were naked and unambivalent. He was 'Emperor and Autocrat of all the Russias'. His other titles ran for thirteen packed lines – 'Sovereign of the Circassian Princes … Prince of Estonia, Grand Duke of Finland and Lithuania … Lord of Turkestan and the Armenian Regions … Lord and Master of All Northern Countries' – before exhausting themselves in a final 'etc …'

The empire was exotic. Much was new; victories against the Turks in the Caucasus, and the great spring campaigns against the descendants of the Golden Horde, the troops marching barefoot through the grasslands to the beat of kettledrums, were well within living memory. The Turcomans were not finally defeated until the 1880s, when the Emir of Bokhara became a dependant of the Tsar. The drive into central Asia was completed in the Pamir mountains only five years before the new century. From Irkutsk, the main Siberian center, gold miners, engineers and fur traders were still pushing into the wilderness. The town reminded the American traveler Basset Digby of San Francisco fifty years before, in the Forty Nine gold rush; it was, he wrote, a 'gilded Gomorrah' where peroxide blondes in tight blue knickerbockers danced double shuffles 'with an incompetence that would leave a Bowery amateur night audience dumb with scorn'. It was difficult to sleep, he complained, because of the local habit of firing revolvers out of the windows in the early hours to frighten off robbers.

Travel was easy only on the railroads, with their slow and lulling broadgauge motion, and by steamboat when the rivers were ice-free. The Volga, greatest of European rivers, was an important artery as it ran its 2300 miles to the Caspian. It had numerous passenger services and the rich took steamer trips for pleasure and for their health. Frozen rivers in winter became highways for sleds. The trains were comfortable – the trans-Siberians were equipped with libraries and pianos – but the network covered only 25,000 miles, the same as Britain, a place fifty times smaller. The trans-Siberian track still had a gap at Lake Baikal, crossed by steamer in summer and by ice in winter. The contractors had skimped on the track, a factor that would play its part in the coming revolution. The rails were half the weight of the American norm, the track bedding was weak and line laid on frozen ground distorted in summer. Derailments were common and 'expresses' steamed so slowly that, an American passenger noted, 'our most comatose cowboy could keep up with this iron horse'.

Few all-weather roads existed, and even now there is no transnational highway. In summer, unsprung carts threw up dust from dirt tracks that hung behind them like the wake of a ship above a grass ocean, the drivers hunched half-asleep, chewing sunflower seeds one by one, the passengers lying on straw behind. In winter, travelers slept in their sleds on long journeys with bearskins wrapped round their bodies, and live dogs curled at their feet for warmth and companionship. Spring and autumn rains brought the mud that Russians call 'roadlessness'. Country roads and village streets became tracts of glistening liquid with the consistency of dough, that could pull boots off with ease and

The bargepullers:
such burlaki were a common sight. These haul a vessel loaded with timber on a tributary of the Volga: human carthorses stumbling along, inching the big barge on its way against the current. At night, they slept on sacks aboard the barge. Russian roads were – still are – few and poor.

Women's work.
Women haul a barge on the Sura river under the eye of a labor contractor. Women have always done hard physical work in Russia: plowing, snow clearing, stone-breaking, toiling on construction sites and in railroad marshaling yards.

Outside the Pale. *A family from the ancient Jewish community in Bokhara in central Asia (above). The Russian empire had the largest Jewish population in the world at the turn of the century. Seven million strong, it included Yiddish-speaking Ashkenazis, Iranian-speaking Daghestanis and the Yehudis of Tashkent and Samarkand who settled before the birth of Christ.*

A million and a quarter had emigrated by 1914, largely to the United States, where the colony in New York was big enough to support two daily newspapers in Russian. They were speeded on their way by vicious pogroms. Violence against Jews was a casual, everyday occurrence in Tsarist Russia. The 'Black Hundreds', roaming gangs who murdered Jews and looted their shops and houses, were often tolerated and sometimes encouraged by local officials; an anti-Semitic riot was preferable to an anti-government one.

Gurians from the Caucasus *(left), the southern mountains and valleys dividing Europe from Asia, inspiration for writers from Pushkin to Tolstoy. Largely conquered from the Turks in a process completed in 1864, the Caucasus was peopled by Georgians, Christians whose orchards, vineyards and crags were annexed by the Russians in 1801; by Circassians, whose beauty made them eagerly sought by the Ottomans as slaves; by Muslim tribesmen, Jews and Cossacks.*

Feuding was a traditional sport in the mountains. Many Caucasian houses had high watchtowers. Another visible sign of centuries of local conflict were the weapons carried by tribesmen, and eagerness to join one of the many Caucasian regiments in the Russian army.

Under one flag. *More than one hundred nationalities lived in the Romanov empire; blond Latvians in the West, Tartar descendants of the Mongol Golden Horde, fur-clad northern Nenets, southern Kirghiz in Muslim robes. Pictured (above) is a group of nomadic reindeer herders of the Tungus Evenks in the area of the Ob river in western Siberia. Only 25,000 people spoke their Manchurian-related tongue; they were spread over the vast area from the Ob to the shores of the sea of Okhotsk and Sakhalin.*

[PHOTO: A. ADRIANOV]

that were to mire the narrow tracks of German panzers in 1941.

Only St Petersburg and Moscow had populations above the million mark. Moscow was the historic capital; Ivan the Terrible, Grand Prince of Muscovy, had proclaimed himself Tsar of all Russia there in 1547. The Kremlin, its red walls jutting above the Moscow river, had been the medieval fortress of Russian power and contained its essentials: palaces, chapels, feasting halls, arsenals and barracks protected by forts and watchtowers.

Government had been transferred to St Petersburg in the eighteenth century, but Moscow retained its grip on the Russian soul. Where the northern capital was elegant and distracted, Moscow was vigorous and crude, a 'mix of piety and dissipation, of religion and self-indulgence'. It was the spiritual center of the Orthodox church, the 'city of forty times forty churches', their gilded onion domes flashing like autumn treetops above its green roofs. The Romanov Tsars ruled and were buried in St Petersburg; they were crowned in the Kremlin.

Moscow was prospering with commerce and textiles. A building boom was in progress, with ornate and turreted mansions thrown up for merchant families. In St Petersburg the rich ate, and often spoke, French. Moscow was Russian; its cuisine, and the Eliseiev foodstore that supplied its ingredients, were becoming known in the West. Spreads of zakouski hors-d'oeuvres included fresh and pressed caviar, herring fillets, salted cucumbers, smoked sturgeon, cold salmon and milk piglet. Winter soup, borsch, was hot red cabbage and meat served with cream. In summer, *okrochka* was ladled with herbs and pieces of fish and ice. Muscovites had a taste for cold; champagne was served almost frozen. Russians were great drinkers of champagne, from the Crimea or from France; the first vintage champagnes, Brut Imperial, were made for the Romanovs. The city's industrialists and merchants, some of them born serfs, were ruthless and hard-drinking. Mikhail Korolyov, the city mayor, would put his top hat on the table of an inn and keep drinking with his friends until the corks had reached the brim. Vodka, flavored with peppers, lemon, aromatic plants and herbs, was drunk by the yard of closely-packed shot glasses. It was a state monopoly, its largest single source of income. It could not be drunk within fifty yards of the monopoly shop, or within a hundred yards of a church. The drinker removed the cork with a sharp blow on the bottom of the bottle, slugged it back between bites of black bread, and returned the empty. The few kopeks deposit it fetched helped him buy another smaller bottle, called a 'cockerel'. If vodka was drunk without a mouthful of bread in a bitter frost, the drinker could collapse and freeze to death.

Restaurants were thriving and cocktail bars were appearing in smart hotels. *Traktirs*, dark rooms with long counters and rough seats, served the ubiquitous salted cucumber, black bread and tea and vodka to poorer Muscovites in a steamy fug. Tea was as important as vodka; the Russian for a tip was *natchai*, 'for the tea'. The rich drank it with lemon; the poor put a sugar lump in their mouth and sucked the tea noisily through it. Coarse Russian tobacco had a sugary, oriental taste and a langorous, musty odor.

Sleds waiting to be hired *in Red Square, Moscow in 1900. Behind its walls in the background, the Kremlin was a sacred place of chapels, banqueting halls, palaces and arsenals.*

The backstreets were packed with wooden shacks, with high watchtowers in each section to look out for fires. The poorest lived in lodging houses, named for their owners, sleeping on two-tiered bunks made of wooden slats. They paid six kopeks for a top bunk, and five for the bottom where there was less air. Nicky's lodgings were for ex-convicts released from hard labor. Iarochenko's was inhabited by failed writers and alcoholic poets who copied theater parts, sending one of their number out in borrowed best boots and cloak to sell the copies at fifty kopeks the act to theater managers. Bounin's housed professional beggars and tailors. At midnight, thieves arrived with stolen capes, coats and dresses. The tailors – 'crabs' who rarely ventured out of doors – worked half-naked by petrol lamp.

St Petersburg was linked to Moscow by a 400-mile railroad, a line engineered by Lieutenant George Washington Whistler, a famous American army railroad man and father of the painter James McNeill Whistler, but built by forced serf labor encouraged by shootings and mass floggings from a special corps of railroad police. St Petersburg itself had been built in similar fashion two centuries before, when Peter the Great had decided, eccentrically, to build a new capital among the marshes of the Neva river on the northwest periphery of his empire. The architects of its palaces of pastel stucco were Italian, French, Scots. The work gangs who had built it, replenished when their number dropped below forty thousand by fresh recruits driven in fetters from provinces a month's march away, were Russian. The city was on the sixtieth parallel, at a level with southern Alaska, subject to ice storms; light for twenty-two hours in the summer 'white night', dark for nineteen in winter. Its serf constructors had died in thousands as they raised its embankments of pink Finnish granite above the waters. The city still flooded, cannon booming to warn basement dwellers when onshore winds raised the gulf of Finland and threatened to drown them.

The fortress island of Peter and Paul dominated the northern aspect, its squat outline lightened by the slender spire of its cathedral. All but one of the Romanov Tsars were buried there, in intimate proximity to the fortress dungeons which had held distinguished prisoners from Peter the Great's own son Alexis to the novelist Feodor Dostoevsky. A gun was fired each noon from the fortress, a reminder to the city that the dynasty shaped its thought as well as its form. The symbols of the city's autocratic power stretched for three miles along the southern side of the Neva. From the dome of St Isaac's Cathedral, a mass of barracks, palaces and ministries met the eye. To the east were foreign embassies, courthouses and the barracks of the crack Pavlovsky and Preobrazhensky regiments. Closer, the dull red façades of the Winter Palace and the Hermitage fronted the river for 500 yards. The Tsar's study looked out over the palace square to the General Staff building, which also housed the finance and foreign ministries in a huge crescent. To the west of the square was the Admiralty, 450 yards long, with a gilded spire. The war office, police prefecture and riding schools were close by. Three in ten adult males in the city wore uniforms.

The city was defined by water, like Venice or Amsterdam. The

A crippled beggar *outside the Sorovsky Monastery (above). Russians were generous to the unfortunate. The foundlings' hospital in Moscow was one of the largest charitable foundations in the world, with 20,000 babies entering each year for a stay of a month before being sent on to foster homes in villages. The new industrial millionaires, and the imperial family, gave generously to charities for the sick and the impoverished.* [Photo: K.E.Hahn]

Passengers wait at a tram stop *(left) in Moscow. The shelter and the newspaper kiosk look Parisian. French influence was strong among the rich, who spoke French among themselves and vacationed in Biarritz and on the Côte d'Azur; it filtered down into the fashions of the new middle classes, though there are more peaked caps in this image than one would have seen in Paris.* [Photo: M. Pariisky]

The Ball of the Colored Wigs *(above) celebrated at Countess Yelisaveta Shuvalova's palace on the Fontanka canal in St Petersburg early in 1914. The wigs were only required of the ladies. The revelers include the leading Society figures, Orlovs, Tolstoys, Gorchakovs and Dolgorukovs. Many of the officers would be dead within nine months, cut down by German machineguns in the sandy forests and marshes of Tannenberg.*

A soup kitchen *(above) for the unemployed on Vasilevsky Island in pre-war St Petersburg. The flood of peasants who came to the city seeking factory work made it socially unstable; there was a predominance of single men, and a majority of those in the city had been born elsewhere. They brought their peasant clothes and habits with them, living off bowls of kasha, a buckwheat gruel, and chewing sunflower seeds whose husks lay on the sidewalks outside the cheap lodging houses like carpets of flies.*

left bank was cut into three semi-circles by canals, where the pastel colors of private palaces were reflected in the sheen of ice and water. The season began with a Christmas bazaar, followed by balls and dances until Lent. At the *bals blancs* for unmarried girls, chaperones in black watched their white-clad charges dance endless quadrilles with young army officers in elkskin breeches. Gipsy music, tangos and waltzes beat out at the vigorous *bals roses* for the young marrieds. Costume balls were fashionable, held in colored wigs, in peasant clothes, or, in the great galleries of the Winter Palace in 1903, in old Russian costume to celebrate the bicentenary of the founding of the city. The Imperial ballet played to packed houses in the Maryinsky Theater; Russians were passionate for dance. Every ballerina had her rich protector. Mathilde Kshesinskaya had been a mistress of the Tsar. When she was to dance in Moscow, the front rows in the Maryinsky were deserted as her admirers took the Moscow train.

Vasilevsky Island, with the soft red façade and birch trees of the university and law faculty, was the intellectual heart of the empire. Its students were held to be a special breed, a university proletariat, shabby and with 'fanatical and prematurely aged looks', made nervous by hunger and the impact of radical ideas. Many of them, wrote the law student Alexander Kerensky, were seduced into revolutionary politics by 'the smoky room, the table loaded with samovar and sandwiches, the group of a dozen men and girls'. The colonnaded stock exchange at the tip of the island, overlooking the Winter Palace, handled four in five of the share transactions carried on throughout the empire. Banks controlling the steel and coal industries of the Donetz basin, the Baku oilfields and the copper and gold mines of Siberia had their

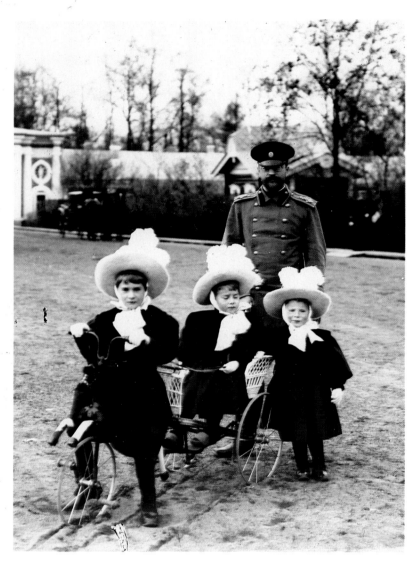

Count Mahlerburg-Streltsky *(above) and his daughters in St Petersburg promenade with a specially-built tricycle carriage.*

Prince Vladimir Orlov *(right), a member of one of the richest families in Russia, tests a 'motor sleigh'. The Mercedes Benz was modified for use in winter snow and for autumn, when rains reduced the roads to liquid mud. 'Fat Orlov', who became so obese that he could not see his knees when he sat down, was later dismissed as director of the military chancellery. His offense was to be one of the few at court to stand up against the Rasputin clique. Lenin and Trotsky were to turn up their noses at Mercedes Benz. Both revolutionaries used Rolls Royces.*

headquarters on the long avenues of the Nevsky and Morskaya.

As Peter the Great had fashioned the city from the swamp, so he structured its society in the *Tchin*, the table of ranks. The empire was obsessed with rank. There were fourteen Tchiny, grading civilians from humble college registrars to the Imperial Chancellor, and the military from Cornet to Field Marshal. The first three grades were addressed as 'Your High Excellency'; from there the title descended through 'Your Excellency' and 'Your High Origin' to 'Your Nobility'. To be a man of substance was to be a Tchinovik, a man with a rank.

Nobility was divided into five ranks: princes, counts, barons, those non-titled gentlemen whose nobility dated from before Peter the Great, and those after. The most senior title, Grand Duke, was reserved for members of the imperial family. There were at least two thousand princes in Russia. It was the only native Russian title; the others were borrowed from the West. Any direct descendant of anyone who had at any stage held sway over any patch of territory in the empire was entitled to call himself prince. After the Caucasus was annexed, Georgian clan leaders were recognised as princes; the same courtesy was applied to the khans of the conquered nomadic tribes and the Armenian and Tartar chieftains. Leo Tolstoy's family butler was the obscure descendant of a long-gone Lithuanian dynasty – and hence a

A relaxing swim (above) after a Turkish bath at Yegorov's Baths in St Petersburg. A century before, an English traveler found the Russians so unwashed that 'I never pass downwind of one if I can help it.' By the 1900s, many peasants took a weekly steam bath in their villages. All the bathers in this picture wear crosses round the neck, as expected of good orthodox believers.

Vladimir Nabokov *(left), later to write the best-selling novel* Lolita *in the United States, admiring butterflies as a boy in 1908. His famous passion for them started during his Russian childhood.*

The four young Romanov princesses *(above)* *were the most eligible girls in Europe before their murder. Photographed in September 1906 in the summer palace at Peterhof, they are, from left: the Grand Duchesses Olga, Tatiana, Marie and Anastasia. Nicholas' devotion to his family was admired by many revolutionaries; not, however, by the Bolsheviks who killed every Romanov they laid hands on.* [PHOTO: K.E.HAHN]

The Empress Alexandra *(right) gives a rare smile whilst cruising with Nicholas aboard the royal yacht* Standart *in July 1910. The revolutionary leader Alexander Kerensky thought Nicholas to be no more than 'a pleasant, somewhat awkward Colonel of the Guards, very ordinary except for a pair of wonderful blue eyes'. But he found Alexandra 'a born empress, proud and unbending, fully conscious of her right to rule'. A granddaughter of Queen Victoria, she spoke Russian with an English accent and her unflagging aim was to preserve the autocracy for 'Baby', the Tsarevich. The imperial couple were close; strong sexuality combined with Alexandra's religious fervor.*

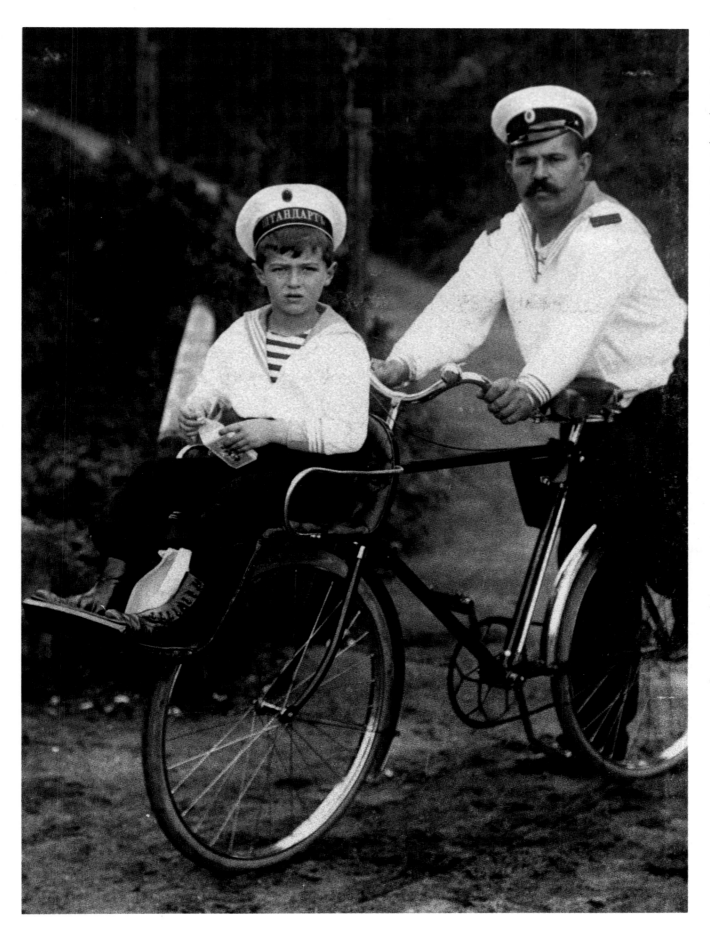

The Tsarevich Alexis *carried on a specially modified bicycle designed to prevent him becoming fatigued by Derevenko, his sailor-factotum. Alexis suffered from hemophilia, and internal bleeding could cause him intense pain. The supposedly loyal Derevenko turned on his young charge after the revolution, mocking Alexis and refusing to carry out any task he thought beneath his new dignity.*

Inspecting the kill: *Nicholas and his cousin Grand Duke Dmitri at Belevezh Pusha, an imperial hunting lodge, in 1912. Dmitri, later to take part in the murder of Rasputin, was one of the few of his fellow Romanovs whom the Tsar liked. Shooting deer, elk, bear and wolves was a favorite entertainment for the rich. Scores of beaters drove the game toward the guns who, dressed in white, were almost invisible against the winter snows.*

prince. Counts were as plentiful as princes. There was no particular to a Russian title, because the *sky*, *ov* and *iev* that ended most Russian names was itself the equivalent of the French *de* or the German *von*. Barons were rarer, often bankers and industrialists and of non-Russian origin: Jewish, Scots, German. In all, some two million souls could call themselves noble. Lenin was a hereditary noble; his grandfather had been a serf, but his father had acquired nobility on his appointment as a senior schools inspector. Many were impoverished by the beginning of the century. The rich – Orlovs, Davidovs, Stroganovs, Yusupovs, Galitzines – were fabulously so, but French-speaking, remote, wintering on the French Riviera and in Italy. They did not provide social stability; they took little part in politics.

The Church provided cohesion. Religion bit deep into the Russian soul. No act of any importance took place without the intercession of an ikon; when a Russian accused another of shamelessness, he would say: 'You have no cross with you'. Each house in the land, however humble, had its 'red corner'; 'red', in its pre-revolution sense in Russian, translated as 'beautiful' and in this space were kept guttering candles and the ikon in its frame, stamped metal for the poor, worked silver for the richer. This ikon was carried to the maternity bed, the betrothal and marriage, to the sickbed where it blessed the water given to the patient. It followed the dead to the cemetery. Almost every dying Russian soldier, their enemies noted, 'clutched at the image of the patron saint he wore about his neck, and pressed it to his lips before

Girls dressed for dancing *at the Smolny Institute in St Petersburg, a boarding school for the daughters of the nobility. They curtsied daily to the portrait of the dowager Empress. The building was to become the Bolshevik headquarters during Red October, and later a shrine to the Party. In 1934 the powerful Bolshevik Sergei Kirov was murdered in a corridor a few yards from where this picture was taken; Stalin used his death as an excuse to unleash his bloody purges on the country.*

drawing his last breath'. The US military attaché found religious ceremonial to be 'almost incredible. The best part of the day is given up to one or other of them four days a week.'

Fasts were kept by all classes, and particularly peasants. They were rigorous, involving total abstinence from all animal produce, including milk and eggs. They were many; five weeks of St Peter's Fast in May and June, a fortnight of the Assumption in August, six weeks until Christmas Eve, and the Great Fast, the seven weeks of Lent. The pious also abstained for two days in normal weeks, on Wednesday, the day of Judas's treachery, and on Friday, the day of the Savior's death.

At the turn of the 19th century, some twenty million Old Believers still clung to the old ritual abandoned by the established Church in the 17th century. Many merchants were Old Believers, in heavy coats of antique cut and top hats, their wives in ornate brocades. These *raskolniks*, like other sectarians, could take matters to extremes. A raskolnik village on the Dniester had believed the first census of 1897 to be the work of the anti-Christ. They dug pits and held their own burial service before, singing hymns, they jumped in and walled themselves up to die of suffocation. Pacifist *dukhobors* stripped themselves naked in protest in front of Cossack recruiting sergeants. *Khlysty* sectarians held mass orgies so that, having sinned, they could gain atonement by beating each other with birch rods.

Holy men, *staretsy*, were sought out in their monasteries or in forest huts like Indian gurus. They would advise on a marriage, a quarrel in the family, a secret crime. The Optina Poustyne monastery, in a clearing in the forests of Kaluga province, with simple huts and whitewashed cells, always had a famed *starets* in residence, like Ambrose, a bearded, ragged figure sought out by Guards officers, high civil servants, literary critics, the great novelists Dostoevsky and Tolstoy.

Orthodoxy had been the creature of the Tsar since Peter the Great. In return, it was made indispensable to ordinary life. It was impossible to exist in an administrative sense without the Church, for it alone registered births, marriages and deaths. Divorce was rare; it could be obtained only through an ecclesiastical tribunal. Each village had its priest, in threadbare cassock and crude boots, his beard and hair hanging uncut in long black and gray locks. He had a near-starvation salary of sixty rubles a year. Factory workers were making three and four times that and the priest was obliged to raise what extra he could from his parishioners, for christenings, weddings and funerals. He ate the produce of his plot of land, working it himself with spade and plow like any peasant. He lived in poverty, and contempt. The peasants, whose fees kept him, thought him grasping. He seemed crude and semi-literate to the gentry, whilst the intelligentsia was almost all atheist. No promotion waited for him. He was a 'White' priest, obliged to marry before he was ordained, so poor a catch that he would most likely marry the daughter of another parish priest doomed, like himself, to spend his life in a single village. Only the 'Black' clergy, unmarried monks, were eligible for the highest reaches of church life; as bishops, archbishops,

A group of monks *at Kerzhensky Monastery, one of five thousand scattered across the great land. Russia was deeply religious. Foreigners were astonished at the amount of time given over to religious ceremonial by ordinary Russians. Almost all kept the Great Fast of Lent, and then attended the climax of Easter Mass, with its triple kiss and echoing proclamation, 'Christ is Risen'. Choirs competed to sing the finest chants and hymns in churches, like the young choirboys in this picture.*
[PHOTO: M.DMITRIEV]

metropolitans. They came from the country's five thousand monasteries, places of contemplation and prayer, with no tradition of healing or teaching, which attracted shoals of wandering pilgrims, their rags tied with string, a burlap sack on their shoulder, hair matted and foul, who progressed by begging across the vast country in search of a shrine or starets.

Intensity of belief was a Russian characteristic. The Empress, Anglo-German by birth and upbringing, was determined to match the faith and the psyche of her new country. In her adoption of Orthodoxy, an ambassador wrote, she mirrored the Russian's 'haunting obsession of the invisible and the life beyond

and the superstitious credulity'. It was a thirst that Russia's new masters – replacing church with Lenin room, cross with red star, priest with political officer – knew must be slaked.

Russians were haunted by sin and punishment. They had an old, pure Christianity, Westerners found, full of pity and belief in ultimate justice. All remembered the robbers next to the crucified Christ. Murderers, thieves, the depraved were thought *neshastnye*, unfortunates. The 'politicals', the prisoners exiled to Siberian villages for political crimes, were astonished at the kindness and sympathy shown to them by the roughest villagers. *Stranniki* wandered the Siberian wilds in birchbark shoes and

Prisoners of the Tsar. *Convicts being chained at one of the prisons on Sakhalin Island in the North Pacific. This photograph was in the collection of the great playwright Anton Chekhov. He visited the penal settlements on the island in 1890, and his subsequent book led to new legislation and improved conditions for prisoners.*

In a letter of September 1890, after leaving North Sakhalin and its 10,000 convicts, Chekhov wrote, 'There is not a single convict or penal settler with whom I have not had a word ... I witnessed a flogging, after which I had nightmares for three or four nights about the flogger and his horrible accessories. I spoke with people chained to their wheelbarrows.' One such can be seen in this photograph. [PHOTO: I. PAVLOVSKY]

ragged coats, hoping to escape from the kingdom of the anti-Christ, living off charity. Begging was not thought shameful; to refuse bread to the beggar was the sin. Russians were generous; there were thousands of charitable organisations across the empire. They supported homes for the blind and deaf-mutes and the aged, for the sick and for foundlings. The hospital for the latter in Moscow was the largest foundation in the world, with an income of a million rubles a year secured from a near-monopoly on playing cards. Its vast building had 2000 windows and corridors 150 yards long.

Less charity was shown to those of other religions. The Catholic millions in Poland, and Protestants in Finland and the Baltic States, looked West and equated Orthodoxy with backwardness. The Moslems in the Caucasus and Central Asia were restless, worried at the influx of Russian settlers and their religion. The Jews suffered most; a strong, creative community, they were periodically devastated by pogroms. A million and a quarter emigrated in the fourteen years before the outbreak of war, mostly to Britain and the United States, where the colony in New York was large enough to support two newspapers in Russian. Constantine Pobedonostsev, tutor and advisor to the Tsar, had given Nicholas his solution to the Jewish question with brute simplicity: 'A third will emigrate, a third will convert to Christianity, and a third will die out'. Violence against Jews was almost casual, a sporadic act of nature, in which Christians released their own tensions in violent riots. As a child, the painter Marc Chagall 'felt at every stage that I was a Jew – people made me feel it'. He described a pogrom. 'The street lamps are out,' he wrote. 'I feel panicky, especially in front of butchers' windows. There you can see calves that are still alive lying beside the butchers' hatchets and knives.' A burly gang faced him with knives – 'Jew or not?' they asked. 'My pockets are empty, my fingers sensitive, my legs weak, and they are out for blood,' Chagall recollected. 'My death would be futile. I so wanted to live.' He denied it. 'All right! Get along!'

Orthodox Jews were supposedly obliged to live within the Pale of Settlement, in eastern Poland, Lithuania, the Ukraine and Bessarabia where they had been trapped by the growth of the Russian empire. Their rights to travel, to exceed a small quota in the better schools and universities, to hold 'any office in government and public establishments', to use their own language were restricted. In practice, though the more traditional remained in the Pale, speaking nothing but Yiddish and wearing the old robes and hats, large numbers of Jewish businessmen, and professional men, doctors, lawyers, lived outside it. Many of the leading financiers, railroad barons, sugar and lumber kings, wheat wholesalers and shipowners were Jews. But, despite their wealth, against them 'everything was permitted, everything was possible'. In the great Kiev pogrom of 1905, the leading banker Alexander Gunzburg shouted at the mob, 'Have you no fear of Christ?', and in reply was beaten with blows 'so powerful that my head was almost driven into my shoulders and my front teeth split'. The Black Hundreds, the gangs of thugs, venal, drunken, who beat up Jews, had tacit support from Tsarist officials. Better to let the poor vent their spite on the Jews, went the thought, than on the regime.

Five further cities had populations above 250,000. None of them – Warsaw, Lodz, Riga, Kiev, Odessa – is Russian today; they are respectively Polish, Polish, Latvian, Ukrainian and Ukrainian. More advanced, and industrialised, than most Russian cities, their workers were in fact better treated than Red myth allowed. By 1902, the empire had 2.5 million industrial workers; 700,000 of them in textile plants, 600,000 in mines and metalworks, 250,000 each in food manufacture and engineering. Women made up almost half the workforce; three-quarters of it in textiles.

A law passed just before the turn of the century set the working day at a maximum of 11.5 hours, with 10 hours on Saturdays. It was forbidden to employ a night shift for more than 10 hours. There were numerous religious holidays; most factories were closed for 90 days a year besides Sundays. In Moscow province, adult males averaged 15 rubles a month, women 10 and adolescents 7 rubles. Children under fifteen made five rubles a month. Specialists made more; cotton spinners and glass blowers 20 rubles, wool and silk spinners 22. The elite in machine tool plants could make 40 to 50 rubles; they rode bicycles, went to theaters in the evenings and horseracing at weekends. Wages were highest in the advanced factories of Lodz, Warsaw and St Petersburg; they were 20 per cent less in Moscow and lower still east of the Urals.

Employers were required to give two weeks' notice of sackings and lay-offs. Fines, at least in principle, were supposed to go into a fund for needy workers and not to employers. An Inspectorate had been set up in 1899 to monitor conditions in factories and mines and encourage education and training programs. Work by children under 12 and by women at night had been banned in 1886. By 1903, the finance ministry had the power to ban 12- to 15-year-olds in plants that could endanger their health. Night work was forbidden for children; and for women and adolescents in textile and match factories, where exploitation had been bad. No women or children were allowed to work in the mines. From 1904, every factory with more than 100 employees was required to have medical services. Often this was no more than a crude ambulance and a nurse to take the injured to hospital. But the Ramensk textile plant in Moscow province, for example, had its own ninety-bed hospital complete with maternity ward.

Many workers were lodged in vast dormitories, barrack-like, with rooms for thirty workers, and in *kamorki*, rooms for several families. In a kamorka, each family marked out its space with blankets and sheets. Beds were simple planks. In the dormitories men slept on plank shelves in tiers going up to the ceiling. Linen was hung to dry from the roof. Each person had two square meters of living space and four cubic meters of air. But to peasants used to living six or ten to an *isba* hut, the conditions were familiar and dormitories were free, while kamorkas cost only a few kopeks a month.

The worst conditions were for those who had to find their own lodgings. A room could cost seven rubles a month, with families

New middle-class Muscovites *(left) round a samovar in 1910. Russia was industrialising rapidly, its growth rate the highest of any major country. It was the world's fourth largest industrial power, and foreign capital was flowing in. These men, burzhui or bourgeois, were to be called 'bloodsuckers' and 'capitalist fiends' by Red agitators.*

The shop floor *(above right) in an engineering works. Conditions were harsh, as in all industrialising countries, but beginning to improve, with wages close to Belgian and French pay in the best plants.*

obliged to take in a lodger who, for 1.5 rubles, got a bed, a lamp and boiling water for his tea. Tenements smelled of sweat, exhausted breath, wet clothes and hanging laundry; 'everywhere dampness and dirt'. Cockroaches and bugs climbed the walls and sticks of furniture during the autumn rains when water lay on the floors.

Workers lived off black bread, cabbage, cabbage soup and buckwheat porridge, with fresh cucumber in summer and salted in winter. Company stores sold goods on credit, their price and quality supposedly checked by factory inspectors. Though not obliged by law, most big factories had their own schools. Educated workers were needed for sophisticated machines imported from France and Germany. Strikes were commonplace and sometimes achieved their end. It was a big textile workers' strike in 1897 that led to the introduction of the 11.5 hour day. There were mutual aid societies in many trades, where contributions were made to the sick and widows and orphans.

The Bund, a powerful league of Jewish workers in Poland, Lithuania and Russia, was well-organised and politically significant.

Workers were not noticeably worse off than in France. French pay rates were higher, but so was the cost of lodgings and food. Disposable income was roughly the same, as was the length of the working week. Indeed, with ninety or more holidays a year, the Russian worker put in less time than his French counterpart. Neither was he tidied away in a ghetto like his Western counterpart. He mingled with smart shoppers and promenading officers and visited central movie houses. He roomed in cellars and garrets in wealthy districts, with the bourgeoisie sandwiched between. Somerset Maugham found that this gave the great Nevsky Prospekt in St Petersburg more character than Fifth Avenue or London's Bond Street.

The Russian soul, at the beginning of the century, was located in the village. Eighty per cent of the English lived in towns;

Village children *(above) play a traditional game with pork knuckles. The village priest gave them some education but, Army service apart, their horizon was limited to the village itself. Its wooden cabins caulked with oakum might straggle for a mile along a dirt road, with only the green-painted dome of the church to break the monotony of bare earth and rough-hewn logs.*
[Photo: N. Svishchev-Paola]

A peasant child *(right) in a cradle and its mother. The poorest* muzhiks *lived in a single room, sleeping on wooden shelves or on the dung-fired stove in winter. Ikons were the only ornament.*

Volga porters *have a break of tea and bread. The tea was sucked through a sugar lump. Poorly fed and shod by pre-war Tsarist standards, these men would have been happy for such rations under Bolshevism. Grain production per head of population did not reach 1913 levels again until the mid-1960s.*

almost two-thirds of Germans and half of Americans did so. Nine out of ten Russians were peasants; the 'dark people', they called themselves. Western travelers found an 'awful sadness' about the immense Russian landscape; forty years later, the enormous sweep, the shallow drifts of mist among the flat hills, dark villages floating on the crests, unnerved an advancing German infantryman. 'A single, severe tone dominated everything,' he wrote, 'so that a solitary horseman might be swallowed up and at the same time remain visible from afar like a thing apart.' Hooded crows and grasshoppers were the only constant companions, with curlews in the wilder parts.

The peasants, an American military attaché wrote, were 'sallow in complexion, lank in figure, with straight yellow hair and a heavy expression of face.' The men wore beards and pudding-bowl haircuts beneath peaked caps, and coarse woollen tunics and trousers; the women had splashes of color on their blouses. The poorest wore crude sandals made of the bark of lime trees, cut in June and plaited during the winter. The better off ran to leather boots, and felt *valenkis* for the snow months. The *muzhiks* were superstitious, slow and fatalistic. 'Go slowly, you will go further,' went the saying. 'If you hurry, people will laugh.'

Village streets ran straight and unpaved, patrolled by geese and lined with cabins made of mud bricks or logs caulked with oakum to keep out draughts. The *isba* roofs were made of lime bark or thatch. The single room had a large stove and oven made of clay on an earthen floor, benches along the walls and a table. An ikon hung in a corner, lit on holy days by a tallow candle in a red or purple lamp. Adults slept on the stove, warm in winter, cool in summer, with children lying on piles of rags on the floor. Only the most prosperous isba had a bedroom, a tin trunk for valuables and a Bible. A gateway led to the farmyard behind the cabin. Most had a round mud hut with a fireplace and a large pan of water above it. A wooden shelf was built beside it. The family would use this simple sauna each week, sweating in the steam from the pan and beating themselves with birch twigs. Nevertheless, the muzhik's odor was so pungent that an English visitor warned that 'to pass to leeward of him is so terrible an event that I always avoid it if possible'.

A central square of bare earth was dominated by the church and its painted domes of pale green. The priest was often as disliked as the state tax-gatherers. A peasant in Tula was astonished to be told that the English Bible was identical to the

The Hungry Year: *a child lies dying from typhus in 1891-2 which saw a lethal combination of typhus and starvation carry off scores of thousands of children. Both were tackled vigorously after 1900. Infant mortality rates fell as hygiene improved and a series of good harvests filled grain stores.* [Photo: M. Dmitriev]

ikons or spun lace. The vigorous worked as sled drivers, pavement layers or hawkers in towns. Others lapsed into a winter lethargy enlivened by drinking bouts. Landlords who could afford it abandoned their estates for city apartments.

Flogging, rent-racking landlords were already largely a myth. The climate and the abolition of serfdom conspired against the gentry. In the other great northern country, Canada, most of the population and almost all the farming is in the belt south of Edmonton. Moscow is well to the north of Edmonton. The southerly lands of the Crimea are on a parallel with Montreal and Minneapolis. The growing season was short; in northern Russia a bare four months. The harvest was correspondingly brief and intense, demanding a labor force three or four times higher than on the American Great Plains. Outside the central Black Earth provinces, where the rich humus of decomposed grass gave the soil its color and trapped the rains, the soil was thin and poor. Yields were low; English and American farmers were getting seven times more wheat to the acre. Livestock had to be wintered from November, and was emaciated when it was released from the yard to the spring pasture. Returns vanished without serf labor. Landowners sold off their arable to their former serfs, holding on where possible to meadowland and forests for rent and timber. By the turn of the century, peasants held four times as much land in European Russia as the gentry. Much of what was left was heavily mortgaged. Estates changed hands frequently or were parceled up between sons. An over-fecund family could be reduced to poverty in two generations; travelers, amazed, found gentry wrapped in sheephide, eating raw turnips and growling at their wives, for all the world indistinguishable from their peasants.

No thriving squirearchy underpinned provincial society against convulsion. Provincial governors were imposed from St Petersburg, isolated from local feeling in their mansions, rotated before they could put down roots. The estates of the big surviving landlords were too scattered to produce local power: the Vorontsov family's 700,000 acres were spread through sixteen provinces; Felix Yusupov, the aristocrat who was to murder Rasputin, only bothered to visit a handful of his family's thirty-eight great houses and estates.

Authority rested on Tsarist officials, ignorant, underpaid and adept at extracting bribes. The peasants treated them with silent contempt or the 'Red Cock' of rural revolt, flagged by rick and manor burning, cattle-maiming and murder. Three hundred infantry battalions and cavalry squadrons were needed to suppress risings in 1902, following a particularly bad harvest. The violence was more orgiastic than political. The peasants called it *ravnenie*, leveling, but they were more interested in burning and land seizure than socialism. Radicals got short shrift in the villages. 'He studied himself into such a state that he began teaching the youngsters that all sorrow came from the Tsar,' a shepherd told Maxim Gorky of a local schoolmaster and revolutionary. 'I don't know how the Tsar had offended him. So Fedka Savin, the village elder, did the right thing – he sent word to the police. Fedka got a gold seven and a half ruble piece for it,

Russian; he had thought that the latter had been invented 'to deceive us'. The miller was the richest village figure, with a pony trap in the yard in place of the crude peasant cart, and his house and windmills substantial affairs with porches and carved beams. He stamped felt for boots and made loans at usurious rates as well as grinding corn. He was often the village healer; water-maidens and sprites were thought to linger in his mill ponds.

Most villages had a *traktir*, a bare wooden bar, where the men amused themselves. In summer, groups with balalaikas met to drink and sing. A visitor noted an undercurrent of violence; sudden quarrels would flare, voices scream and then as suddenly subside, the balalaikas 'tinkling in the darkness again'. On market days, the square filled with traveling drapers, saddlers and bootmakers. Pedlars were dressed all in black, black frock coat, black waistcoat with glass buttons, black hat. The melancholy of the landscape was matched by its people. How strange it was, an English traveler noted, that 'their word for "harvest" should be strada, "Suffering"'! In the ice months, the blank whiteness of the steppe appeared to reach into the villages for there were no hedges or fences to break its monotony. No field work was possible. Some families made wooden spoons and forks, painted

and the teacher was dragged off to gaol by the policeman that night. That was the end of him and his learning.' The shepherd had little regard for the ruling classes, either: 'Among gentlemen, who's not a hound is a beast.' But he sympathised with their methods. 'Beat your own people,' he said, 'and others will fear you.' Every peasant, it was said, was 'proud to be the pike that gobbles up the carp.'

Even the most naturally high-spirited of men fell prey to the melancholy. 'In the summer our lives were made wretched by midges,' wrote Leon Trotsky of his exile in a Siberian village. 'They even bit to death a cow which had lost its way in the woods … In the spring and autumn the village was buried in mud.' In the winter, cockroaches 'filled the cabin with their rustlings'. Trotsky's killer, Joseph Stalin, wrote from his own exile: 'Nature is reduced to stark ugliness – in summer the river, and in winter the snow.'

Most peasants, only a generation away from serfdom, died in the village of their birth. Few strayed further than the nearest town, which could be a two- or three-day journey by cart. The low gray houses in the poorer provincial towns seemed like 'heaps of refuse' to the writer Maxim Gorky. The white walls of the churches stood out against them 'like clean patches on dirty rags'.

Simbirsk, a more thriving town on bluffs above the middle reaches of the Volga, shared with the countryside the 'torpidity of peace, the calm on land which is found at sea'. Its courtyards were overgrown with grass, the novelist I. A. Goncharov wrote; from time to time 'someone sticks his head out of a window, looks around, gaping in both directions, spits and disappears'. Its two hills were dominated by the twin symbols of Tsarism, the governor's residence and the cathedral; and by a library and high school whose alumni included two great leaders of the coming revolution, Alexander Kerensky and Vladimir Lenin, as well as Goncharov. Apple and cherry orchards ran down to the river and the quays for the bustling steamboats on the mile-wide river.

In spring, Kerensky remembered the waterside white with fragrant blossom and the nights 'breathless with the songs of nightingales'. Below the city, the watermeadows were flooded with snowmelt in spring and with hay mowers in summer. Manor houses stood in the woods and thickets along the shore. It was, Goncharov said, 'a picture of slumber and stagnation'. A goat and chickens rested in the shade of a fence and the dust of carriage wheels made patterns in the street. Kerensky recalled the social rigidity, the 'Olympian gods of the nobility', the country gentry who wintered in the town and the 'common citizens', merchants, clerks and clergy.

He remembered, too, the carriage with drawn blinds that drove through the town at night and 'took people into the unknown at the behest of Sonia's stern father'. Sonia was a young playmate; her father was the head of the secret police. Beneath the calm was terrorism; Lenin's elder brother Alexander had left Simbirsk to study in St Petersburg and plot to assassinate the Tsar with a bomb concealed in a dictionary. He had been hanged.

Father and son *on a street in provincial Russia, a place as uneventful and unchanging as the surface of the moon. The duckboards were laid for the spring or autumn mud. In summer, every pedestrian pulled a little cloud of dust behind him; in winter, the streets filled with ice.*

2
EASTERN FRONTS

The great naturalist painter Ilya Repin *reads of the death of Tolstoy in 1910 whilst the children's writer Kornei Chukovsky sits for his portrait. Repin's famous portrait of Tolstoy and his wife is on the easel. After the revolution, Stalin sent Chukovsky to try to persuade Repin to return from his estate in Finland. Repin refused; none of the letters he sent to friends was delivered because he could not bear to write Leningrad in place of St Petersburg on the envelopes.*

RUSSIA BURNED WITH ENERGY BEFORE ITS SPINE WAS SNAPPED in the Great War. In the arts, St Petersburg was the most dynamic city on earth; the country's sciences, and increasingly its industry, were world class; only in politics was it mired in the sloth and absolutism of its past. The economy was booming as capital and skills flowed in from the West. 'Russian Fives', high-yielding government bonds, were held by tens of thousands of French and British investors. Russia was a favorite posting, a British banker said, because 'all things seem possible'. The Russian economy was fourth in the world, after the US, Britain and Germany. A muzhik family, the Khrushchevs, moved to the coal town of Yuzovka when their shepherd son Nikita was fourteen. It was named for John Hughes, the Welshman who sank the first pits. When Nikita visited the 20th Century Fox lot in Hollywood fifty years later, the Soviet leader told the assembled stars how he had left the pastures to work 'in a factory owned by Germans, in coal mines owned by Frenchmen and in chemical plants owned by Belgians'. Yuzovka would later be renamed Stalino, after the young revolutionary now known as Koba who was running an illegal printing press in Batum, a grimy half-Turkish city on the Black Sea where Rothschild and Nobel had oil refineries.

It might rankle to work for foreign capitalists, but they were a vital part of the modernisation of the ramshackle empire. So was literacy. The 1897 census showed that 70 per cent could read and write in the cities and it was increasing quickly elsewhere. Primary education for all children between 8 and 11 was introduced by law in the first decade of the century. By the outbreak of war, more than half of children were getting at least primary education; universal literacy was expected by the early 1920s.

The flourishing universities had low fees, waived entirely for the half or more of students who came from poor families. Such government generosity was not reciprocated; Russian students were notoriously radical, and assassinated three Tsarist ministers in the first four years of the century. There were also 'People's' and 'Peasants'' universities, voluntary institutes which attracted many women (and which the Bolsheviks were to close down). Russian women, the novelist Ivan Turgenev had noted, were stronger in character, decision and temper than their menfolk. The 'pretty girl with bright, hard eyes under her astrakhan cap' was a standard part of revolutionary cells; several were serving life sentences for political murders.

Russians were great readers – the liberal newspaper *Russkoye Selo* had a circulation of 2.5 million copies, among the highest in the world. An English traveler on a pre-war trans-Siberian train, Maurice Baring, found the soldiers reading Gogol and Pushkin – 'they begin anywhere in the book and stop anywhere, and always find it interesting.' Every station bookstall from Moscow to Harbin had a copy of Jerome K. Jerome's *Three Men in a Boat*, and 'every peasant seemed to have read Milton's *Paradise Lost*.' Baring thought the Russian middle class to be 'extremely well educated – so much better educated than the average educated Englishman that comparison would be silly.'

St Petersburg scientists were world leaders in soil science, petroleum chemistry and hydrodynamics. Dmitri Mendeleev had formulated the Periodic Law of the chemical elements at the university and Alexander Popov first used the aerial in radio experiments. Ivan Pavlov won an early Nobel prize in 1904 for his study of conditioned responses in dogs. Igor Sikorsky was soon to produce the world's first four-engined aircraft at the Russo-Balt plant. Tchaikovsky's earlier achievement in music was being vigorously upheld. Sergei Rachmaninov was composing his rich, romantic piano music; his fellow student at the St Petersburg Conservatory, Alexander Scriabin, had become professor of the pianoforte and was writing sonatas deeply affected by his search for the 'mystic chord'. The precocious Sergei Prokofiev had already composed two operas by the time he entered the St Petersburg Conservatory in 1904 at the age of thirteen. There he was taught by Nikolai Rimsky-Korsakov, who was turning to opera after his orchestral masterpieces *Capriccio Espagnol* and *Scheherazade*. Igor Stravinsky, another pupil, had dropped his

Peasant and cow pose in St Petersburg. *The movement against academic tradition in the 1860s saw peasant life as the true subject matter for painting. It gave full scope for the prevalent nationalist, anti-Western, socially idealising feelings. By 1900 it had become the new orthodoxy.*

The aircraft designer Igor Sikorsky *at the controls of an experimental aircraft, when barely out of his teens. He produced the world's first four-engined aircraft, the Grand. The 400 hp craft cruised above St Petersburg for six hours, with sixteen people and a dog aboard. Its passenger compartment had a sofa and washroom. During the war, Sikorsky built and flew large bomber aircraft. Russian design and airframes were excellent, but engines were poor. After the revolution, Sikorsky emigrated to the United States, becoming a leading designer and manufacturer of helicopters.*

law studies to start writing his first symphony. Serge Diaghilev was editing *Mir Iskousstva*, 'World of Art'. Like Stravinsky, he was also a law dropout; he and his Ballets Russes would soon storm Paris with Stravinsky's enchanting ballets, *The Firebird* and *Petrushka*.

The *World of Art* movement, so Diaghilev's friend Alexander Benois claimed, covered 'the whole of life'. Benois was a case in point; Peter Ustinov's great-uncle was a painter, art critic and historian, theater producer and the designer of many sets for Diaghilev. Costumes and decor were also designed by Leon Bakst, the self-styled 'Russian Velasquez'; Mikhail Larionov, who created Rayonnism (a fusion of Cubism, Futurism and Orphism) with his wife Natalia Goncharova, worked on ballet designs for Diaghilev too. Businessmen in Moscow competed against each other in building great collections of Russian and French art. It was in Moscow that the finest collections were found – of French impressionists and post-impressionists, *fauvistes* and cubists, Picassos, Braques, Gauguins, Cézannes. More than a score of Matisses hung in a salon in the city's Trubetskoy Palace, the spoil of Sergei Shchukin, one of six tycoon-collectors; Manet's sketch for 'Le Déjeuner sur l'herbe' adorned his dining room. Marc Chagall was still a schoolboy; he and Vassily Kandinsky, deeply influenced by Russian ikons, were to bring the surreal and the abstract to painting. Kasimir Malevich was to launch Suprematism, devoted to the purity of geometric form, circles, crosses, triangles.

St Petersburg had four opera houses; permanent companies ran nine-month seasons in Moscow and the great provincial cities. The great bass Fedor Chaliapin, born in a Kazan slum, was bringing the crafts of the actor to opera for the first time. Russians were passionate balletomanes. Ballet nights were held in the Maryinsky Theater in the capital each Sunday and Wednesday; each box was subscribed months in advance, by regiments, by the membership of the Yacht or English Club, by industrialists, who dissected and praised or damned the performance of each dancer. Every ballerina had a rich protector; the exquisite Mathilde Kshesinskaya had been the mistress of the Tsar and had now transferred her affections to a Grand Duke. The incomparable Tamara Karsavina was training at the Imperial Ballet School in St Petersburg; so was Vaslav Nijinsky, the greatest male dancer of the century, soon to take the title role in Stravinsky's *Petrushka*, before sliding into paranoid schizophrenia. The choreographer Michel Fokine was teaching at the school and injecting a sense of drama and role into the stylised ballet of the old century; his pupil Anna Pavlova would soon enslave audiences in performances of his 'The Dying Swan'.

Anna Pavlova *rests after a rehearsal (above). The ballerina became world famous for her roles in works by Fokine, particularly 'The Dying Swan' (right). She choreographed a dozen works herself, including 'Autumn Leaves'. She introduced the first pedigree bulldogs into Russia and was often photographed with them.*

The dancer and choreographer Michel Fokine *being sculpted (above). Fokine trained at the Imperial Ballet in St Petersburg and joined Diaghilev's Ballets Russes in 1909 as a choreographer. He destroyed the artificial, stylised dance of the late 19th century, creating something more natural and expressive.*

The Ballets Russes. *Serge Diaghilev's troupe (left) dine in St Petersburg after a performance in 1909. They soon took Paris by storm. The famous ballerina Tamara Karsavina sits with her elbows on the table in the foreground whilst Lydia Lopokova, who would later marry the renowned British economist John Maynard Keynes, stands opposite her. The great Kiev-born Vaslav Nijinsky stands extreme right.*

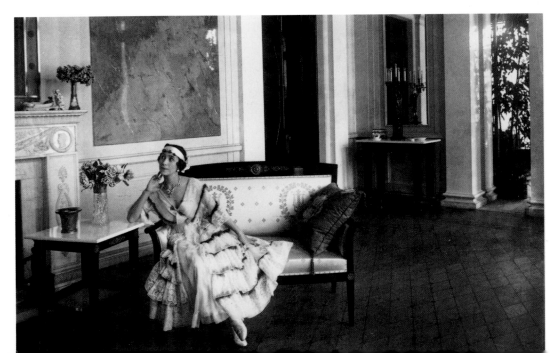

Mathilde Kshesinskaya *(left), the ballerina and Tsar Nicholas' mistress before his marriage. Her Petrograd mansion was sacked in the February 1917 revolution. She left Russia in 1920 and married Grand Duke Andrei, the Tsar's cousin. Margot Fonteyn was among many she later taught in Paris.*

Maxim Gorky and his mistress Maria Andreyeva *posing for Ilya Repin in the summer of 1905. Gorky spun tales of the dossers and down-and-outs he lived with in his early life. His best known play on slum life,* The Lower Depths, *appeared in 1902. Maria Andreyeva was in the original cast and she exchanged her first kiss with Gorky* on the first night of the play, though he had first met her with Chekhov in 1900.

A passionate leftist, Gorky was a man with 'no power to inflict harm or suffering.' Shortly after this picture was taken, he was imprisoned for inciting strikes and supporting the abortive 1905 revolution. On his release, he traveled in the United States and Britain, where he met Lenin. He had uneven, off-on relations with Bolshevism, a dogma he found suspicious because it made proletarians 'sweet and reasonable – I had never known people who were really like this.'
An ecstatic witness of the February Revolution, by the time of the Bolshevik coup he thought that Lenin and Trotsky were

Maxim Gorky and the great singer Fedor Chaliapin, *two products of the lower depths, hamming it up in Yalta in 1900. Chaliapin escaped to France in the 1920s.*

The dramatist and doctor Anton Chekhov *poses with his dog Khiva on the steps of his home in Melikhovo. He resigned from the Moscow Academy of Sciences when the writer Maxim Gorky, whom he much admired, was expelled for left-wing views on the orders of the Tsar. He died in 1904 of tuberculosis, the year in which he had written* The Cherry Orchard. *He was 44 years old. Gorky and Chaliapin went together to his funeral.*

'poisoned with the filthy venom of power'. He was abroad from 1922 to 1928, but then returned to sponsor 'social realism' in Soviet writing. Stalin showered him with honors, but he died under virtual house arrest in 1936. Stalin probably had him murdered.

In the theater, Anton Chekhov, serf's grandson, doctor and playwright, in a creative burst spurred by the tuberculosis that was killing him, produced three masterpieces in a six-year burst, *The Seagull, Uncle Vanya,* and *The Three Sisters.* They were performed at the Moscow Art Theater under the brilliant actor-producer Stanislavsky. Maxim Gorky, one-time scullery boy, dockhand and chronicler of slum life, was working on his best-known play, *The Lower Depths,* which Stanislavsky would also produce. Leo Tolstoy, though his great novels were behind him, was still active enough to infuriate the Church by straying into what the Holy Synod thought was heresy with *Resurrection*; he was excommunicated in 1901, denouncing the worship of Christ as blasphemy and his own works, *War and Peace, Anna Karenina,* as worthless. Leonid Pasternak, the painter who illustrated Tolstoy's works, had a young son named Boris, who would win his own reputation as a poet and novelist; other teenagers would soon break into print and fame, Vladimir Mayakovsky, the nobleman's son with an earring and painted geometric shapes on his powdered face; the beauty Anna Akhmatova; the doomed poet Osip Mandelstam. The poet Alexander Blok published his first book of poems, *Songs about the Fair Lady,* in 1904; other poets were the Symbolist Andrei Bely, the Catholic convert Vyacheslav Ivanov and Valery Bryussov, translator of Verlaine and Mallarmé.

This freethinking vigor took the West by storm; Russia became the rage, its ballet, its exquisite Fabergé jewelry, its caviar and chicken Kiev, its vodka, imported for newfangled cocktails. At home, it ran full tilt into the autocracy; into Cossack patrols with saber and knout – a length of raw elkhide that could cut through a back to the intestines – secret police with their provocations and infiltrations, provincial governors with powers to stretch a neck at whim, into an apparatus of government stiff with inertia when not oiled with corruption.

There was no national legislature, no parliament, no layer of responsible peers or elected representatives to cushion shocks. Tsar Nicholas himself embodied authority – at his coronation, he

Tolstoy on his horse, Demir, in 1908, *every inch the aristocrat in spite of the peasant dress he affected. The great novelist was also soldier, landowner, philosopher and mystic. He began to write as an artillery officer in the expansionist Russian drive into the Caucasus in the middle of the 19th century. He served as a battery commander in the Crimean war and later settled on the large family estates at Yasnaya Polana in Tula province. After* War and Peace *and* Anna Karenina, *he turned to propagating his own code of ethics, based on nonresistance to evil.* [PHOTO: K. BULLA]

Nicholas relaxes *(below right) in the study of a hunting lodge in 1894. He rarely wore civilian clothes, even when not on official duty. The German Kaiser, Wilhelm II, a relation like much of Europe's royalty, thought he was best suited 'to be a country gentleman growing turnips'.*

placed the crown on his own head for none other was worthy enough. Yet Nicholas, said Gregory Rasputin who knew him as well as any, was a man who 'lacked insides'. He was short, while his Romanov uncles were gargantuan; his eyes were wistful and worried; he had no luck – hundreds had been crushed to death in the first moments of his reign at his coronation fete, the superstitious remembered. His heir the Tsarevich was a hemophiliac. The occult and the supernatural were in vogue; the lines on the Tsar's palms, the superstitious whispered, were those of the doomed. The effects of his natural shyness were worsened by security constraints. The Romanovs were not universally loved; Nicholas as a boy, 'deathly pale in his blue sailor's suit', had watched his grandfather Alexander II, 'the Liberator' of the serfs, dying with his right leg torn off after he had been bombed on a St Petersburg street in 1881; his father cheated would-be murderers, who included Lenin's brother, by dying prematurely in his bed of fever. Nicholas had virtues; he was modest, patient, courteous, loyal. Rasputin thought him 'made for family life and

to enjoy his children.' Other qualities – ruthlessness, the ability to exploit and inflict pain, an instinct for danger – are needed by an autocrat. His gentle qualities, his devotion to his family, turned against him in crisis; his empress Alexandra increased his isolation. She despised St Petersburg society. 'Poor, humble, peasant Russia' – that, to her, was the 'real' Russia, instinctively pro-absolutist, wary of any constitutionalism. The imperial couple saw only those they were obliged to; foreign ambassadors, ministers, court officials, bureaucrats, high priests. When ultimately searching for advice on the revolution, the only 'ordinary subject' Nicholas was conscious of knowing was his dentist.

They were rarely in St Petersburg; they loathed the endless rooms and corridors of the Winter Palace. They spent most of the year in Tsarskoe Selo, the imperial retreat beyond the city's western suburbs. They shunned Catherine Palace, a glittering fantasy of crystal, polished parquet and marble, where flowers brought from the Crimea blazed in huge Chinese vases against curtains of sapphire brocade. They lived instead in the simpler, ocher-washed Alexander Palace, their apartments furnished like an English country house. The doors to the Tsar's study and Alexandra's mauve boudoir – the twin hearts of autocracy – were guarded by 'the Ethiopians', four enormous blacks, one of them an American named Jim Hercules, in scarlet breeches, white turbans and pointy shoes. The royal children, four girls of striking slim beauty, Marie, Tatiana, Olga, Anastasia, and the boy Alexis, had few playmates beyond an occasional visiting cousin. Even these were rare; Alexandra disliked her husband's family, a feeling that was mutual. The dynasty needed change, fluidity, maneuver to survive; industrialisation, new wealth, new classes were siring tensions that demanded at least the appearance of constitutional compromise. Nicholas believed in autocracy; beyond that, he was empty. The vast and venal bureaucracy, which mixed centralised bungling and petty tyranny to a degree an American found 'defies all belief and comprehension', was headless as the regime slipped toward its first great crisis in 1904.

That February, the Japanese made a surprise attack on the

Russian fleet off Port Arthur: a Manchurian precursor of Pearl Harbor. Unable to overrun the town, the Japanese laid siege to it. The garrison held out and in October Nicholas ordered the Baltic fleet to sail to the Pacific to relieve Port Arthur. Its slow voyage across the globe was marked by huge incompetence. The commander referred to his number two as 'the sack of shit'; the obese commander of cruisers was known as 'the vast space'. Barely out of the Baltic, the fleet opened fire on British fishing smacks in the North Sea; its gunnery officers mistook them for Japanese torpedo boats, in reality two oceans distant. Mutiny broke out on the prison ship that accompanied the fleet. Before Christmas, the Japanese were close enough to Port Arthur to bring the harbor within artillery range. The ships and the city the fleet was steaming to relieve were doomed before it rounded the Cape of Good Hope.

Revolution rode in with the humiliations in Manchuria. The interior minister V. Plevhe was murdered. 'He carried autocratic theory and practice to lengths which even in Russia seemed abnormal', the London *Times* reported. 'He shut every tap and screwed down every safety valve; and at last the world learns without surprise that the boiler has burst.' Assassination, the terrorists said, was necessary to 'force out the rusty nails that keep our coffin shut.' Workers at the huge Putilov arms and engineering works in St Petersburg went on strike. A priest, Father Georgy Gapon, seized on the unrest and multiplied it. On January 8, 1905, 200,000 were on strike. Gapon drew up a petition seeking 'justice and protection' from the Tsar. It asked for an eight-hour day, a basic wage, the release of political prisoners. It received 150,000 signatures.

On Sunday, January 9, a crowd of 100,000 led by Gapon assembled outside the Winter Palace, the 'Tsar's house', carrying ikons and banners. They wished to present their petition to the Tsar, not knowing that he was twenty miles away in the Alexander Palace. The last paragraph of the petition was more prophetic than Gapon had planned; 'If you do not respond to our prayer', it told the Tsar, 'we shall die, here, on this square, in front of your palace'. As they pushed forward, a cordon of Cossacks and Hussars opened fire. The official death toll was ninety-two; the snow on the Nevsky Prospekt was stained where the wounded dragged themselves away.

A wave of strikes and demonstrations broke out from Warsaw to the Urals. Three hundred were killed in the Polish city of Lodz. In an obscure industrial town, Ivanovo-Voznesensk, the workers set up the first known 'Soviet', a council or committee of workers that demanded 'the right to assemble freely to discuss their needs and elect delegates'. The Baltic fleet steamed on, deaf to the world. It entered the Strait of Tsushima between Japan and Korea on May 27. The Japanese Admiral Togo was waiting and, in the greatest sea battle since Trafalgar, the Russians lost their full complement of twelve battleships, sunk or surrendered, seven out of twelve cruisers and six out of nine destroyers. The navy was humiliated. In the Black Sea port of Odessa, police, Cossacks and the anti-Semitic gangs of the Black Hundreds fought against

Revenge for Bloody Sunday. *Father Georgy Gapon, the priest who led the crowds to massacre in 1905, was lynched a year later by a group of former comrades at his summer cottage in Oserki outside St Petersburg. Exposed as an agent provocateur for the Okhrana secret police, he was hanged with a clothesline.*

strikers and massacred Jews. On June 15 the city was put under martial law. The same day, the battleship *Potemkin*, the pride of the Black Sea fleet, put into Odessa with the Red flag flying. The crew had mutinied, throwing some of the officers overboard and locking the rest in her brig. As fighting continued ashore, the sailors fired salvoes at the city. Their rangefinding was inaccurate; they gave up the bombardment and steamed back into the Black Sea, eventually scuttling the battleship at Constanza in Rumania.

Naval mutinies spread to Kronstadt, the big naval base off St Petersburg, and Sevastopol. In the countryside, peasants began burning manor houses and maiming cattle. Along railroad tracks, passengers could see the steppe illuminated by burning crops, whilst 'cows, horses or sheep roamed the fields with ripped stomachs, mooing or bellowing with pain'. Soviets mushroomed in the cities. By October, a general strike had spread through the empire. Ominously, the strikers were joined by students and supported by their professors. Even the corps de ballet at the Maryinsky Theater joined in.

But the unrest was largely leaderless. The senior revolutionaries were abroad, indulging in émigré squabbles, reading of the distant events in newspapers. The Marxist Social Democrats had held their first meeting in secret in a log cabin on the outskirts of Minsk in 1897. The infant party mounted its

Young Marxists pose in St Petersburg *before being exiled to Siberia in 1897. Prematurely bald, Vladimir Lenin in the center dominates the group. Yuli Martov is on his right. Lenin had arrived in St Petersburg to practice law. The police left the Marxists alone, assuming their interest to be in economic theory, not practical insurrection, until they were involved in a wave of strikes in 1895. Martov, real name Cedarbaum, was a Jewish intellectual from Odessa. After Siberia, they moved to western Europe. They were an odd couple. Martov ate with his followers at the bustling La Rotonde bistro in Paris, a city he loved. Lenin loathed Paris – 'What the devil made us come here!' – and took his disciples to a miserable café on the Avenue d'Orléans, where they drank sickly grenadine and soda. They soon split, into Lenin's Bolsheviks and Martov's Mensheviks. In 1918-19 Martov was a fearless denouncer of Lenin's terror and went on trying to halt the Bolshevik tide when driven into exile, until his death in 1923.*

A group of political exiles in Siberia *in 1916. They lived in villages in a vast arc around Irkutsk, sometimes 700 miles from the nearest railhead. Joseph Stalin is third left in the back row with his hat pushed back; the generalissimo of the Second World War escaped compulsory service in the First because of the childhood withering of his left arm. His fellow Bolshevik Lev Kamenev, whom Stalin would later execute, is on his left in the back row. Yakov Sverdlov, who ordered the murder of the imperial family, is immediately behind the cloth cap in the front row. He escaped the fate of most Old Bolsheviks; influenza got to him before Stalin. Political opponents exiled to Siberia were incomparably better off under the Tsarist than the coming Bolshevik system.*

second congress six years later in a rat-infested warehouse in Brussels and, having been moved on by the Belgian police, in a London church. The two main figures, Vladimir Lenin and Yuli Martov, soon split. Lenin called for an elitist organisation with membership restricted to professional revolutionaries. Yuli Martov thought this a 'siege mentality'. He argued for a broader and more democratic party than that allowed for by Lenin's dictatorial elite. Lenin, due to the small attendance in London, narrowly won the vote. The Social Democrats divided into two factions – Lenin's Bolsheviks, for 'majority', and Martov's Mensheviks, for 'minority'.

Lenin was in Geneva, an 'awful hole', reading up the tactics of streetfighting. 'It horrifies me to find that there has been talk about bombs for over six months, yet none has been made!' he wrote to Party cells in St Petersburg. 'Form fighting squads at once everywhere.' He was appealing to a phantom force since the Bolsheviks played almost no part in the 1905 revolution. Lenin did not return to Russia until November when he made little impact; his courage was suspect. Tatiana Alexinskaya, the wife of a ranking Bolshevik, watched him when Cossacks charged a St Petersburg demonstration. 'Lenin was the first to flee,' she said. 'He jumped over a barrier. His bowler hat fell off, revealing his bare skull, perspiring and glistening under the sunlight. He fell, got up, and continued to run.'

The Menshevik Leon Trotsky, more determined than most, returned early from his Western exile to St Petersburg. Here he dominated the new Soviet, the council that attempted to coordinate the rising. Witty and attractive, he was open to debate

with all. Speaking to a group of Guards officers at a political soirée in the house of a baroness – 'the butler waited for my visiting card but, woe is me, what visiting card should a man with a cover name produce?' – he told them that it was their duty to hand over the keys to the arsenals to the people. The rich were fascinated by radicals whose aim it was to destroy them; *Pravda*, the Bolshevik newspaper, was to be founded and funded by Victor Tikhomirnov, a shipping magnate. Savva Morozov, one of the wealthiest men in the empire, was a Marxist. He loved the philosophy, he said, for its energy; he sided with the Bolsheviks against the Mensheviks, explaining that extremism was a natural condition for Russians. He financed Party publications; everything Lenin wrote, he chuckled, was 'a political punch in the face'. In 1905, however, he went to the French Riviera and shot himself in a hotel bedroom; his nephew N. P. Schmidt, heir to a furniture fortune, did for himself in similar style the following year as the Bolsheviks beat the Mensheviks to his legacy.

Guards officers could flirt with Trotsky, the navy could not be trusted, but the mass of peasant infantrymen stayed loyal to the Tsar. Without their support, or at least disinterest, no revolution could succeed. Nicholas conceded the principles of freedom of speech, conscience and association in October. A *Duma*, or assembly, was established that had some power for the first time in Russia. But the Tsar retained supreme power; both the franchise and the assembly's authority were severely limited. This was no democracy, which Nicholas regarded as 'senseless and criminal', but it was enough for liberal Constitutional Democrats, the influential 'Cadets', to call off their support for the general

Lenin. *A British secret agent thought he looked 'more like a provincial grocer than a leader of men'; while the French ambassador found him 'crazy with vanity'.*

Lev Kamenev, *a 'quick-moving little man with a wide vivacious face', leading Bolshevik moderate who was shot after a show trial in 1936.*

Joseph Djugashvili, *aka Ryaboi or 'Pockmark', aka Koba, aka Zakhar Melikyants, aka Nisharadze, aka Joseph Stalin.*

Maria Ulyanova, *Lenin's sister, an enthusiastic but incompetent revolutionary whom the Okhrana secret police tailed without difficulty.*

Alexander Ulyanov, *Lenin's much loved elder brother who was hanged on a gibbet in 1887 after plotting to murder the Tsar with a bomb concealed in a medical dictionary.*

Nadezhda Krupskaya, *Lenin's wife. She later developed bulging eyes because of thyroid problems, and was known as 'the Fish'.*

A fancy dress ball *in St Petersburg, c 1910. The Grand Duchess Yelena Vladimirovna, the Tsar's sister-in-law and a noted beauty, sits in front of the man in the colonial pith helmet. Nicholas and Alexandra seldom went to balls or parties. The Empress raged at a 'corrupt and godless society' that 'thinks of nothing but dancing and dining.'*

strike. The London *Times* claimed that 'the people have won, the Tsar has capitulated, the autocracy is no more'. That was twelve years premature. As Trotsky said, the Tsar had granted everything and given nothing; 'we want neither the wolf's snout nor the fox's tail.' The struggle went on. In December, districts of Moscow were destroyed in heavy streetfighting. Rifles were smuggled in for the rebels from the United States, where Mark Twain caught the mood: 'If such a government cannot be overthrown otherwise than by dynamite, then thank God for dynamite.'

The army and the ever-eager Cossacks slowly restored control. By year end, the St Petersburg Soviet, though it would later give its name to the country, was over, having lasted only fifty days, and Trotsky was in the Peter and Paul Fortress, lying back on his cot in his cell, reading French novels. The far-right, anti-Semitic, anti-liberal Union of the Russian People snowballed to more than a million members, encouraging pogroms, accusing Jews of the ritual murder of Christian babies, inflaming the successful reaction.

Peter Stolypin became prime minister in the spring of 1906, a sturdy, vigorous country squire, big as a bear and as brave. The British ambassador thought him the 'most notable figure in

Europe'. He treated revolutionaries with a monarchist's contempt. 'You want great upheavals,' he roared, 'but we want a great Russia.' More than 2000 rebels had been shot or hanged in the Baltic provinces alone in the immediate aftermath of the crushed revolt. He followed on with such gusto that the noose became known as the 'Stolypin necktie'.

Terrorism remained endemic. Prisoners were tried within twenty-four hours of arrest and executed at once. It was common for a terrorist to be tried and hanged before his victim was buried. Stolypin was himself a target. In 1906, his house was blown apart by a bomb, crushing his daughter's legs. Yet, an observer said, 'he gave no impression of ferocity. He left an impression only of cold gentleness, of icy compassion, of saddened self-control.' Convinced that the monarchy could only survive with more responsible government, he persisted with a series of sweeping reforms. He sold off state-owned land, including the vast Siberian crown-lands. He lifted legal restrictions on land ownership and travel from the peasants. Individuals were encouraged to consolidate their land holdings away from the backward and impoverished village communes. Stolypin wanted to create from the most energetic peasants a sturdy yeoman class as a counterweight to revolution. It was, he

A picnic *in the last full summer of peace. Outdoor living was becoming fashionable though informality had limits kept on it, a duty performed here by the table-cloths and carpets. Russian cuisine, with its cold spreads of pressed caviar, smoked sturgeon and salted cucumber, was ideally suited.*

said, 'a gamble not on the drunken and feeble but on the sober and the strong'. He succeeded well enough to throw the distant revolutionaries into depression. If land reform continued, Lenin admitted, the Bolsheviks might be forced to renounce any agrarian program at all. In the southern oilfields, an agitator named Stalin felt that the tide was flowing against revolution. Two decades later, he would take a grisly revenge on Stolypin's new class.

On September 14, 1911, Stolypin went to a performance of Rimsky-Korsakov's *Tsar Sultan* at the Kiev Opera House. He was seated in the stalls and Nicholas was in the imperial box. During the second-act interval, a young man in evening dress approached the prime minister and then pulled out a Browning pistol. 'We heard two sounds as if something was dropped,' wrote Nicholas. 'Women were shrieking and directly in front of me in the stalls Stolypin was standing. He slowly turned his face towards me and with his left hand made the sign of the Cross in the air ... He slowly sank into his chair and began to unbutton his tunic.' He died five days later.

He left a Russia that, barring cataclysm, had a good chance of avoiding revolution. The countryside was pacified and thriving; the 1913 harvest was a record not to be matched until the 1960s;

industrial production had more than doubled in the previous seven years.

St Petersburg glittered; though the imperial couple were rarely seen, being frequently closeted, so the rumors said, with a peasant starets with insane eyes, Gregory Rasputin. His influence over them came from his unique ability to help the sickly Tsarevich. The black cocktail barman at the Hôtel de l'Europe acknowledged orders for cocktails in a soft Kentucky accent, while in the 'phosphorescent, crazy, voluptuous summer nights', the rays of the midnight sun glided into the gardens where they discovered 'long-haired students discussing with girls the transcendental values of German philosophy'. Archbishops parked their carriages outside the Stock Exchange. Fortunes of millions of rubles, the novelist Alexei Tolstoy wrote, had 'appeared as if out of thin air. People doped themselves with music ... with half-naked women ... with champagne. Gambling clubs, houses of assignation, theaters, picture-houses, amusement parks cropped up like mushrooms.' The magnate Nikolai Ryabushinsky sponsored exhibitions of Van Gogh, Braque and Rouault. Stravinsky smashed the musical mold with *The Rite of Spring*. V. Khlebnikov had written the first Futurist poem, of one word, *Smekh*, laughter, and its derivatives. Futurist poets had

Peter Stolypin, who ran Russia for six dynamic years *in the aftermath of the 1905 revolt. He transferred land to the peasants with the same gusto as he hanged revolutionaries. Another twenty years of peace would have turned Russia into a stable peasant society. As it was, a terrible future awaited Stolypin's landowning peasants in Bolshevik Russia. A terrible future awaited him as well. He was one of the prime targets for Social Revolutionary murder squads in 1906. They managed to place a bomb outside his dacha, killing 33 people, but Stolypin escaped the blast. At (left) is the wreckage a few minutes after the explosion. Four thousand people were killed by terrorists in the troubles that followed Bloody Sunday. A double agent shot him in the Kiev opera house in 1911. The Tsar was in the imperial box and so witnessed the end of the only statesman who might have prevented revolution.*

issued their manifesto, calling for language itself to be smashed. Mayakovsky wandered the Moscow streets with Futurist painters dressed in cardboard clothes with flowers painted on their faces. But the actual Future had other plans.

THE GREAT WAR

On August 2, 1914, crowds cheering 'For Faith, Tsar and Country' gathered in St Petersburg to share the ecstasy of Berlin, Paris and London as Europe embarked light-heartedly on destroying itself. The French ambassador, Maurice Paléologue, watched Nicholas repeat the oath taken by his ancestor Alexander I in 1812 during the Napoleonic invasion, swearing at a solemn mass not to make peace until the last enemy was driven from Russian soil. The Empress, the ambassador noted, 'every now and then closed her eyes, her livid face reminding one of a death mask'. Guards officers, foreseeing a victory parade down the Unter den Linden in Berlin, asked whether they should pack their dress uniforms. Mobs sacked the German embassy and the name of the city was changed to the Slavonic Petrograd. In Austrian Galicia, Lenin was briefly arrested as a Russian spy. The irony of being taken for an Imperialist agent escaped him. Once he was released, Lenin moved to Switzerland because he feared the outpouring of Russian patriotism would mean the end of Socialism.

The Russian army was a colossus, comfortably the largest in the world. Mobilisation added 3.1 million reserves to the pre-war regular strength of 1.4 million within a few weeks. More than 15 million men would eventually be harnessed to what her Western allies called the 'Russian steamroller'. Only a few felt what was in

Nicholas stands on the balcony *of the Winter Palace to be greeted by cheering crowds at the declaration of war in August 1914. He had just prayed before the famous Vladimir ikon of the Virgin, which was reputed to have turned back Tamerlane and to have been worshiped by Kutuzov before he faced the French in 1812. The war was to become a catastrophe for the nation and for the dynasty.*

Count Sergei Witte, a former premier, *was one of the few to argue against war with Germany. Defeat, he said, would destroy Tsarism. But victory too, by undermining the German and the Austro-Hungarian empires, would finish the Russian autocracy.*

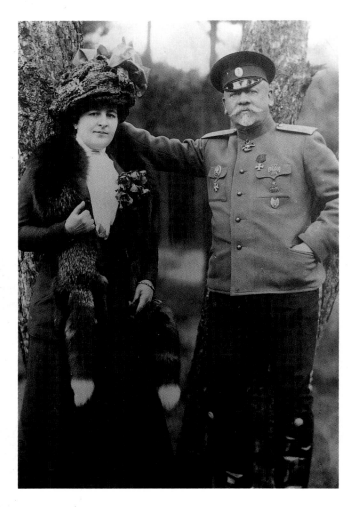

The minister of war, *General Vladimir Sukhomlinov, poses in 1915 with his wife, thirty-two years younger than himself. This 'drawing-room soldier, scented, pomaded', was also corrupt, keeping his wife in fancy clothes by fiddling his official expenses. He was shortly to be sacked and accused of treason.*

The 'Russian Steamroller', *as the imperial army was known to its British and French allies, was easily the largest force of men under arms in the world. Cocooned in the confidence of its own size, its mass had become vulnerable to the machinegun and rapid-firing artillery.*

Russian dead awaiting mass burial, *and then being thrown into hastily dug pits. 'In the Great War ledger,' the German commander Hindenburg wrote, 'the page on which the Russian losses were written has been torn out. No one knows the figure. Five millions or eight millions? We too have no idea. All we know is that sometimes in our battles with the Russians we had to remove the mounds of enemy corpses in order to get a clear field of fire against fresh assaulting waves.' The trauma led first to withdrawal – living soldiers, a trooper wrote, became simply 'men who were going to die' – and then to 'a terrible anger' that erupted in revolution.*

store. A trooper from Kiev told the British military attaché : 'They say it is a wide road that leads to a war and only a narrow path that leads home again.' Count Sergei Witte, the shrewdest of Nicholas' advisors, thought the war to be 'madness ... Even if we assume a complete victory, it means not only the end of German domination, but the proclamation of republics throughout central Europe. That means the simultaneous end of Tsarism.' As to defeat, he preferred 'to remain silent'.

Most of the millions who were to be tested beyond the breaking point in the coming slaughter were muzhiks. They were subject to a constant and harsh discipline that found its most savage expression in the knout. It was accepted as part of the natural order of things that the Russian needed to be driven. Despite the emancipation of the serfs by Alexander II in 1861, the serflike treatment of soldiers continued under Nicholas. A recruit first learnt unquestioning obedience, his NCOs beating him on parade with swagger sticks, a ritual compared to a valet beating dust from a curtain. He stood at attention, his hand at his cap, through any conversation with an officer. Yet he was known for his courage and endurance. 'The Turks are tumbling like ninepins,' went a bittersweet Russian saying, 'but through the grace of God our men stand firm, though headless.'

Russia had mass, but the impact of manpower was being offset

Cooking at the front. *Russian cheerfulness under physical hardship impressed British observers. The Russian soldier could live off the land, scouring the fields for vegetables and livestock, a sack slung across his back to carry a twist of salt and scavenged potatoes. His ability to move without logistical support would still astonish the Germans thirty years later when, his rations supplemented by American Spam, he thought himself living in luxury.*

Troops pumping out a trench *at the front, March 1917. Most experienced officers and NCOs were killed early in the war. Their replacements were badly trained and had poor morale. British liaison officers found Russian trenches to be 'poorly built and badly planned'. Rifles were in 'very poor condition' and officers 'gave the impression of being lazy and hard drinkers.' Artillery batteries were 'frequently unconcealed, without pits or shelter for the men'.*

A field nurse, Elena Tsebrzhinskaya, *poses after being decorated for bravery. She volunteered as a male nurse in November 1914. Her sex was discovered when she was wounded, but she was allowed to remain with her nursing unit. Nicholas personally intervened to allow several women to continue serving in combat posts; later, women's combat battalions were raised.*

Heroes selected for photographs, *which were then circulated among the regiments to raise morale. By mid-1916 Russian artillery units were being ordered to fire on their own infantry to force them into the attack. Thousands surrendered: 'We throw our rifles away and give up, because things are dreadful in our army, and so are our officers.'*

by quick-firing artillery and the machinegun. The essence was how it was handled in battle and the omens were not good. A chasm separated men from officers whose promotion was based more on patronage and social and financial standing than on merit. The higher echelons of the officer corps were stuffed with over-age generals who were kept on the active list regardless of performance. The war minister, General Vladimir Sukhomlinov, had last fought against the Turks thirty-six years before; he thought the machinegun and rapid-firing artillery to be newfangled and cowardly. 'With his sly look, his eyes always gleaming watchfully under the heavy folds of his eyelids,' the French ambassador wrote, 'I know few men who inspire more mistrust at first sight.'

Within a year, four million had been killed, wounded, captured or were missing. 'The regular army vanished,' said General Alexei Brusilov, a senior commander. 'It is replaced by an army of ignoramuses.' The Russians were short of telephone wire, so orders were passed by radio. Code books were also scarce, so many radio messages were sent in clear. The Germans intercepted the commands for the first great battle of the war, at Tannenberg; it helped them to destroy two armies in four days. The Russians fought successfully against the Austro-Hungarians, but the Germans were another matter. A British observer, Sir Bernard Pares, witnessed a German artillery attack in southern Poland. 'The elementary Russian trenches were completely wiped out and so, to all intents and purposes, was human life in that

area,' he wrote. 'The Russian division stationed at this point was reduced from a normal 16,000 to 500 men.' Without supplies and ammunition, the Russians fell back in Galicia and Poland. 'You know, Sir, we have no weapons except the soldiers' breast,' a private told Pares. 'This is not war, Sir, it is slaughter.'

The war committee of the Duma sent the Tsar a list of 'what we have learned': that the Russians were short of artillery, machineguns and ammunition, with which the enemy was plentifully supplied; that every enemy soldier had a rifle, whereas 'hundreds of thousands of our men are without weapons, and have to wait until they can pick up the rifles dropped by their fallen comrades'; that 'trenches are not prepared in sufficient numbers'; that 'neither bravery, nor talent, nor competence, nor military worth' influenced appointments, and that the able were rarely given important commands. A divisional commander said that the Germans literally plowed up the battlefield with shellbursts, burying the defenders in the process. 'They use up metal,' he said. 'We use up human life.'

The Germans overran Russian Poland. Warsaw fell on August 5, 1915. General Polivanov, the new war minister, reported that: 'The army is no longer retreating, it is running away … The appearance of a small German patrol evokes panic and results in the flight of whole regiments.' No matter how bad things were at the front – he put his trust in 'the impenetrable spaces, impassable mud and the mercy of Saint Nicholas' – he feared there was 'a far more dreadful event threatening Russia.' The

Wounded in a field hospital. *Censors dealing with field mail were convinced that references to losses were hysterical and untrue. Checking a sample regiment, they found that its strength had fallen from 2389 to 665 in ten days.*
[Photo G. Fried]

The Empress, dressed as a nurse, *with Alexis. Rasputin's influence, based on Alexis' illness, grew when Nicholas became Commander-in-Chief and left for army headquarters in Mogilev. The* nemetskoe zasilye, *the 'German plague', was replacing anti-Semitism in the Russian soul and attaching itself to the Darmstadt-born Empress. A mocking café joke had the young Tsarevich weeping in the palace. 'What's the matter, Alexis?' a visiting general asks. 'Well, when the Russians lose, my father cries,' said the boy. 'When the Germans lose, my mother cries. When am I to cry?'*

Tsar dismissed his uncle, Grand Duke Nicholas, and replaced him as Commander-in-Chief. It was, Polivanov said, a 'stunning blow' which he rightly thought would result in the Tsar taking personal blame for future disasters.

Fourteen armies held a front in 1916 that stretched from Riga on the Baltic to the Black Sea and across it to Erzerum and Persia. 'Colorless, expressionless, endless regiments marching through dead cold,' a trooper wrote. 'They were not individual Russians any more; they were not men who were going to die for their country, they were just men who were going to die.' The high morale of 1914 had gone. 'Under the mask of servile submissiveness lies terrible anger … Just strike a tiny little match and everything will go up in flames.' Trains of wounded from the front slid daily into the Warsaw Station in Petrograd. In the hospital of St George, they lay in the quiet white and blue wards with 'tired suffering eyes.' Thousands of refugees from the lost territories were crammed into wooden sheds and cellars near the station, often shoeless, the children still in the thin cotton frocks of their summer flight. The bread queues in the capital stretched for blocks. Bakeries had their windows smashed at night. Speculators flourished. 'The sharks are working their gigantic jaws,' a financial paper reported as the cost of bread quadrupled and that of aspirin increased almost one hundred times. Cabarets and cafés flourished; prohibition had been introduced at the start of the war, crippling government finances, but the rich slipped bootleg vodka into pineapple juice and drank it from teacups. The suicide rate tripled. Hotels were filled with officers who should have been at the front: 'there is no disgrace in being a

The Winter Palace *(opposite) awaits the arrival of the latest batch of casualties in 1914. The wounded filled the wards and then the corridors of Petrograd hospitals; the overflow ran into private houses, hotels and then into the vast Palace.*

Gregory Rasputin
with a group of society admirers in about 1915. The mystic healer was introduced to the imperial family by Anna Vyrubova, the confidante of the Empress, a woman as 'commonplace as a bubble in biscuit dough'. Rasputin was skillful at exciting wellbred ladies with his foul language and manners.
[PHOTO: K.BULLA]

shirker'. The young Boris Pasternak found life 'gay with the brilliance of a florist's window in winter.' Dmitri Merekhovsky thought that the Romanovs had reduced Russia to the 'fifth act of a tragedy played in a brothel'.

With Nicholas away at distant army headquarters, Alexandra became the autocrat. At the insistence of her 'Friend' Rasputin, the country had five interior ministers and three war ministers in ten months. A general was overheard at the ballet to warn that the city's inflated military garrison was 'good for nothing but to supply recruits for the army of anarchy.' No one was in any doubt that there would be a revolution. 'No one is even talking about it,' said Zinaida Gippius, a baroque beauty and poetess. 'We have gone numb.' The general said that the revolution 'will be started not by the people, but by the army'. *Okhrana* secret police agents in the city warned that the 'mood of opposition has gone very far' – far beyond 1905.

Rumors swirled round the Empress and Rasputin; they were German spies, people whispered, they were traitors, they were lovers. 'I first heard people speaking of the emperor and empress with open animosity and contempt,' wrote Zinaida Purishkevich, the sister of a rich, far right Duma deputy. 'Rasputin, Rasputin, Rasputin, it was like a refrain; his mistakes, his shocking personal

conduct, his mysterious power. This power was tremendous; it was like dusk enveloping all our world, eclipsing the sun.' Her brother Vladimir was a Jew-baiter, an eccentric who appeared in the Duma with a red carnation sticking out from his fly buttons, a reactionary who was prepared to murder to save the autocracy. Felix Yusupov originated the plot to kill Rasputin for the same motive; to save the autocracy from itself. Yusupov was heir to the greatest fortune in Russia; the family estates included a 125-mile stretch of Crimean coastline rich in oil, and thirty-eight palaces and manors. The family's exquisite palace on the Moika canal in Petrograd had an art gallery rich in paintings by Rembrandt and Fragonard, and a miniature Louis XV theater where Felix, given to transvestism, enjoyed dressing up. It was to this palace that he invited Rasputin on the night of December 16, 1916.

Rasputin was a reluctant victim. Yusupov gave him poisoned drink and cakes, and shot him in the heart; his 'green viper eyes' had opened and he had rushed at Yusupov with a roar. Purishkevich then shot him in the head and back, and kicked him in the head. The body was then dumped into a hole in the frozen Neva river. 'The bullet which killed him reached the very heart of the ruling dynasty,' wrote Alexander Blok. It had been fired, not by a revolutionary, but by a crypto-fascist and a fop.

Co-conspirator Grand Duke Dmitri *was the Tsar's cousin, 26 at the end of 1916, a 'flighty and impulsive' young officer and a heavy drinker. Felix Yusupov recruited him to help in the murder of Rasputin. He is seen here with Nicholas and Nicholas's daughter Tatiana.*

Rasputin's killer: *Felix Yusupov with his wife Irina, a niece of the Tsar, in 1910. Yusupov came from the richest family in Russia with an annual income equivalent to a ton of gold. He was a fop, who experimented with transvestism as a boy. 'By day I was a schoolboy and by night a fashionable woman.' He lured Rasputin into the trap with the promise that he would meet Princess Irina. Anna Pavlova said of Yusupov that he had 'God in one eye and the Devil in the other.'*

The eyes of a maniac. *By the autumn of 1916, the government of Russia was dominated by Rasputin. His hair was long and matted, his beard a greasy napkin, his teeth black with neglect. The ballerina Tamara Karsavina passed him in the street and recognised him immediately through his 'eyes of strange lightness, set close, inconceivable in a peasant face, the eyes of a maniac.'*

3
THE YEAR OF REVOLUTIONS

RASPUTIN'S CORPSE WAS FOUND ON MONDAY, DECEMBER 19, and people knelt in the snow outside the Moika Palace to give thanks to God and Felix Yusupov. On Tuesday, the Empress prayed over the corpse, smothering it with flowers and ikons. On Thursday night, it was buried in a plot of ground on the edge of the imperial park at Tsarskoe Selo. His murderers could not be executed; they were too popular, and Felix was married to the Tsar's niece Irina. He was exiled to his family estates in the south. Vladimir Purishkevich went to the front.

The Tsar, at army headquarters in Mogilev, walked his English collie dogs in the afternoons and watched a twenty-reel Pathé serial called 'The Streets of New York', in the evenings. He was too weak to survive, they said in Petrograd, power 'hung over him like a shroud.' Most venom was reserved for the Empress. The crowds called her 'the German woman'. Her melancholy evenings were passed listening to a Rumanian chamber orchestra and gazing silently into the fire. Each day, sometimes several times, she poured out her simple political philosophy in letters to the Tsar; the Russians loved 'to feel the whip – it's their nature – tender love and then the iron hand to punish and guide'.

February 1917 began bitterly cold, the streets filled with ice. Food lines lengthened. 'Never before has there been so much swearing, argument and scandal,' Okhrana agents reported. There were 170,000 troops in the city, double the peacetime garrison, but the secret police thought them to be 'raw, untrained material, unfit to put down disorders'. The best troops were at the front and the capital was manned with reservists, shell-shock victims and the poorest Cossacks. On February 14, police agents reported that army officers had for the first time mingled with crowds demonstrating on the Nevsky against the war and the government. 'Behind the white columns of the hall grinned Hopelessness,' a conservative said of the mood in Duma debates. 'And she whispered: "Why? What for? What difference does it make?"'

Food hoarding was under way. A small helping of potatoes, fifteen kopeks before the war, was now difficult to find at 1.20 rubles. Wood for heating was beyond the means of the poor and the temperature in middle-class apartments was kept barely above freezing. Grain trains were blocked by heavy snowfalls. International Women's Day was held on Thursday, February 23, which gave an excuse for women from textile plants to stream into the streets, shouting: 'Down with hunger! Bread for the workers!' They pelted the windows of engineering shops with snowballs to bring the men out. Nikolai Sukhanov, the crotchety, radical civil

Cossacks, key players in the Revolution. *With a truss of hay tied to their saddles for their wiry horses, they could roam the streets for twelve hours at a time. Traditionally they were volunteers and fiercely loyal to the Tsar, breaking up demonstrations and strikes during the troubles of 1905, but those in Petrograd in 1917 were drafted from the most impoverished regions of the Kuban and the Don. Police agents saw them urging the crowds on and realised that these historic forces of reaction had turned revolutionary.*

Political prisoners *freed in the first days of the February Revolution from the Shlusselberg Fortress in Petrograd. The Bolsheviks were incompetent conspirators, easily infiltrated by the Tsarist secret police. Thirty-six hours before the Revolution started, the last big group of them in the capital had been arrested, including Lenin's sister. So they played little or no part, and Lenin and Trotsky only arrived back from exile after it was all over.*

The banners read: 'Long live the People who have opened the prison doors', and 'Everything for the People – factories, land and freedom'.

servant who was to become the great diarist of the revolution, and its victim, thought the disorders no different to scores he had watched before except, he noted, that the authorities seemed irresolute this time. The crowds felt it. They began overturning tramcars and sacked a big bakery. The 'Pharaohs', street slang for police, did nothing. Okhrana agents noted that *masterovye*, skilled craftsmen, had begun to join the strikers. The agitators working the crowds no longer bothered to hide their faces by pulling down their caps. The troops did not have their normal stomach for dispersing the crowds. A Cossack officer shouted at some strikers led by an elderly woman: 'Who are you following? You are being led by an old crone!' The woman retorted: 'No old crone, but a sister and wife of soldiers at the front.' The troops lowered their rifles. Someone yelled: 'Cossacks, you are our brothers, you can't shoot us.' The horsemen turned away.

Alexandra thought there was no more to it than youngsters running about for excitement: 'If the weather was cold, they would probably have stayed at home.' She did, however, write to Nicholas that she hoped that a young Socialist lawyer, Alexander Kerensky, would be hanged. In a Duma debate, Kerensky had called for someone to do to the Tsar what Brutus had done to Caesar. She misspelled his name 'Kedrinsky'. In fashionable circles, the main talk was of the party Princess Leon Radziwill was throwing the following Sunday.

As luck would have it, the weather stayed warm on Friday. Demonstrators were out again in force. Something was afoot with the Cossacks; startled onlookers noticed that the crowds had begun to cheer their traditional tormentors. A Cossack unit on a main boulevard was ordered to charge. Its officers, eyes bloodshot, forced a way through the crowd. The troopers rode their horses delicately in single file through the narrow gap opened up by the officers. 'Some of them smiled, and one actually winked,' a demonstrator recollected. The few Bolsheviks at large in Petrograd read the situation wrongly and thought that, as ever, the troops would soon have the measure of the strikers.

Killing started on Saturday, February 25. The demonstrators were back, running into officers returning to barracks after a night in the gipsy houses. There were few of the familiar smoke plumes above the city. All factories had closed. Police opened fire on a mob that was beating a police officer with an iron tramcar lever, and fired a volley into a mob near the Nikolaevsky railroad station. Canes, hats and galoshes littered the snow as the demonstrators fled. A cavalry squadron shot down nine people on the Nevsky. But slowly the people began to command, forcing officers to abandon their carriages and rescuing those who had been taken by police snatch squads. The police were melting away, disguising themselves in army greatcoats. Politics played little part. There were no leaders. 'What do they want?' Nikolai Sukhanov heard a bystander ask of the crowds. 'They want bread, peace with the Germans and freedom for the Yids,' his companion replied. Sukhanov thought the man had scored a bullseye.

Sunday started with deceptive calm and a pleasant light frost.

Soldiers pose on a commandeered car *with red flags on their bayonets on February 27, 1917, the first day of full revolution, when cars and trucks added to the hazards of gunfire as they raced round the streets, overloaded with ecstatic troops. Mutineers seized the Rolls-Royce that was used as shore transport for the Royal Yacht, and drove about, tooting its horn.*

Churches were full. A large crowd started for the Nevsky, crossing the ice to avoid police on the river bridges. They ran into an infantry unit near the Moika canal at 1 pm. The troops knelt and fired two volleys into them. Then there was general firing in the Nevsky area. Ambulances raced along the boulevard and students in Red Cross armbands and white aprons gave first aid to the wounded. On Znamenskaya Square, the training unit of the Volynsky Regiment was ordered by its commander Captain Lashkevich to fire volleys into the crowd, killing a score. At a nearby school for young ladies of the nobility, the girls heard a mistress use an unfamiliar and thrilling word: 'Revolt'.

As the crowds were cut down, Alexandra was visiting Rasputin's grave. 'It seems to me that it will all be all right,' she wrote to Nicholas at 3.30 pm. 'The sun shines so clearly and I felt such peace and quiet at His dear grave. He died in order to save us.' An Okhrana agent was less certain. The game depended entirely on the behavior of the army, he reported. 'If the troops turn against the government, then nothing can save the country.' A long line of carriages and blazing lights marked the venue of Princess Radziwill's glittering party. The regime still had a few hours left.

The Volynsky guardsmen who had shot down demonstrators on the orders of Captain Lashkevich held a meeting on Sunday night. They decided that they would not act as 'executioners' and would 'join the people'. At 7 am on Monday morning, cartridges were issued and the unit formed up on parade in battle order. Lashkevich arrived with orders. He was met with mutiny. 'We won't kill any more. Enough blood!' From a barracks window a shot rang out and Lashkevich fell dead.

The Volynskys had to spread their mutiny quickly to evade the firing squad. Rifles were seized from the battalion stores and the men fired in the air, the shots audible from the British embassy. No response came from the officers. Colonel Viskovsky, the commanding officer, suggested that his officers go home and took his own advice.

A grey disorderly mass spread from the barracks, carrying ragged banners. The wedge of the city round it was the sacred place of Russian arms. It held artillery and engineering schools, cavalry stables, parade grounds, guards regiments and their chapels, museums of the Napoleonic and Turkish campaigns, and the Nicholas Military Academy. An Academy officer, Sergei Mstislavsky, looked over clotheslines and their freight of frozen shirts and uniforms to small gray figures at the entrance to the Volynsky barracks. Rifle barrels glinted in the sun. He could hear shooting. Fleeing NCOs and officers made for sanctuary in the Academy. Other refugees arrived. They reported that the Preobrazhenskys, the oldest regiment in Russia, founded by Peter the Great, had bayoneted their colonel.

The Volynsky mutineers ran into a nearby engineer battalion barracks, shouting: 'Hurrah, comrades, get your rifles!' Voices cried: 'Cartridges too!' The locked doors of the storerooms were broken down, a shot rang out, and the quartermaster was killed. The engineers joined the uprising, marching to the Liteiny Prospekt, where their band played to cheering crowds and a soldier flapped his arms like a bird, screeching: 'We're going forward into the unknown!' The law courts were set ablaze. The gates of the main arsenal were battered in and the depot commander killed. Thousands of revolvers were handed out to the crowds. Teenagers swirled out of side streets, shouting and firing their new weapons at the pigeons on the streetcar wires.

The city governor, jaw trembling, demanded a plan from the police chief. The existing security plan divided the city into sectors, each under the control of a unit that was now mutinying. News came in that a squadron of armored cars, which had supposedly been disabled, were rumbling down the Nevsky with red pennants flying from them. A shock detachment was organised under a much-decorated officer, Colonel A. P. Kutepov. He scraped together six companies of riflemen, fifteen machineguns and a squadron and a half of cavalry. Kutepov said he needed at least a brigade. 'We're giving you all we've got,' he was told. Many officers, frightened of their troops or contemptuous of the government, made themselves absent, reporting 'sick'. Kutepov set off, an oil slick in a mutinous ocean.

Mutinous troops in Petrograd *at the height of the February Revolution. Their refusal to obey orders transformed a commonplace strike into one of the century's greatest events. Some murdered their officers; but most were good-humored. One group of soldiers approached a lieutenant and begged him to command them. 'We have to have a gentleman to give us orders', they explained.*

The wheels of change: *the courtyard of the Technological College in Petrograd during the February Revolution, with some private cars commandeered by the revolutionaries.*
[PHOTO: K. BULLA]

Civilians began to urge regiments to come out. 'Comrade soldiers!' they shouted to a battalion of the Moscow regiment, 'Come out: join the people.' The crowd broke down the picket fence and surged on the troops. The commander ordered his men to fire volleys and drew his revolver, shooting in the air. He was felled and beaten to death. The troops began to shoot at their own barracks while the crowd broke into the armory and helped themselves to rifles and cartridges. The Kresty prison was taken, and its 2400 prisoners were freed. Women convicts shuffled out of the Litovsky castle in prison gowns and carpet slippers. Policemen, identified by their long greatcoats and gray fur hats, were lynched. Station houses were set afire. Other potential targets of the mob fled. The prima ballerina Mathilde

Kshesinskaya, the former mistress of the Tsar, abandoned her art nouveau mansion with her fox terrier under one arm, and a case full of jewels in the other.

By late afternoon, with smoke from the burning law courts and prisons drifting across the darkening sky, only a handful of strongpoints remained in loyal hands. The American naval attaché reported a cavalry regiment riding quietly away and leaving the city to the mutineers. A lone police machinegunner was holding out on the roof of a house opposite the British embassy. The noise of automatic fire stopped with startling suddenness as he was found and killed by the soldiers. Hooligans and professional thieves celebrated the absence of police by careering round in hijacked cars, firing in the air, and stopping to break into bourgeois apartments. Countess Kleinmikhel was dining with Prince and Princess Kurakin five minutes from the embassy. They had started the first course when servants burst into the dining room. 'Run! Run!' they cried. 'Bandits' had broken into the building, wounding two doormen, and were making their way through the rooms. The countess led her guests out into the night to refuge in a house opposite. From there they watched fascinated as a group of soldiers and sailors were served their meal on silver plate and ordered up dozens of bottles of wine from the countess's cellar.

Alexander Kerensky was woken by his wife Olga at 8 am on Monday, February 27th. Kerensky was thirty-six, a Duma deputy and 'noisy lawyer flying high' who had found his moment. He was born in Simbirsk, which he remembered with affection. He had become involved in radical politics at St Petersburg in his teens, but had no time for fashionable terrorism or Marxism; he was 'unquestionably humanitarian and utterly Russian in every respect'. On graduation, he started a legal aid office in the city, advising workers on their rights and representing them without fees. In 1904, he married Olga Baranovskaya, the daughter of an army officer – his own mother was a general's daughter. During the 1905 revolution, he founded a socialist newspaper and served four months in the Kresty prison after a friend's revolver was found in his apartment. Kerensky was thrilled with his luck. 'The stigma of "bureaucratic descent" was removed under the showerbath in prison,' he said. 'I was now "one of us" in radical and socialist circles.'

In 1912, troops shot dead 170 striking miners in the Lena goldfields in Siberia. The massacre caused deep revulsion throughout Russia, and Kerensky made a national reputation

when he was appointed to the enquiry commission. He was elected to the Duma a few months later. The heavyweights in the smoking room thought him a 'puppy', for his speeches were emotional and left his 'whole body trembling with sweat pouring down the pale cheeks', but the gallery adored him. Almost alone, he denounced anti-Semitic atrocities. The war was a catastrophe for the Jews; scores of thousands fled from the combat zones and wandered in the snows, 'driven like cattle by platoons of Cossacks'. Not a day passed without Jews being hanged on trumped-up charges of spying, the French ambassador wrote – 'yet there are 240,000 Jewish soldiers fighting, and fighting well, in the ranks of the Russian army.' Kerensky went in person to Kuzhi, a small town near the front in Kovno where Jews were being lynched for supposedly hiding Germans in their cellars so that they could surprise Russian troops at night. He examined the cellars and proved the charge a nonsense.

His Okhrana nickname was 'Speedy' – and on the 27th he hurried through the mutinous city to the Tauride Palace where the Duma met. At about 1 pm, a flood of soldiers and workers, scraps of red on their coats, arrived at the palace. Kerensky greeted them. He had a quality of decision and emotion; an onlooker whispered: 'He is their *vozhd*, leader.' By mid-afternoon, two provisional committees were in existence in separate wings of the palace. One was dominated by moderate bourgeois members of the Duma, and would develop into the Provisional Government. The other was the first Petrograd Soviet to meet since 1905. Kerensky was a member of both. The Soviet elected a permanent executive committee drawn from all socialist groups; the Bolsheviks had two members out of the fourteen. It decided to publish its own daily newspaper, to be called *Izvestiya*.

At 8 pm on Monday evening, the Tsar was cabled a warning that only a handful of his troops remained loyal. A state of siege was proclaimed; the notices were skewered on railings, for lack of glue, and blew away in the night breeze. Kutepov's counterforce melted away into the crowd, and he walked home and ordered the door locked. But the mutineers also felt their position desperate. They feared that loyal troops would be sent from the front to crush them. The defenders of the Tauride Palace, the center of the revolution, had no weapons heavier than four non-functioning machineguns. A volunteer sent out to buy lubricants for them returned empty-handed because he had thought it rude to wake shop-owners late at night. But mutineers slipped into the deserted Maryinsky Palace. Grand Duke Mikhail demanded that loyal troops still holding the Winter Palace be withdrawn. He did not want the people to be fired on from the House of the Romanovs: no repetition of 1905. The disgruntled loyalists were turned out of their beds into the freezing Palace Square, and slipped away to their barracks. Exhausted politicians, wrapped in fur coats, sprawled on the armchairs and benches of the Tauride. Kerensky, his frock-coat spread out about him, was draped over a small couch, bent like a pretzel, his mouth wide open and snoring gently. A pair of soldiers cut Repin's famous portrait of Nicholas out of its frame high above the debating chamber with their bayonets. Mutiny, unparalleled in its rapidity and scope, had won.

The mutineers had the run of the city on Tuesday. Trucks with rifles and bayonets sticking from them 'like enormous hedgehogs' cruised the streets whilst looters broke into the palaces. Maurice Paléologue, the French ambassador, saw one of the Tsar's gigantic Ethiopians, his uniform discarded, shuffling in civilian clothes with tears pouring from his eyes. The ambassador sensed it was the end of an era stretching back to Catherine the Great. Nicholas himself spent the day on the imperial train, steaming slowly to join the Empress at the Alexander Palace. Shortly after midnight, the train was flung into reverse ninety miles short of the capital; the next station up the line was in rebel hands. In the early hours of Wednesday, March 1, after 303 years, a Romanov was fleeing from his people. The train halted at Pskov station. Here, in the silk-hung drawing room car, late on Thursday evening, March 2, 1917, Nicholas signed an act of abdication. He did so in pencil, 'as others do when they make a list of dirty laundry'.

The official death toll was 1224, the equivalent of a few hours-worth of casualties in the Great War; as well as those killed in Petrograd, Baltic fleet sailors had murdered scores of officers and petty officers, flinging them overboard into holes cut in the harbor ice. The Americans hailed the revolution as a 'fitting and glorious successor' to their own. US ambassador David Francis, a poker-playing banker from St Louis, said that it was the realisation of an American dream – 'I mean government by consent of the governed.' But there were effectively two governments in Petrograd; the Provisional Government, dominated by middle-class members of the Duma, and the Soviet of workers' and soldiers' deputies. They represented different classes and sharply different policies. The Soviet wanted an eight-

Limbless veterans *outside the Kazan Cathedral in Petrograd in the summer of 1917. Trucks and ambulances carried them through the streets in an attempt to arouse anti-German sentiment before Kerensky launched a final offensive in June.*

hour day, land hand-outs to the peasants, an army with voluntary discipline and elected officers, and an end to the war. The Provisional Government wished to continue the war and to keep social change to a minimum. The first prime minister of revolutionary Russia was Georgy Lvov, a prince and a landowner with the air of a country doctor.

Flag-bedecked 'revolution specials' returned political exiles from Siberia to triumphant receptions in Moscow and Petrograd. A consortium of banks raised half a million rubles for the welfare of the ex-terrorists, many of whom were committed to the overthrow of the banking system. Capitalism welcomed the revolution; London stockbrokers urged clients to buy oil and gold shares, whilst the *Economist* charted the rise of Russian 'Fives' on the bond market.

Lenin learnt of the revolution in Zurich. He did not at first believe the news. Stuck in miserable lodgings whose windows could only be opened when the neighboring sausage factory closed for the night, he had recently told a meeting that he did

not expect revolution in his lifetime and now his Bolsheviks had, for all practical purposes, played no part in it. The Party was marginal, riddled with informers, and he, its leader, spent his energy in internecine dispute with fellow socialists, attacking them with the violence that was his peculiar quality as 'ugly scum … blisters … pus'. But Lenin had great potential for the Germans. He was opposed to the war; return him to Petrograd, and he was certain to undermine the Russian war effort. Lenin had exhausted himself with wild schemes to return to Russia by aircraft, disguised as a Swede, pretending to be a deaf-mute. The Germans could return him in comfort, by railroad. 'It was with a sense of awe,' Winston Churchill wrote of Lenin's German paymasters, 'that they turned upon Russia the most grisly of all weapons. They transported Lenin in a sealed truck like a plague bacillus into Russia.' He arrived at Petrograd's Finland Station late at night on April 3 and gave a speech on the platform, a 'bright, blinding, exotic beacon'. In three sentences, it outlined the Bolshevik appeal and the growing contempt for the Provisional Government: 'The people need peace. The people need bread and land. And they give you war, hunger, no food, and the land remains with the landowners.'

In May Trotsky returned. Sentenced to life in Siberia for his part in the 1905 revolution, he had fled across the Arctic taiga in a reindeer-sled, guided by a local Zyrian so drunk that Trotsky had to kick him and take off his fur hat to keep him awake. After a week, taking notes on the wild life and the social habits of the few raw fish-eating inhabitants, he reached a railhead and was soon safely in Paris. He was deported during the war to Spain and then went to New York a few days after Rasputin's murder: 'It is dark. Cold. Wind. Rain. On land, a wet mountain of buildings,' he wrote. 'The New World!' News of the revolution came to him in the $18 a month apartment he was furnishing on the installment plan on 164th Street in the Bronx. He left with regret; he thought the city the 'fullest expression of our modern age'.

The war continued, 'a great pump which sucks out the strength of the country'. Alexander Kerensky had become war minister in early May. He was idolised at mass meetings for the war effort where women in a 'hysteria of emotion' threw their jewelry at his feet. Bruce Lockhart, British diplomat and secret agent, thought him the most powerful speaker he was ever to hear – and that included Hitler. By the end of June, Kerensky's summer offensive was a disaster. Regiments dissolved as thousands of deserters streamed away from the front, killing any officer who tried to stop them. Behind the front, the few civilians left had faces 'idiotic with fear' and the women 'snatched their greasy skirts and fled' when they saw soldiers. Further back, trains were so overloaded with deserters that car axles caught fire from the weight. The stations, swarming with uniforms, resembled 'open hives of gray-brown bees' and stank like vast

Bolsheviks involved in the 'July Days', *their first abortive coup in 1917, await sentencing (left). Lenin fled to Finland; others, including Leon Trotsky, were arrested and imprisoned. Nikolai Krylenko is sitting in the middle of the front row. Four months later, this former ensign, a 'degenerate of the most repulsive type', would be commander-in-chief of the Russian armed forces.*

The men who ended an empire. *The soldiers' section of the Petrograd Soviet meet in the State Duma (right). The Soviet, containing representatives of all shades on the Left, was not yet the tool of the Bolsheviks, as proved by the banners in this picture. The one top left reads 'Down with Lenin'; another, 'War for freedom of Nations ... to complete destruction of German militarism'.*

A Women's Death Battalion, *so-called, takes an oath of allegiance on flag and ikon in Moscow in June 1917. They were formed, to shame the male deserters who were destroying the Russian army as a fighting force, by the remarkable Maria Bochkaryova. She had slept with the governor of Yakutsk to save her husband from being exiled for terrorism after the 1905 revolution. To rid herself of the humiliation, she successfully petitioned the Tsar to join the army in 1914, and was a three times wounded sergeant. In the event, the women saw little combat; the 'storming' of the Winter Palace by the Bolsheviks was the nearest most came to action. In the picture above volunteers for the battalion queue to have their hair cut to military length.*

latrines. The men of a bomber squadron sabotaged the aircraft by weakening the struts since they did not want the pilots to annoy the Germans.

The fiasco at the front hurried the Bolsheviks into a premature rising, the July Days, as it was called. The men of a machinegun regiment infiltrated by Bolshevik agitators marched through the capital, urging the overthrow of the Provisional Government and the hanging of Kerensky. A mob joined them, whose 'insane, dumb, beastlike faces' terrified bourgeois Petrograd. Regiments loyal to the government were drafted into the city and the attempt to force an issue failed. Details of German payments to the Bolsheviks were leaked to the press; headlines screamed that Lenin was a Berlin agent. He fled, hiding up in a haymakers' hut before crossing the border into Finland. Trotsky was arrested, and returned to the Kresty prison.

On July 21 Lvov resigned and Kerensky formed a new government which busied itself with foreign relations and constitutional reform, whilst Russia disintegrated. Food was scarce and money flooded off the presses, 476 million rubles had been printed in April, a billion were printed in July. Inflation was reaching 1000 per cent. Government printing plants could no longer guillotine individual notes; they were issued in sheets and people cut out notes with scissors. In the factories, the men 'come to work drunk, speak at meetings drunk … They drink methylated spirits, varnish and all kinds of other substitutes'. In Tambov province, peasants ran Prince Boris Vyazemsky off his estate and looted his house. At the railroad station, deserters discovered him. They ran him through with bayonets and finished him off with iron ties. Then they cut off his head.

Power, Sukhanov recalled, was 'hanging in the air'. Kerensky had the trappings of authority – he used the imperial train, he lived in the imperial suite in the Winter Palace, he slept with his mistress in Alexander III's bed – but not the substance. His commander-in-chief, General Lavr Kornilov, a wiry Cossack, mounted a confused Rightist coup in early September against the Government, with a division of Caucasian mountain troops. It did not reach Petrograd; the rail line was cut, agitators worked on the men as they milled round the track. The 'counter-revolution' collapsed; Kornilov was placed under house arrest whilst the general who had led the troops on his behalf shot himself.

The Bolsheviks were rehabilitated by the blundering Cossack reactionary and Kerensky was isolated. Officers, tainted with Kornilov's counter-revolution, lost all control of their men. Louise Bryant, a young American correspondent, arrived at the docks in Vyborg to watch soldiers on the adjacent railroad platform shouting: 'The officers! The bright, pretty officers!' 'They threw them in the canal,' she filed to the *Philadelphia Public Ledger*. 'They have just finished it now. They have killed fifty and I heard them screaming.' In the rear, two young officers disguised as soldiers were flung from a train into a gorge, 'falling like dolls', betrayed by the *burzhui* hairbrushes in their kit. At the front, troops fraternised with the Germans, who gave them tobacco and wine. Russia was breaking up. Nationalist

Antiques and paintings *are packed up in the Catherine Palace, after Nicholas II and his family were transferred in August 1917 from Tsarskoe Selo outside Petrograd to Tobolsk in Siberia. The train carrying them was marked 'Japanese Red Cross Mission' for fear that deserters or Leftists would attack them.*

movements rolled through the Ukraine, Finland, the Baltic States. Cossacks, Bashkirs, Siberians, Buryats declared themselves independent. Racial hatreds stirred. Jews felt the 'bloodstained specter of the Middle Ages' to hang over their heads. 'The pogrom movement is mounting,' the *Russkiye Vedomosti* correspondent in Bessarabia reported. 'Talk is heard of shifting all the blame onto the Jews.'

Kerensky took brandy and morphine. 'He really is hysterical,' his secretary told Louise Bryant. 'He weeps and he is so dreadfully alone. I mean, he cannot depend on anyone.' There had still been no elections for the Constituent Assembly, the parliament promised since March; a pre-parliament was the nearest point reached. Committees had examined the American, Belgian and Swiss constitutions in their search for perfection;

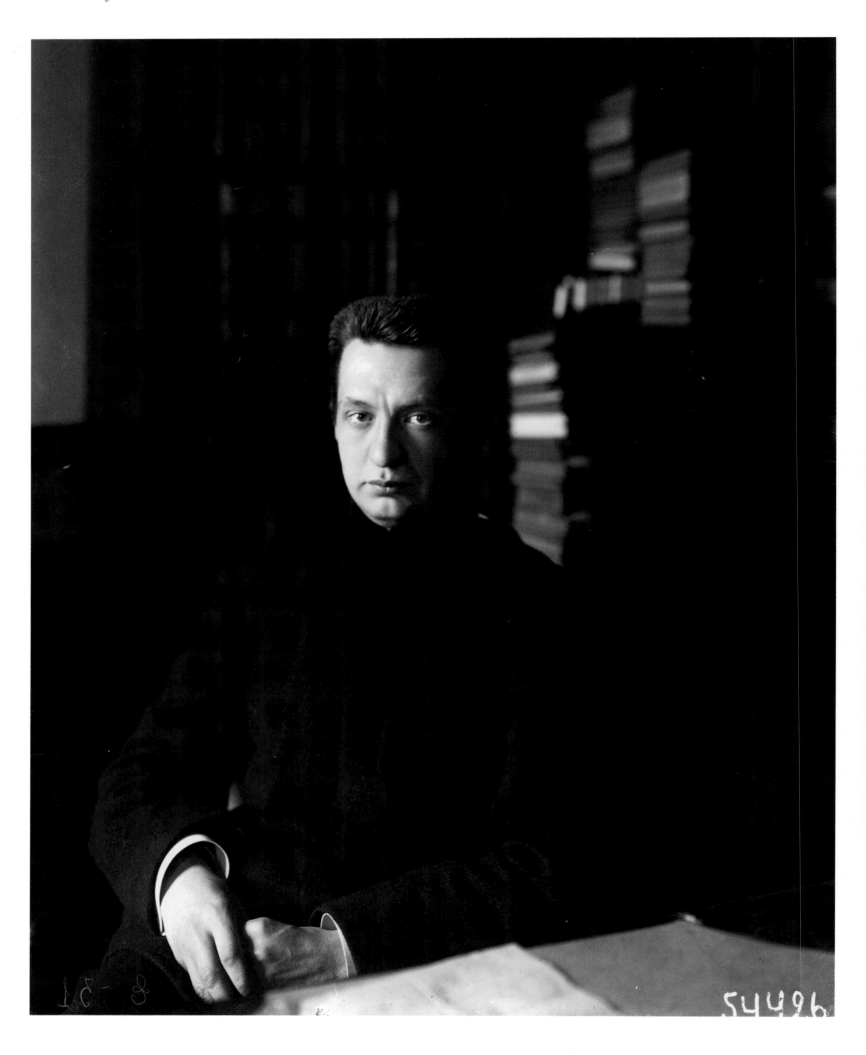

Alexander Kerensky
(opposite) was a 36-year-old lawyer, who specialised in defending difficult political cases, when the Revolution hurtled him upward to become Russian leader, first as war minister, then as prime minister of the Provisional Government.

'Famous leader of the bandits and hooligans' –
Leon Trotsky (right), with Lenin the leading spirit of the Bolsheviks, so described by the British secret agent Robert Bruce Lockhart: 'The very incarnation of a bourgeois caricature of a revolutionary ... all temperament.'

Lenin in disguise *(left) after the collapse of the July Days in 1917. The telltale beard has gone and he is wearing a wig to hide his balding dome. He was not an effective conspirator; his wig fell off and he was easily recognised by fellow politicians.*

Leon Trotsky in uniform *(opposite), with his trademark pince-nez, salutes at a celebration of the October coup. Lenin is on his right. Trotsky inspired the coup; his energy and his oratory saw it through. His fluent pen later turned it into the heroic myth of Red October. In reality, only the odd armored car gave evidence to the indifferent masses that the government was being overthrown.*

they discussed the merits of proportional representation and an upper house – 'all Russia, it seemed, was just talking, talking.' Leon Trotsky, 'a four-kind son of a bitch but the greatest Jew since Jesus' in the eyes of the American Red Cross representative, was also a doer, and he had been released from prison.

RED OCTOBER

Chill rain fouled the streets with mud and slush, which lay untouched by municipal clearance gangs. Trams ran only intermittently. Damp winds blew off the Gulf of Finland, but there were no warm clothes in the shops, just window after window full of flowers, corsets, dog collars and false hair, bourgeois objects for which there was no demand. Queues started at 4 am, for bread, sugar and tobacco. On September 25, Kerensky appointed a new cabinet. It was the fourth Provisional Government, the third coalition and the seventh major reshuffle since the revolution. Reval, the last stronghold between the Germans and Petrograd, was evacuated by the Russians on October 3. It was asked daily when the government was going to

evacuate the city. Barges were filled with the treasures from the Hermitage and sacks full of papers from the ministries. One sank. 'Nichevo,' said watching soldiers as it went under, 'It doesn't matter.' Every day hundreds of thousands of 'hungry, tired and angry people' listened to Bolshevik propaganda. It was the simplest message, as paraphrased by Sukhanov: 'The rich have lots of everything, the poor have nothing. Everything will belong to the poor ...' It did not matter that it was lies. 'After all,' wrote the young poet Boris Pasternak, 'what everybody needed were not empires, but bread, salt and paraffin.'

Trotsky, the 'famous leader of the bandits and hooligans', caused a sensation at the pre-parliament. He accused the government and the bourgeoisie of encouraging the 'bony hand of hunger' to strangle the revolution. He said they were preparing to surrender the capital as part of a government 'conspiracy'. That drew fury from the right, shouts about Germans, sealed trains and a cry of 'Bastard!' Then he and the Bolsheviks walked out. Sukhanov thought that they were 'now taking up arms against the entire old world'. In 'ruined, half-wild, petty bourgeois, economically shattered' Russia, this small party was trying to create an unheard-of proletarian state and a new society. They had 'put an end to the united front of the democracy for ever'. Civil war would surely follow. Bloodlust and class hatred were running strong. Manors were burning, figures of the old regime were being casually murdered by mobs. In a village near Baku, half a dozen ragged deserters bayoneted an elderly general, who had told them: 'This is my single fault. I love Russia, I love my people, I demand that you let me go!' They did not like his use of the word *demand*. The mob turned on the two ladies with him and trampled their bodies 'like a manure heap.' The civil war implicit in the walk-out would, all those concerned knew well, extend throughout Russia.

Deception was essential for a Bolshevik takeover; Trotsky was brilliant in formulating its tactics. The country was in no mood for single party power. An uprising carried out under the slogan of the Soviet, Trotsky realised, was 'something quite different'. So, 'whilst moving forward all along the line,' he later explained, 'we maintained an appearance of defensiveness.' He could not do this with a properly convened Soviet Congress; there was not the slightest chance of a Bolshevik victory in a national Soviet election, so the existing Congress was cynically and illegally packed with Bolsheviks.

The decision to mount the coup was taken on October 10. Lenin had returned to the city, possibly disguised as a train driver. At 10 pm, he crossed the city for the first Central Committee meeting he had attended in three months. It was held in Sukhanov's snug flat in an art nouveau building at the Karpovka. The great diarist's wife, Galina, was a Bolshevik and had ensured that her husband would be late back that night. Twelve members took part, in wigs and make-up, glued-on mustaches and false beards. Lenin wore a wig of gray hair that came down deep on his domed brow. It had been ordered from a Helsingfors wigmaker who had worked for the Maryinsky Theater and whose normal clientele were aristocrats. He had been puzzled why Lenin insisted on a gray model, for most of his customers wanted to look younger. Lenin wore glasses and had shaved his beard. Zinoviev, his shock of hair a trademark, reversed the process by shaving his head and wearing a false beard. The Provisional Government's chance to arrest those plotting to overthrow it – the already famous Trotsky, Zinoviev, Kamenev, Kollontai, Lenin; and those who would only later stir the human conscience, the secret policeman Felix Dzerzhinsky, the Tsar-killer Yakov Sverdlov, the mass liquidator Joseph Stalin – was missed. Towards 3 am, Lenin took a child's squared exercise book and wrote a resolution in pencil stub in it: 'Recognising ... that an armed rising is inevitable and that its time has come, the Central Committee suggests that all party organisations be guided by this.' The exhausted conspirators broke off for a breakfast of black bread and cheese before setting off to pass the word, that now was the time to seize power.

Party agitators were not the only ones privy to the conspiracy; the newspapers 'shrieked it'. When the cabinet met on October 16, there was no deep alarm. They assumed that a coup was unlikely, since it had lost any element of surprise. Lenin was

exhausted by the strains of the conspiracy, the late hours. He dropped his wig returning to his hideout near the Finland railroad station and it had to be scrubbed with soap and water. He never got the hang of wearing his wig. 'He kept trying to straighten it,' said his Bolshevik landlady, Margarita Fofanova. 'And he was always asking people if he had got it on properly.' Everything played on his nerves. Sukhanov thought that Lenin's notions – the smashing of the credit system, the seizure of banks, parity of wages, factory workers administering a state – were 'so disproportionately few in comparison with the immensity of the tasks, and so unknown to anyone outside the Bolshevik party, that you might say that they were completely irrelevant.' Maxim Gorky described the coup plotters as 'crazed fanatics'.

On October 22, the commissar for the western front cabled Kerensky that: 'There is nothing left but to give up. Disintegration has attained its limit.' The newspaper *Russkiye Vedomosti* apologised to its readers that it could run only a fraction of the stories about mutinies and pogroms that flooded its newsroom each day. Kharkov, Tambov and Ostrog 'merge into one dark picture of murders, pillages, arsons and debauch.' Mobs ferreted for axes and crowbars to break into liquor cellars.

Landowners and shopkeepers suspected of speculation were beaten to death with clubs, and the 'same fate awaits Jews, just because they are Jews'.

In Petrograd, everything could be had for big money. The ten-minute cab ride from the French embassy to the Hôtel de l'Europe cost twenty times the pre-war rate. Soldiers were hired by the hour to stand in queues, and sold off their chocolate rations at twelve rubles the pound. Felix Yusupov, back in Petrograd from his brief exile in the south, found social life 'agreeable once more' and gave parties in his palace. Chaliapin was singing and the ballerina Karsavina was appearing in a new ballet at the Maryinsky. If the Bolshevik coup came, most thought it would fail. 'I only wish they would come out,' Kerensky told the British ambassador, 'and then I will put them down.' David Francis, the US ambassador, thought that an opportunity was being lost. 'Beginning to think the Bolsheviks will make no demonstrations,' he cabled Washington. 'If so, shall regret as believe sentiment turning against them and time opportune moment for giving them a wholesome lesson ...' No serious plans were made to cope with a coup.

At 5 am on October 24, military cadets acting on Kerensky's orders broke the page molds of Bolshevik newspapers and sealed the offices. Trotsky was jubilant: 'Kerensky is on the offensive.' He could accuse the government of counter-revolution. 'Although an insurrection can only win on the offensive,' he said, 'it develops better the more it looks like self-defense.' A few hours later, Bolshevik troops retook the offices without incident. The molds were re-poured and the papers came out four hours late. Kerensky cabled the front for additional forces, but hoped they would not be needed. He had 2000 cadets, 200 women soldiers and 134 unattached officers for policing duties. Trotsky was at the Smolny, the Bolshevik and Soviet HQ. A delegation from the city hall arrived during the afternoon to ask on behalf of the mayor whether the rising was taking place. Trotsky assured them that it was, though they could see little evidence. The rest of the city had come to a decision: that here there was to be no coup. Elegant figures in evening dress settled to watch Alexei Tolstoy's play *The Death of Ivan the Terrible* at the Alexandrinsky Theater. Opera buffs were in the Maryinsky listening to Chaliapin in *Boris Godunov*. The Restaurant de Paris was turning away diners without reservations. Cinemas, bars and night-clubs were all full.

Lenin paced the floor in his hideaway. At 6 pm he scribbled a note: 'Now everything hangs by a hair ... We must at all costs, this very evening, this very night, arrest the ministers ...' Shortly after 10 pm, he determined to make his way to the Smolny. He wore his wig and had added a large pair of spectacles, but had forgotten his make-up in his excitement. He wrapped a handkerchief round his face as if he had toothache, then he caught a tram part of the way, arriving at the Smolny shortly before midnight. The sentries at first refused to let him in; his pass was out of date. He contacted Trotsky, who found he looked 'quite odd'. Socialist opponents had no difficulty in spotting him. 'They have recognised us, the scoundrels,' Lenin said forlornly.

'A kindly old gent'. *US Ambassador to Russia David Francis was a St Louis banker whose 'knowledge of anything beyond banking and poker is severely limited.' He thought the Bolsheviks had no chance of retaining power after their coup, since they were 'altogether too crazy'; most observers agreed with him.*

The mood in the Smolny was far from revolutionary. It was 'gray. Faces were tired, dull, even gloomy.'

Small groups of Bolshevik troops moved out of their barracks in the early hours of Wednesday, October 25. They were visibly relieved at the lack of resistance. They took the Neva bridges, the main telegraph office, post offices, the railroad stations, the Central Bank and the power stations. It was unnecessary for them to attack a target – 'at best,' an onlooker noted, 'they surrounded them.' Not a shot was fired. When Kerensky woke, he found his telephone had been cut off and saw that the Winter Palace bridge was controlled by Bolsheviks. He decided to leave the city to raise loyal troops at the front to put down the coup. The government motor pool was out of action; Bolsheviks had removed the distributors during the night. An ensign was sent out to see if he could requisition an automobile that worked. The British embassy turned him down. So did Vladimir Nabokov, the cabinet secretary, who was having his morning bath, but the Americans were more generous. An embassy official, Sheldon Whitehouse, lent his, a Renault complete with chauffeur. Whitehouse was assured that he would have the car back as soon as Kerensky returned from the front with enough troops to put down the coup – 'within five days.' Kerensky's American driver became lost and had to stop for instructions. The route took the car through Bolshevik cordons that were supposedly sealing the city center. Kerensky, sitting in the open back of the tourer, was recognised by scores of pedestrians and rose to acknowledge them with salutes. On the outskirts, Kerensky said, a patrol of Red Guards 'came rushing towards our machine from all sides, but we had already passed them.'

Government ministers arrived at the Winter Palace by cab, whilst in the Smolny Lenin announced their overthrow. The city ignored Lenin's claim. Trams were running, the banks were open and factories were working. Troops in the cordons were bored, smoking and at ease. Sukhanov found the atmosphere 'quite frivolous' and unwarlike. The soldiers looked as if they would scatter at the first blank shot – 'but there was no one to do any shooting'. At 2.35 pm, Trotsky felt compelled to hold an extraordinary session of the Petrograd Soviet to prevent the Congress delegates drifting away in boredom from the Smolny. He claimed that the government had 'ceased to exist', as the

The partisan chronicler, John Reed *(below). This great, if hardly impartial, witness of Red October was born in Oregon, the son of a judge, and educated at Harvard. He helped to found the Communist Labor Party, later the Communist Party of the United States. He died of typhoid in Moscow in 1920 and is buried on Red Square.*

result of a movement of 'such enormous masses' for which there was no parallel in history. These were passing almost unnoticed in the streets as he spoke. The only sign of revolt was the odd armored car, siren blaring, with Bolshevik initials splashed in red paint on its gray body. Sukhanov was so unimpressed by it all that he went home to eat supper by the stub of a candle. He thought that any Bolshevik regime would be 'ephemeral'.

The 'siege' of the Winter Palace was so sloppy that the American journalists John Reed and Louise Bryant were able to stroll into the building during the afternoon. Palace servants in their Tsarist blue uniforms took their coats, and cadets were glad to show them round. Louise Bryant found them 'poor, uncomfortable, unhappy boys', reared in genteel isolation and now 'without a court, without a Tsar, without all the tradition they believed in'. Packing cases and mattresses littered the floors, with cigarette butts and empty wine bottles. Many of the defenders were drunk. A captain greeted the journalists, smelling of alcohol. 'I am very anxious to get away from Russia,' he said. 'I have made up my mind to join the American army.' Two cyclists arrived with a Bolshevik ultimatum threatening to open fire if the palace did not surrender by 7.10 pm. The ministers still had hopes that Kerensky would appear with reinforcements, and declined to give themselves up.

The coup did not interfere with the evening life of the city. The ministers in the Winter Palace supped on soup, fish and artichokes, and then ordered the palace lights to be put out. In the resulting confusion, among both besieged and besiegers, four cadets from the Constantine Academy were slightly wounded, probably by their own side. The Bolshevik-crewed *Aurora*, moored on the Neva, was ordered to open fire on the palace when a red light was shone from the Peter and Paul Fortress. The cruiser was fresh out of the dockyard after repairs, however, and had only blank ammunition. The fortress garrison could not find a red lamp, but at 9.40 pm, a purplish flare was seen going up from it and the *Aurora* turrets opened up with blanks. The cadets replied with machinegun fire until they realised that, for all the smoke and noise, no shells were falling on them.

The women's battalion loyal to Kerensky, declaring that its function was to fight Germans, left the palace. At about 11 pm, two live rounds were fired at the palace from the six-inch guns of the Peter and Paul Fortress. The explosions startled Vladimir Nabokov, the 18-year-old son of the cabinet secretary, and later the author of *Lolita*, who was writing a poem in the family house on the Morskaya. One shell missed the 1500-room target by several hundred yards. The other hit but did little damage. A few minutes later, the three-inch guns joined in with thirty-five rounds. Most fell in the river. Only one hit was recorded, which chipped a cornice. Ministers catnapped in the palace, or fielded telephone calls from well-wishers urging them to hold out until morning. Bolsheviks were found wandering in palace corridors, and disarmed without resistance. 'How many of them are there in the palace?' a minister asked. 'Who is actually holding the palace – us or them?' Nobody knew.

At 2 am on October 26th, a friend rang the justice minister
Malyantovich to ask how he was. 'Not bad, in cheerful spirits,' he
replied. He lay back on a divan to get some sleep, but shortly a
noise began to rise and draw nearer. The ministers grabbed their
overcoats. A cadet rushed in, drew himself up to attention and
saluted, excited but determined. 'What are the orders of the
government?' he asked. 'To fight to the last man?' Wearily, the
ministers shouted: 'It's not necessary! Its useless. No bloodshed!'
A little man, a wide-brimmed artist's hat pushed back on his long
red hair, flew into the room like a 'chip tossed up by a wave.' An
armed mob behind him 'filled up the room like water.' He
shouted in a shrill and jarring voice: 'I inform you, all you
members of the Provisional Government, that you are arrested. I
am Antonov-Ovseenko, a representative of the Milrevkom.'
Petrograd had fallen to the Bolsheviks.

Defending the Malachite Room: *Military cadets in the Winter Palace (above) and a women's battalion were almost the only forces to remain loyal to the Provisional Government in the capital during the Bolshevik coup on October 25, 1917. The barrel of a machinegun can be seen, bottom left. During the evening, groups of Bolsheviks gradually infiltrated the building. It was so large that defenders and attackers rarely caught sight of each other in its 1500 rooms.*

A group of telephone operators *(left) during the coup. The Bolsheviks forgot to cut off the telephones in the Winter Palace so the government ministers were able to keep in touch with supporters in the capital and in Moscow throughout the siege.*

Sailors who took part in the 'storming' of the Winter Palace *(top). There is also one soldier in the middle of the group. The Bolsheviks miscalculated how long it would take Red sailors to arrive in Petrograd from the Baltic Fleet so they were too late to play much of a role in Red October.*

Vladimir Antonov-Ovseenko *(above) at the time of the October coup. A former Tsarist officer who avoided a death sentence for inciting mutiny in 1905 by fleeing to Paris, he was in charge of Bolshevik strategy during the coup. He forgot to defend his own headquarters – but he did arrest the ministers in the Winter Palace. Two decades later, he was recalled to Moscow from Spain where he was serving as a commissar in the civil war, and shot.*

Electors cast their votes *(above) in November 1917 for the Constituent Assembly. Since February the Provisional Government had been promising free elections with universal suffrage for this Assembly, which was to be Russia's new parliament. When the Bolsheviks carried out their October coup, the elections were less than three weeks away and they did not dare cancel them. But they had no intention of abiding by a result which they knew would not favor them. Sure enough, they won only 24 per cent of the vote while the Social Revolutionaries got 40 per cent.*

The first – and only – sitting of the Constituent Assembly *(above) lasted for a few hours in the Tauride Palace in Petrograd on January 5, 1918. Lenin, 'excited and pale like a corpse', ostentatiously lolled in his seat before armed Red sailors broke up the session. Russian democracy was dead from this moment for three-quarters of a century.*

A Bolshevik propaganda truck *(left) during the elections for the Constituent Assembly.*

4
RED ON WHITE

In the weeks after the October coup the Bolsheviks strengthened their grip on first Petrograd and then Moscow, while openly telling the Russian armies to fraternise with the Germans. Anti-Bolsheviks drifted southward to the valleys of the Don and the Kuban, as did Kornilov, whose imprisonment had ended. The first units of the White counter-revolutionary volunteer army paraded at Novocherkassk on November 26, 1917. On December 2, the volunteers took Rostov in street fighting, the first major action of the civil war.

White recruiting was at first informal. Serge Obolensky, commanding a small group of volunteers in Yalta, came across a friend dressed in felt hat, dark suit, high buttoned boots, gloves, and a fine cane. He urged him to join the White cause, which he did, 'cane and all'. The Reds enlisted sailors from the Black Sea fleet and convicts freed from Yalta prisons. Both sides found it difficult to identify one another, since at this stage both wore old Tsarist-designed uniforms, and civilian clothes. Two men with rifles challenged Obolensky: 'Who are you?' 'We're Whites,' Obolensky observed. At that, the two opened fire and ran. 'We shot back,' said Obolensky. 'They missed and I think we missed.' He jumped over a wall for cover, and landed on top of a plump gipsy guitar player who had serenaded him at Petrograd parties.

Large units of sailors from Kronstadt and the Baltic Fleet were sent by the Reds to track down Whites. Felix Yusupov was visited by sailors at his estate in the Crimea. They came with a banner reading 'Death to the burzhui', the bourgeoisie, and Yusupov noticed that one was wearing a diamond bracelet. When they discovered that he was Rasputin's murderer, they congratulated him and insisted that he sing to them on his guitar. He was lucky. The Reds were not usually sentimental with class enemies. When they took Yalta, they threw fifty White prisoners off the jetty that stretched out into the bay. Stones were tied to their feet, and on sunny days the corpses could be seen from the terraced slopes of the town, waving their hands with the currents. Burzhui learned to soak their hands in alcohol to crack the skin, and to rub dirt into them. Bolsheviks at checkpoints could shoot a man if his hands were soft. The Whites were as free with atrocity. An officer who found a prisoner wearing Obolensky's looted overcoat — it had the English maker's label sewn in it — shot him on the spot.

The Red army was formally established by a decree signed by Lenin on January 28, 1918. The Red air force was formed from the Russian Flying Club in Petrograd, with electricians from the local tram depot drafted in as mechanics. Trotsky became commissar of war in March. Together with Dzerzhinsky's Cheka, the props of Bolshevism were in place. Trotsky's task was 'to arm

Speaking for the Revolution, *Leon Trotsky addresses the faithful from a makeshift podium of park benches in Red Square, close to the site of the mass grave of those killed in the fighting in Moscow which followed the Bolshevik coup. Trotsky became the main Red commander in the civil war unleashed by the coup. He traveled from front to front in a special train rallying and bullying the Bolshevik troops. The Reds relied heavily on bourgeois officers and specialists. 'Some came over to our side out of fear, some came for the novelty; others came because they had no alternative – they had to earn a living,' wrote Nikita Khrushchev. 'And some came out of treachery.'*

Labeled a Traitor: *the Red Cossack Mironov under guard shortly before his execution. He was one of the best Red commanders in the civil war, and popular with his men. But he was too independent and clashed with Trotsky, among others. He was accused of treason and then shot. He is still wearing the Order of the Red Banner that he had been awarded.*

the revolution', from a shabby room with a desk and a couple of cheap chairs, 'partitioned off like a poor artist's studio', on the top floor of the Smolny. He had to build his new army from scratch. Few former officers volunteered to join the Reds, so Trotsky conscripted them as *voenspets*, military specialists. The Red army was to have more than 40,000 of these bourgeois officers, more than the Bolsheviks could create from their own workers and peasants, and 250,000 former Tsarist NCOs. Many thought the voenspets to be untrustworthy class enemies; they were accepted only on the basis that the Party would 'squeeze them like lemons and then throw them away'. Political commissars were appointed to preserve ideological purity, and to spy on them; Trotsky called it the 'iron corset'. Every professional officer down to company commander was shadowed by a commissar; no order was valid unless it was signed by both. The commissar could have his commander shot on suspicion of treason. Officers had no insignia and no official rank. Harsh discipline and the death penalty made it clear, however, that the heady days when soldiers' committees had run their units and elected officers were over.

By the summer of 1918 only the inner core of European Russia, roughly the area of the medieval Grand Duchy of Moscow, was firmly under Bolshevik control. The Germans had moved through the Baltic states and were helping the nationalist Gustav Mannerheim defeat the Red Finns. In the Kuban, General Kornilov had been killed by a Red shell at Ekaterinodar. The Reds dug up his body, hung it from a tree and kicked it round the streets before burning it in a slaughterhouse. General Anton Denikin had taken command of his volunteers. Groups of Whites set up provisional governments in Siberia, where a corps of anti-Communist Czech legionnaires was loose. They numbered 40,000, and included ex-POWs and deserters taken on the Austrian front who had been released and armed to fight for Czech independence from Austria. Trotsky had agreed that they could travel to France to resume fighting the Germans, Austria's allies, by way of the Trans-Siberian railway and the Pacific. The Germans objected to this. Czech relations with the Bolsheviks degenerated into outright hostility after a local Soviet arrested a group of them in May 1918 for brawling in Chelyabinsk, a Urals town. The Czechs seized part of the railroad and linked with Admiral Kolchak, a former Black Sea fleet commander, and his Whites. The Western Allies were aiding the Whites, hoping to recreate a Russian front against Germany. British, French, American and Japanese troops were landed on the Russian periphery, near Archangel in the north, in Vladivostok in the east, and on the Black Sea and Caucasus to the south.

A small force could saunter through swathes of the toppled empire, its towns starving, packs of deserters roaming the countryside. The Czechs made a formidable strike force against incoherent Red units; former colonels served as platoon commanders and Junker cadets as ensigns in experienced White all-officer battalions. Revolutionary was distinguished from reactionary by the five-pointed stars and pointed hats of the Reds,

Ex-Tsar Nicholas saws wood in captivity at Tsarskoye Selo with Pierre Gilliard, his children's tutor. Nicholas had always enjoyed physical exercise. He and the family volunteered to work during their captivity. 'At two o'clock we all went into the garden,' he wrote in his diary. 'Everyone set about digging with great zeal and even joy, and worked without noticing the time until five o'clock.'

chosen by Trotsky after a design competition, and the epaulettes of the Whites. Within two months, stiffened with Whites, the Czechs controlled most of the Trans-Siberian.

Their success was a death sentence for Nicholas and his family. The Bolsheviks had transferred them in April for safekeeping to Ekaterinburg, nine hundred miles east of Moscow on the far slopes of the Urals. The Party did not want to give the Whites any 'live banner to rally round'. They had begun to murder every Romanov they could find, starting with Grand Duke Mikhail on the night of June 12. He and his English secretary were taken by Cheka agents from the hotel in Perm where they were being held, and murdered in nearby woods. The body of the Romanov who had been Tsar for a few hours fifteen months before was then thrown into a smelting furnace.

By mid-July the Czechs had outflanked Ekaterinburg. At 2.30 am on the morning of July 17 the imperial family were awoken in the 'house of special assignation' where the Cheka was keeping them, a merchant's home. They were told that they were being moved away from the approaching Czechs. Nicholas and Alexandra, their crippled son and four daughters, with three servants, the family doctor and Anastasia's pet King Charles spaniel, were led into the basement to wait for motor cars. A truck was parked outside the house. Its engine was running and served to muffle the firing and shouts as a Cheka execution squad shot and bayoneted them to death. The girls had jewels sewn into their clothes which deflected the bullets. The process may have taken several minutes. The bodies were dismembered and dumped in a mine shaft. Feeling it was not deep enough to hide their handiwork, the Chekists returned and were removing them

to another shaft when their truck got stuck in mud. The bodies were doused in sulfuric acid and thrown in a shallow grave. When they were identified by DNA testing in 1993, after being exhumed, it was found that the Tsarevich and Anastasia were missing. Ekaterinburg fell eight days after the murders.

On the same day that the ex-Tsar died, Cheka squads seized other Romanovs ninety miles away at Alapayevsk. Grand Duchess Elizabeth, Grand Duke Sergei Mikhailovich, and the three sons of Grand Duke Constantine were beaten and thrown, still alive, down a mine shaft. A peasant heard hymns being sung from the shaft, before they died of exhaustion and starvation. When the Whites found the bodies, the injured head of one of the boys was found to have been carefully bandaged with a handkerchief. In January 1919, four more Grand Dukes were executed in the Peter and Paul Fortress. Maxim Gorky pleaded for Nikolai Mikhailovich, a liberal and respected historian. 'The revolution does not need historians,' Lenin replied. Charles I of England and Louis XVI of France were brought to trial before execution. The Romanovs died, with their children and their pets, as in gangster massacres.

On August 6, 1918 the retreating Reds fled Kazan. Open plain lay between the Whites and Moscow. Trotsky steamed off to do battle in his armored train; he was to travel 65,000 miles in it over the coming three years, as his armies swelled to five million men. It mounted machineguns and light artillery, a printing press, radio for contact with Moscow, a sleeping car, horse boxes, ammunition wagons and a flat-bed for his Rolls-Royce command car. He thought the train to be the key to turning Bolshevik amateurs into soldiers. 'It needed good commanders, a few dozen

The imprisoned princesses: *Olga, Tatiana, Anastasia, and Marie after working in the gardens of Tsarskoye Selo in May 1917. Following the February Revolution they were confined here where they were expected to share the work of the household. After the October coup this period of house arrest changed to one of close imprisonment. In April 1918 they were moved to Ekaterinburg, where 'the Protocol of Execution' was sent in code on July 16.*

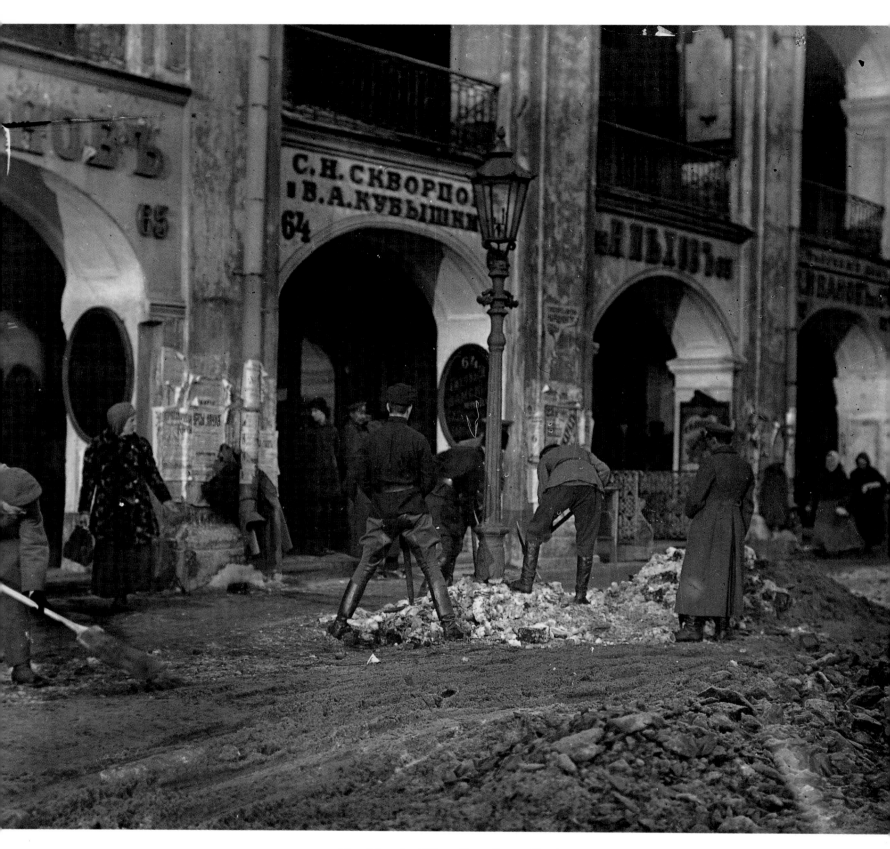

Humbling the Officer Class. *Former Tsarist officers are forced to clear the streets under guard. Public humiliation was part of a policy aimed at destroying the self-respect of the 'former classes'. 'Priests, officers, bankers, industrialists, monks, merchants – it's all the same,' the Cheka announced. 'Neither cassock, nor uniform, nor diploma can give them* *protection.' Many were taken to work camps sited behind the secretive walls of northern monasteries. One of the first was opened in 1919 at Khologory in the far north near Archangel. Many of the prisoners were executed; the survivors 'perished slowly and surely, of ill treatment and neglect'.*

experienced fighters, a dozen or so Communists ready to make any sacrifice, boots for the barefooted, a bath-house, an energetic propaganda campaign, food, underwear, tobacco and matches,' he wrote. 'The train took care of all this.' It pulled into Svyazhsk, a small town on the western bank of the Volga opposite Kazan. Reds were streaming west from the river, unkempt, rifles and uniforms filthy, eyeing their commanders murderously. Trotsky, dramatic with his shock of black hair, his black leather coat, his pince-nez, cried: 'I issue this warning. If any detachment retreats without orders, the first to be shot will be the commissar, the second the commander.' The joint leaders of a regiment that had pulled out were shot; the commissar, commander and every tenth man in a unit which had hijacked a steamer to flee were similarly disposed of. Trotsky could cajole, too; he carried large amounts of tobacco and a brass band aboard the train to perk up morale. The scattered Red forces in the Volga valley were rounded up into 'armies', though under strength and ill-equipped. Control of 1st Army was given to Mikhail Tukhachevsky, a 25-year-old aristocrat and former Guards officer who had escaped from a German POW camp at his sixth attempt the previous October. Trotsky counter-attacked in the middle of August, so short of troops that his leather-jacketed escort was pressed into the line. The Reds stormed Kazan on 10 September, with the help of Kronstadt sailors, and two days later Tukhachevsky took Simbirsk.

The terror meted out to the Romanovs became general policy in September after Lenin was shot in the chest and neck by a young SR, Fanya Kaplan. 'I have long had the intention of killing Lenin,' she said before her execution. 'In my eyes he has betrayed the revolution. I was for the Constituent Assembly and still am.' She was partly successful; Lenin never recovered full health, but the attack was the pretext for Red Terror. The decree proclaiming it, on 5 September 1918, stated that all those involved with the Whites were to be shot. It was not necessary to have proof to condemn. 'We are not waging war against individuals,' a Chekist commander told his men. 'We are exterminating the bourgeoisie as a class. Do not look for evidence that the accused acted in deed or thought against Soviet power. The first questions that you ought to put are: To what class does he belong? What is his origin? What is his education or profession?' It was on this basis that a Cheka detachment led by a future prime minister of the Soviet Union, N. A. Bulganin, had already shot fifty-seven people in Yaroslavl.

The terror was ubiquitous for, amid the ceaseless regulations as Pasternak put it in *Dr Zhivago*, 'everyone had reason to feel he was guilty of everything, that he was an impostor, an undetected criminal ... People slandered and accused themselves, not only out of terror but of their own free will, from a morbidly destructive impulse ...' In 'dumb, dark, hungry Moscow' people were dependent on the illegal black market and its *meshochniki*, its bagmen, to survive. Men and women of the old regime offered artificial flowers, black net evening dresses and uniforms of offices that had been abolished. Simpler people dealt in more useful things, 'spiky crusts of stale rationed black bread, damp,

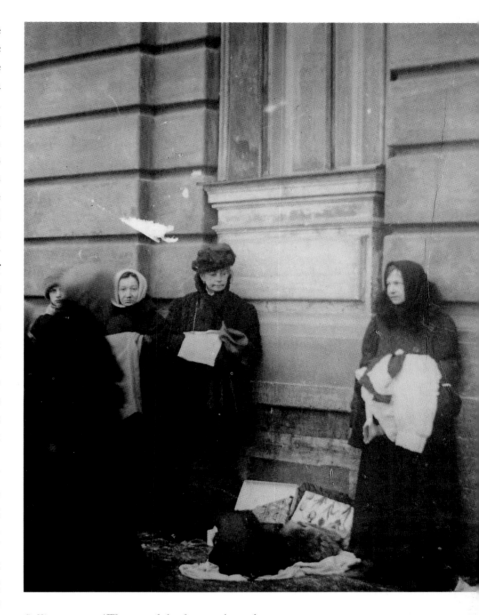

Selling to eat. '*Women of the former classes*' *sell their possessions on the streets of Moscow. During the civil war, people depended on the black market to live. Women of the old regime sold artificial flowers, silver thimbles and buckles, Court medals and other mementoes of their former lives to earn enough to eat.*

dirty chunks of sugar and ounce packets of coarse tobacco …' Typhus added to the horrors of starvation; millions of acres of grain were left unharvested to rot in the autumn, amid a plague of mice. Industry collapsed under enforced nationalisation and regulations that were 'ever more lifeless, meaningless and unfulfillable as time went by'.

The war went better. The Germans and Austrians pulled out of Russia and the Ukraine after the armistice on the Western front, selling their rifles to the Reds for a mark each and their field guns for 150. The Allies continued to support the Whites. 'Having defeated all the tigers and lions,' Winston Churchill said, 'I don't like to be defeated by baboons.' Trotsky's reputation soared after Kazan, to the disgust of the Reds downstream on the Volga in Tsaritsyn. The local commander, Voroshilov, and his commissar, Joseph Stalin, had driven off a White attack; unimpressed, Trotsky recalled Stalin to Moscow. The humiliation was not forgotten; Trotsky and countless 'Trotskyites' would be murdered in one of the most violent hatreds of the century. Tsaritsyn would be renamed Stalingrad.

Nineteen nineteen was the decisive year. The Whites launched four offensives; from the south under Generals Denikin and Wrangel; from out of Siberia under Admiral Kolchak; from Estonia under General Yudenich; and from Archangel with the British-backed troops of General Miller. The attacks were uncoordinated, allowing Trotsky to switch troops from front to front by rail; and, as the Reds were compressed into their Russian heartland, their lines of communication grew shorter as the Whites outran their strength. The fighting was bitter, desertion and treachery commonplace. At Kharkov, the Reds nailed the epaulettes of captured officers into their shoulders. The writer Mikhail Sholokov, who experienced the civil war in the Don country, described how an escort of Red Cossacks murdered its officer prisoners. A cry went up: 'Cut them down … Damn them!

The decisive year *of the civil war. Wounded Reds (right) in 1919 in western Russia. The Whites moved toward Moscow and Petrograd on several fronts, but weakened as they advanced beyond their base areas, whilst the Reds were strengthened as their fronts compressed and the distance between them was reduced.*

Armored trains in defense of Petrograd *(below). In October 1919, Nikolai Yudenich's Whites were so close to the city that they could see 'even the trains pulling out of the Nikolai station'. But Trotsky rallied the Reds and the Whites were driven back. Trotsky's own armored train was only derailed once, although this was what made the trains most vulnerable.*

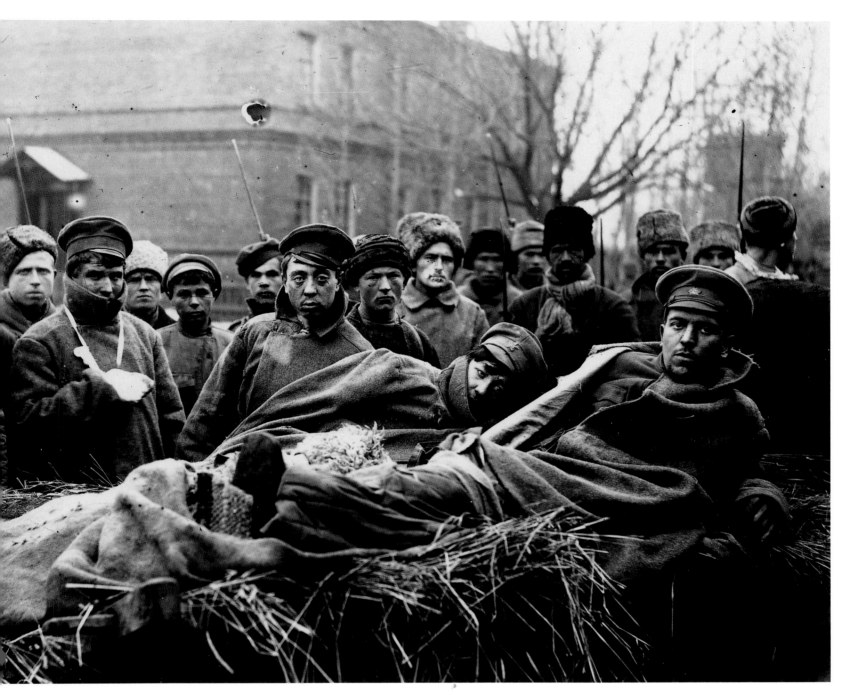

Damn all of them! We take no prisoners!' An officer fell on his knees while 'flying blades played over his face.' Another was shot through the back, 'running with his coat flapping in the wind', then 'squatted down and grabbled with his fingers at his breast until he died …' The White general Peter Wrangel shot 300 of the 3000 Reds he captured at Sevastopol, to encourage the rest to desert to his cause.

Gangs of 'Greens', independent looters, savaged areas in which no Red or White writ ran; 'a comet with a filthy tail of robbery and rape' said Trotsky of a Don Cossack band. Anarchists under the Ukrainian Nestor Makhno swore to exterminate both the 'rich bourgeoisie and the Bolshevik commissars'. Regiments changed sides; so did cities, Kiev more than ten times. Individual White governments issued their own currency notes; the areas on the periphery proclaimed their independence, Georgia, the Ukraine, the Baltic states, Azerbaijan, Armenia. Wars were fought on the

railroads between 'dreadnoughts', heavily armed trains that steamed to seek one another out across the plains.

Trotsky thought that Kolchak's advance from Siberia was the greatest threat. He installed himself at the front, returning briefly for a dramatic appearance in full uniform straight off his train at the founding congress of the Communist International. The Comintern, devoted to the global spread of Communism, was more menacing on a Moscow stage than in reality.

The Whites were making gains on all fronts as the congress opened. By the late spring, however, Kolchak was overextended and the Reds had outflanked him to seize the passes through the Urals. They consolidated their positions with trenches dug by forced labor gangs made up of trainloads of 'former persons' sent to the front.

Kolchak fell back into Siberia, pursued by young Tukhachevsky. 'Twenty or thirty thousand resolute,

'All Russia was waiting for trains.' *Families moved from region to region looking for bread. Pedlars known as 'bagmen' swarmed along the railroads and rivers in tens of thousands. They bartered tools, nails, hinges and cloth for food in the villages. They kept Russia alive in the civil war; more than half the grain eaten in the cities came from them, buying and selling at prices tens of times higher than those officially set by the Bolshevik government. Labeled from late 1918 as 'enemies of the people' because of their 'petty bourgeois greed', they fell victim to the Cheka for breaking Bolshevik regulations.*

ю. з.

322203.

29.ОКТ.19

Red victors near Vladivostok (*left*). *In 1920, as the Americans withdrew from the extreme east, a raggletaggle detachment of Red Guards reached Vladivostok. Their equipment had been picked up from retreating Whites. They lived off the land with no need for logistic support. The Whites sold off Allied aid to civilians. The prostitutes in towns held by Whites wore British nurses' uniforms and stockings.*

comprehending, well-armed Europeans could, without any serious difficulty or loss, have made their way very swiftly along any of the great railroads which converged on Moscow,' Winston Churchill complained. True, no doubt; but Kolchak's forces were disintegrating through typhus, hunger and lack of will. A regiment went over to the Reds en masse after murdering its officers.

Trotsky was free to turn his attention to the south. The British repaid the compliment by sending a British-crewed bomber to kill him at a meeting he should have attended in Tsaritsyn, but the commissar was not in town that day. Wrangel broke into the future Stalingrad on June 30, supported by British-supplied tanks and armored cars. A victory Te Deum was sung in the cathedral, which the Reds had used as a store dump. On October 13, grinding down Trotsky's 'barefoot, naked, hungry, lice-ridden army', Denikin took Orel. The Whites were less than 200 miles from Moscow.

They were closing on Petrograd, too. Though the British were not formally at war with the Soviet government, they were determined, in Churchill's words, to 'strangle at birth' the infant Bolshevik state. Royal Navy torpedo boats sank the Red cruiser *Oleg* in the Baltic and, under cover of a bombing raid by British aircraft, sank two battleships and a destroyer in the Kronstadt naval base that guarded the approaches to Petrograd. Two forts went over to the Whites; Joseph Stalin, the ranking Bolshevik in the city, had sixty-seven officers of the Kronstadt garrison executed as an example.

At a Politburo meeting on October 15 Lenin proposed abandoning Petrograd to concentrate remaining Red strength round Moscow. The possibility of deserting Moscow for the Urals was also discussed. Trotsky argued that Petrograd, 'cradle of the revolution', could not be deserted and set off for it in his train the next day, as Whites moved down the long avenue, strewn with yellow leaves, in the park of the imperial palace at Gatchina, twenty miles south-west of the city. The city defenders were panicked by the rattle of Yudenich's British-built tanks on the city outskirts on October 20. The Whites could see the whole city, 'even trains pulling out of the Nikolai station, the white plumes of their steam trailing across the brown landscape as they hurried toward Moscow.' Trotsky harangued his men from horseback: 'This beautiful Red Petrograd remains what it has been. The torch of revolution.' They fought with what Yudenich called 'heroic madness' and within three days he was retreating through Gatchina.

In the south, the Whites were collapsing, too. The Reds took Kursk in early November as Denikin fell back toward the Black Sea. Defeat was as much moral as military. Pogroms of Jews took place in areas under White control. 'The inner soul festered in an atmosphere of hatred,' Denikin said. 'They affected the spirit of the troops, warped their minds and destroyed discipline.' Wrangel said that, although his men still had Allied supplies and Cossack bread, their 'moral bases had already been destroyed.' In the nightclubs, the Red writer Ilya Ehrenburg saw drinking bouts ending with White officers 'shooting at fellow customers, at mirrors, or in the air ... The more they shouted about their strong nerves, the more it was clear that their nerves were giving way; and the goal was vanishing behind a fog of alcohol, hatred, fear and blood.'

The British abandoned Kolchak; the prime minister, David Lloyd George, said that anti-Bolshevism in Russia faced a 'prolonged and sanguinary struggle' in which the Allies should play no further part. Kolchak in turn fled Omsk on November 14, with his mistress and the imperial gold reserve. He moved east on the Trans-Siberian, a slow journey since the line was choked with broken locomotives and flatcars filled with Czech booty. Firefights broke out between Whites and Czechs over the pumps where water had to be thawed out before it could be transferred into the locomotives. On the *trakt*, the rough road along the line, refugees and soldiers toiled on foot with typhus and the cold thinning their ranks. On January 15, 1920, the Reds caught up with the admiral at Irkutsk. They had done a deal with the Czechs who, in return for safe conduct to move east, handed over Kolchak, his mistress, staff officers and the remains of the gold reserve. The following day, as the Czech trains steamed on for Vladivostok, the Allies lifted their blockade of Soviet Russia. In the pre-dawn gloom of February 7 Kolchak was taken from prison and shot by the headlights of a truck on the banks of the Angara. His body was pushed into a hole in the ice.

Twelve days later, the White front at Archangel collapsed and General Miller left the city on an icebreaker. The Whites in Murmansk fled into Finland. To the south, Odessa fell on February 7, Allied evacuation ships steaming out of the port with Whites clinging to their gangplanks. Denikin's force in the Kuban fell back on Novorossisk, hoping to be evacuated by sea to the Crimea. Cossacks shot their horses and tore at them for food whilst they waited for Royal Navy ships. Red guns were shelling the port as men were clubbed off overloaded destroyers with rifle butts and drowned trying to swim out to the ships. Officers abandoned on the quays shot themselves as 50,000 steamed off for the Crimea. The town fell on March 27, the Reds taking 22,000 prisoners.

The remnants of Denikin's army fought on in the Crimea under Wrangel, tall in high Cossack hat, the 'black Baron' of Bolshevik agitprop. He was given new life when the newly independent Poles attacked the Bolsheviks, sweeping through the Ukraine to take Kiev on May 7. Trotsky transferred the bulk of the Red army to the west, where it pushed forward against the Poles under Tukhachevsky. The Reds were less than fifteen miles from Warsaw on August 14, and foreign diplomats were evacuated from the city. Then a Polish counterattack outflanked Tukhachevsky and three Red armies broke up in shock. Driving the Reds back to Minsk during September, the Polish leader Josef Pilsudski, a former Siberian exile, negotiated an armistice: the Russians would wait until 1939 to take their revenge.

The full Red force was now applied to Wrangel. The Whites, shivering on the steppes, their shirts stuffed with straw and moss, fell back to the Crimea and the narrow isthmus at Perekop. The assault began on the third anniversary of Red October. Although White machineguns firing on fixed lines took a terrible toll, the Reds crossed the frozen marshes and broke through into the Crimea. A quarter of a million White soldiers and refugees escaped by ship to Istanbul and on the afternoon of November 4, 1920, Wrangel himself climbed aboard a motor boat on the Sevastopol quayside and was ferried to a waiting White cruiser with the name of the dead General Kornilov. 'We are going into exile,' the last White commander told his men on the quay. 'We are not going as beggars with outstretched hands, but with our heads held high …'

The flight into exile continued until a total ban was placed on emigration in 1926. How many millions of the vulnerable fled is not known; so many were vulnerable in Soviet Russia – priests, landowners, judges, police, civil servants, bankers, factory owners,

Aftermath of a massacre: *Kolchak's Whites' handiwork at Omsk before their defeat in 1919. Both sides committed atrocities undreamt of during the battles of the First World War. The civil war affected all who fought in it. 'Not only did the experience cripple the body,' General Denikin said, 'It deformed the soul as well.'*

A Red Hero of the civil war, *machinegunner Anton Bliznyak, in 1918. He was wounded thirteen times and lost an eye, as the stripes on his sleeve indicate. The cigar is a reward; Trotsky's armored train had special stowage for tobacco and cigars, rare items during the war, which he would hand out to troops who distinguished themselves.*

officers, stockbrokers, shopkeepers, grain merchants, oilmen, mineowners, 'speculators', the cocktail barman at the Petrograd Astoria, anyone who could qualify as burzhui, anyone who disagreed with Bolshevism, anyone who fought for the Whites, whether noble or peasant.

Many escaped through the port of Odessa, before it fell to the Reds, and made their way to Yugoslavia. Others got out through the Baltic states to Germany, where 'Russian Berlin' was the lively émigré capital. With a million per cent inflation, life was cheap for Russians who had escaped with gold and jewelry. The émigré writer Vladimir Nabokov was first published in Berlin; his father was murdered in the city by a right-wing Russian ex-officer. The cost of living rose sharply in 1924, when the mark was stabilised, and many Russians moved on to Paris, where they supplied a generation of cab drivers and artists. The great bass Fedor Chaliapin fled in 1922, declaring: 'The practice of Bolshevism proved even more dreadful than its theories … Bolshevism has become completely saturated with that awful intolerance and bigotry, that obtuse smugness which is Russian philistinism.'

A smaller number, including the young Nabokov, and the aircraft designer Igor Sikorsky, sailed to the United States and fame. Alexander Kerensky and the composer Sergei Rachmaninov were also to die in the US. Rachmaninov escaped

A pogrom perpetrated by Whites *(above). They carried on the Russian tradition of Jewish persecution and took pains to point out the number of Jews among the Red leaders, as did the Nazis later.*

Marc Chagall *(left), the painter (in front), survived the anti-semitic pogroms only to seek refuge in the West after he became disillusioned with the Bolsheviks. He left shortly after this picture was taken in 1923.*

via Sweden with a single small suitcase containing the score for his *Monna Vanna*; Red customs officials, searching for gold, thought the manuscripts were children's exercise books and let them through. Whites in Siberia fled to Manchuria, where the railroad city of Harbin acquired a huge Russian population. They moved on to China, where there were large Russian colonies in Sinkiang, and then on to Hong Kong and the US, Australia and Brazil. Romanov survivors, and Felix Yusupov, escaped aboard British warships. They included the Dowager Empress Maria and her daughters Xenia and Olga, the last of whom died above a barbershop in Toronto in 1960, and Nicholas II's first cousin, Grand Duke Cyril, who declared himself 'Tsar of all the Russias' in France and held court in a Breton village.

The battleship Petropavlovsk, *Kronstadt 1921. A commander at the salute among his men, while the band plays. This ship's crew played a large part in the Kronstadt tragedy.*

[PHOTO: A.M. SEDYAKIN]

KRONSTADT

The Bolsheviks had little to celebrate; the country was in ruins. Inflation led to a barter economy, where wages were paid in kind. Orphaned children wandered the streets in muggers' gangs. Spoil from pillaged apartments was sold in thieves' markets: amber, silver chains, Bristol glass, Bokhara rugs, cameos. In the countryside, 'iron detachments' of Bolsheviks seized grain and the horses and carts to transport it to the cities. The Volga had risen in revolt in 1919. In the Ukraine, the Grigoriev rising called on 20,000 men and six armored trains; as many as 40,000 marched under the black flag of the anarchist leader Makhno who, the Whites having fled, now transferred his attention to the Reds. In August 1920 the Antonov rebellion began overrunning Tambov province, demanding a return to the Constituent Assembly. Antonov was a former police chief who had acquired a hoard of arms and was leading a 'Green' revolt of 40,000 against the Reds who, the peasants felt, were destroying Russia. Antonov's men enjoyed dealing with captured Bolsheviks, especially Chekists; they would flay them, bury them alive, crucify them or throw them to wild dogs. They tore up railroad track to prevent Red troops from reaching them, and Lenin confessed that, 'We are barely hanging on.' He appointed Antonov-Ovseenko, the victor of the Winter Palace, as Commissar for Repression and sent him to the countryside. The new commissar reported in January 1921 that the peasantry was starving, living on acorns and nettles.

The peasant thought his dream had been achieved in 1917; it was one 'of living anarchically on his own land by the work of his hands, in complete independence,' as Pasternak's Dr Zhivago put it. But he found that he had only traded the old Tsarist oppression for 'the new, much harsher yoke of the revolutionary super-state.' The peasants reacted to food requisitioning by sowing less, so that food output by 1921 had fallen to less than half the 1913 level.

Disbanded Red army men, with axes, bludgeons and pistols, roamed for food and plunder, setting up camps by railroad tracks amid old tree stumps overgrown with wild strawberries. Famine swept the Volga in 1921; in that year and the one following, it and the diseases that rode with it – typhus, typhoid, dysentery and cholera – would kill perhaps five million.

The towns were in crisis too. Industrial production in 1920 was a fifth of pre-war levels, despite the creation of Trotsky's 'labor armies'. Transport was chaotic, with bridges brought down in the civil war and coal-burning locomotives ruined by being run on wood. Skilled metal workers in Petrograd were thought pampered on 800 grammes of black bread a day. The norm was 200 grammes. Cities were depopulated as people fled to the countryside for food. Abandoned houses were dismembered for firewood. Trains were packed with families aimlessly foraging for food. When a train stopped, the noise of the crowds outside 'rose to the pitch of a storm at sea' as people rolled down the banks 'like marbles' and jumped on the buffers or hauled themselves in through the windows. Between Red October and the high summer of 1920, the Moscow population halved. In Petrograd, it fell from 2.5 million to 750,000, a drop of two thirds.

Severe weather in the opening months of 1921 disrupted freight trains of food. A cut of one third was announced in the bread ration. Checkpoints were set up to prevent 'speculators' and bagmen from bringing in food to barter for gold rings, watches and ornaments. Zinoviev, the Party boss in Petrograd, used military cadets to break up food demonstrations. Many Red army men were thought unreliable and were disarmed and confined to barracks.

Kronstadt is the naval base on the eastern tip of the fortified island of Kotlin, lying in the Gulf of Finland, two hours' steaming at an easy ten knots from Petrograd. The shores of the island were – still are – protected by forts and batteries. It had a long tradition of revolt. The bomb which had assassinated Alexander II in 1881 was made by a Kronstadt naval officer. A mutiny in October 1905 was succeeded by a full-scale, but poorly planned insurrection the following July. A harsh regime of flogging and incarceration under Vice-Admiral Robert Viren followed, but during the night of March 1, 1917 he, together with fifty of the most hated naval officers and thirty police and their spies, was shot by firing squad. Kronstadt's Red sailors became Trotsky's 'pride and glory', black-uniformed heroes flung like shovels of concrete to stiffen the crumbling fronts of the civil war.

They were now on the verge of mutiny, because 'life under the yoke of the Communist dictatorship has become more terrible than death.' They objected to the suppression of freedoms, to the mass arrests that were following the big strikes in Petrograd, to the way that Bolshevik commissars and functionaries lived high on the hog in a hungry land. They were the stuff of revolution. To repress them would mark the final subjugation to the Party of the 'revolutionary battlers' of whom Bolshevik agitprop made so much, and of the industrial poor in whose interests they were protesting. Kronstadt marked the point at which Soviet rule solidified; the moment when the 'Socialist morality' became no more than the elevation of force into a system.

The vagrant dogs fared well. *A terrible famine raged on the Volga in 1921. Armand Hammer, the American industrialist who traded with the infant Soviet Union, recorded 'children with their limbs shriveled to the size of sticks and their bellies horribly bloated by eating grass and herbs.' The Americans were able to send aid – the Bolsheviks did not deny this famine, as they were to with later periods of mass hunger – but millions starved to death. Peasants who rose against Bolshevik rule in Tambov province were shot in batches.*

Orders for the assault *(top). Cadets and infantry were to advance across the ice to storm the rebel sailors in Kronstadt. The first attack failed, despite the Chekists shooting troops who wavered.*

Members of the press corps *who covered the storming of Kronstadt (above). The reason for the revolt – 'the nightmare rule' of Bolshevism – was suppressed. But the system of War Communism was relaxed; the labor armies were disbanded and private commerce was re-established in the New Economic Policy.*

On February 26, 1921 the crews of the dreadnoughts *Petropavlovsk* and *Sevastopol* sent a delegation to Petrograd to report on conditions in the city: 'One might have thought that these were not factories but the forced labor prisons of Tsarist times.' Two days later, a squadron meeting was held on the *Petropavlovsk*, a ship whose memory was to become as blank as the *Potemkin* was cherished. The men demanded freedom of speech and the press, free trade unions, and the liberation of political prisoners. A further mass meeting was called for March 1 in Anchor Square, a huge open space close to the Seamen's Cathedral, known as the 'Free University' for its tradition of fiery speechmaking. Kalinin, the president of the Soviet republic, was shouted down at the meeting and by midnight on March 2, the rebels had taken control of Kronstadt and its docks.

A three-man delegation from a naval air squadron based at Oranienbaum on the mainland crossed the ice to make contact with the mutineers. The squadron elected its own provisional revolutionary committee. In the early hours of March 3 a trainload of reliable military cadets surrounded the Oranienbaum barracks. Forty-five members of the squadron were led out and shot.

The mutineers in Kronstadt remained confident. The city had 135 cannon and 68 machineguns. The two battleships had a dozen twelve-inch guns apiece; three heavy cruisers and fifteen gunboats were also in port. Trotsky, by contrast, was far away, applying himself to the suppression of a peasant rising in western Siberia. Attackers would have to advance across a flat expanse of ice against heavy artillery and automatic weapons in strongly defended positions. The ice was the key; the conduit for liberal demands to move out, or for repression to close in. A few volunteer propagandists were arrested on reaching the mainland shore. Artillery experts advised the sailors to shell the ice to create a moat against invading forces. Nothing was done, the ice remaining thick and firm, the warships icelocked.

The rebels, militarily soporific, were ideologically busy enough to seal their fate. Political officers were dismissed, and a free trade union declared. A radio station and a daily newspaper, the Kronstadt *Izvestia*, were started. The latter poured scorn on the 'nightmare rule of communist dictatorship.' 'Lenin said that "Communism is Soviet power and electrification,"' ran one leading article. 'But the people are convinced that the Bolshevik form of communism is commissarocracy plus firing squads.' They wanted elections to the Soviet by secret ballot on an equal franchise, with all socialist and anarchist parties legalised and able to compete equally. They demanded an end to the 'serfdom' of peasants and workers, with the right to move jobs. Communist political departments, commissars, Chekists and 'all the privileges of Communists' should be scrapped. Rationing should be equal; workers should be paid 'in gold and not in paper trash.'

Trotsky rushed back to Petrograd by special train on March 5. He had leaflets airdropped over Kronstadt, warning the sailors, who had followed him 'to his prison cell at Kresty, to the walls of Kazan on the Volga', that if they did not capitulate within twenty-

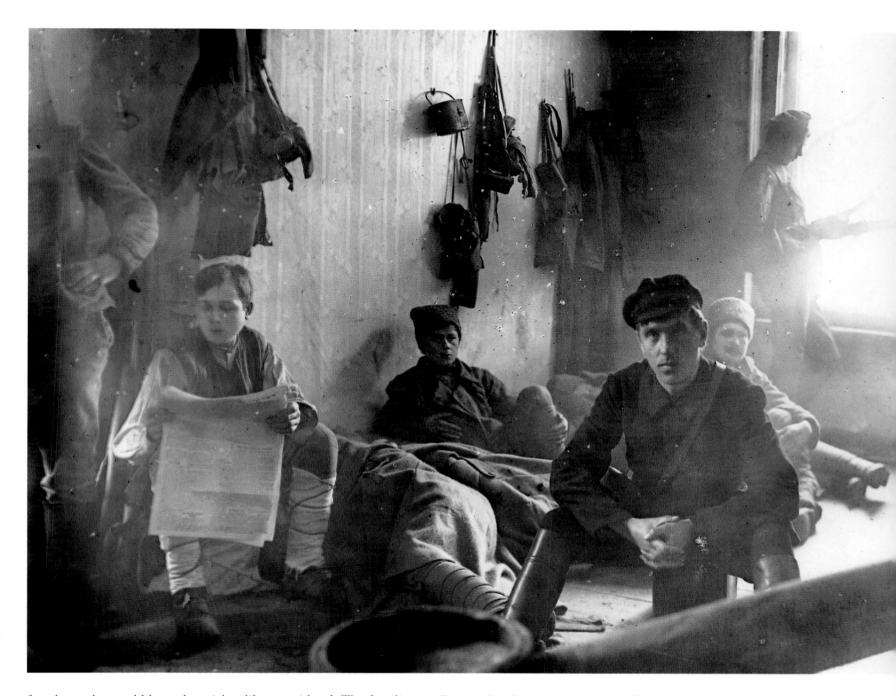

Troops after the successful assault. *They were later sent to remote postings, as the Bolsheviks sought to forget that they had turned on the sailor-heroes of the civil war.*

four hours he would have them 'shot like partridges'. The families of Kronstadt men in Petrograd were rounded up as hostages. An army force, with military cadets and Chekists for stiffening, was put under Tukhachevsky's command. Trotsky attacked when his ultimatum expired. Mainland batteries opened fire after dark on the evening of March 6, attracting counter-fire from the twelve-inch guns of the *Sevastopol*. Early the next morning, military cadets, their uniforms covered in white linen sheets, attacked across the ice. Cheka machinegunners brought up the rear to discourage deserters, but still the assault failed. Some scrambled to the Kronstadt shore and joined the rebels; 500 were left dead on the ice.

The onus was on Tukhachevsky to finish the rebels off before the ice melted. Once ice-free, the sea would prevent an assault on Kronstadt from the mainland whilst freeing the battleships and cruisers to shell Petrograd. He gathered a force of 50,000, well larded with Tartars, Bakshirs and Letts who had no sentiment for

John Reed *with the propaganda train (top right) 'October Revolution' in 1919 shortly before his death in Moscow of typhus. The American author was a skilled propagandist himself. His bestselling book* Ten Days that Shook the World *gave a brilliant but biased account of the Bolshevik seizure of power. His wife, the journalist Louise Bryant, was a more accurate witness.*

Actors of the 'Living Newspaper' Group *spell out Stanok, 'Sickle' (right), in a Petrograd theater in 1920 to attract engineering workers to the Party. The propaganda effort by the Party, ceaseless, all-embracing, was to lead to the coining of the word 'brain-washing'.*

Steamships as well as trains *were used to spread the Party message (right). Nadezhda Krupskaya, Lenin's wife, leads the team aboard the river steamer* Red Star *in 1921.*

The propaganda train 'Lenin' *(left) carries a team of actors and orators round the Ukraine in 1919. The Bolsheviks placed great emphasis on 'agitprop', the combination of agitation and propaganda at which they excelled. The message was carried on posters, pamphlets and in plays performed by the theater group attached to the train.*

the predominantly Russian rebels. The second assault began before dawn on March 17, in a freezing fog that reflected the defenders' searchlights. Delegates to the Tenth Party Congress meeting in Petrograd helped drive the troops forward. During the morning the fog dispersed before brilliant sunshine. Shells pierced the ice, and the attackers drowned or froze. It was not until 1 am on March 18, twenty-two hours after they had left their start lines, that Tukhachevsky's troops took the island forts. They broke into the city, with fierce street fighting continuing into the afternoon. The defenders were demoralised by the flight of their leaders over the ice to Finland, and by the presence of families in their midst. The battleship crews refused to blow up their ships, and these 'counter-revolutionary nests' fell to Tukhachevsky.

The price of a direct assault on prepared positions was high. So many corpses lay on the ice that the Finnish government, fearing epidemics if they washed ashore during the icemelt, officially asked that they be removed. Of his 50,000 men, Tukhachevsky may have lost 20,000 killed and wounded. A mass funeral was held in Petrograd on March 24. The dead included fifteen Congress delegates. The rebels had 600 killed and 1000 wounded. Some 2500 were taken prisoner; 8000 escaped over the ice to Finland. There was no public trial. Thirteen alleged ringleaders were tried in camera and executed. Several hundred sailors are believed to have been shot out of hand on the island. The remainder were ferried to Cheka prisons on the mainland. Some were shot in batches, others were sent to labor camps on the White Sea. The assault troops were scattered across remote postings; within a month, Tukhachevsky was fighting Antonov's peasants in Tambov province, finally subduing them in May, shooting prisoners by the batch. Kronstadt was Trotsky's affair. Stalin played no part in it, a fact that would later be a factor in the death or disappearance of almost every principal involved in it: Congress delegates, Tukhachevsky, Zinoviev, Trotsky. Even Stephan Petrichenko, the seaman-leader, apparently safe across the ice in Finland, was returned to the Russians in 1945 and died in a camp. Bolsheviks had long memories.

MAN OF STEEL

The regime could not afford multiple Kronstadts, more Tambovs. Fear of counter-revolution persuaded the Party Congress to revert more closely to economic normality. Forced requisitioning of food was abolished; free trade was again permitted. This New Economic Policy, NEP, was a grudging affair; Lenin said it was a tactical retreat the better to prepare for the eventual Socialist advance. The 'NEPmen' it bred, small shopkeepers, traders, middlemen, anti-Communist to their core, improved living standards enough for the Bolsheviks to survive and, in due course, to kill off them and the Policy. As the economy went more liberal, politics became less so. The Congress voted to outlaw all opposition to the Party line. The surviving republics in the south,

Azerbaijan, Armenia, Georgia, were brought back into the Soviet Union. Joseph Stalin was commissar for nationalities, dealing with the lives of 65 million non-Russians, hostile Catholic Ukrainians, primitive Ostyak fur hunters, Moslem nomads. He had no time for 'bourgeois nationalism'.

Stalin was not a man who was much noticed; it eased his progress. Nikolai Sukhanov thought of him as a 'gray blur, looming up now and then and leaving no trace.' The British secret agent Bruce Lockhart remembered only his 'sallow face, black mustache and heavy eyebrows … I paid little attention to him.' He was, as Trotsky put it, 'soporific' in public, monotone and flat. Trotsky, mercurial, brilliant, underestimated the Georgian's crafty ambition and capacity for toil. Bolshevik bureaucracy sprouted after the civil war; the dull Party workhorse, the hack who presented no apparent challenge to the high achievers around him, worked his way slowly to the top.

As well as nationalities, Stalin was commissar of the workers' and peasants' inspectorate, the *Rabkrin*. Theoretically a means for 'toilers' to check at will on the performance of Soviet civil servants, the *Rabkrin* in Stalin's hands was a force that pried into all areas of bureaucracy. It gave him a wide brief to supervise the functioning of government. That was not all. Within the Politburo, Stalin was responsible for the daily running of the Party, as linkman between Politburo and *Orgburo*, which gave orders to Party personnel. Dull routine and the dull people who performed it were at the heart of the party organisation; Stalin had an unequaled grasp of both. Trotsky's armored train, that 'vital shovelful of coal that kept a dying fire alive', was parked in a museum. The Red army had been reduced by two thirds since the end of the civil war. Trotsky's power base was much reduced and his rival now ran the engine room of Bolshevism. On April 3, 1922 Stalin was appointed general secretary of the Central Committee, extending his power over the careers of functionaries and the decisions of the Politburo.

Lenin, who had been prey to severe headaches for several years, suffered a stroke at the end of May 1922. He returned briefly from convalescing in the country in mid-autumn, before a second stroke and then a third in March 1923 left him a wheelchair-bound half-vegetable. In a brief political testament at the end of 1922, a sour document that picked holes in all his colleagues, he noted Trotsky and Stalin as the two most able leaders. Trotsky, he carped, had 'too far-reaching a self-confidence'. The venom was reserved for Stalin: 'too rude', a man who should be replaced as general secretary by someone 'more patient, more loyal, more polite and attentive to comrades, less capricious'. This hostility would have ruined Stalin had it not been stifled by the third stroke, which left Lenin speechless. Stalin deepened his control of the government machine and its personnel; 'Comrade Card Index', he was called. He formed a triumvirate within the Politburo with the big city bosses, Grigori Zinoviev from Petrograd and Moscow's Lev Kamenev. Its main purpose was to block Trotsky; few thought that Stalin would become a leader. They did not realise that he was already listening

A broken man. *Lenin suffered a series of strokes and was confined to a wheelchair; he was incapable of work by the time this picture was taken in the summer of 1923. A team of forty doctors and nurses looked after him. He was also nursed by his favorite younger sister Maria Ulyanova, who leans over him whilst a neurosurgeon stands behind. The picture was taken by a gardener at the Lenin dacha.*

in to his colleagues' conversations on the Kremlin's internal telephone system.

Stalin was developing a modest, warm image; pipe smoker and careful listener, a man who 'loves neither money, nor pleasure, neither sport nor women', who lived quietly with his wife and young family in lodgings in the servants' quarters of the Kremlin. Trotsky, by contrast, was served his food by a former court butler on plates that still bore the Romanov double eagle. Stalin had another edge; as its fixer and patron, its chief bureaucrat, he embodied the Party. Living in a nation they had swamped with

blood and incompetence, with a gimcrack 'new society' devoted to class hatred, but still convinced that they represented the way of the future, Soviet Communists were devoted to the Party. Everything should be sacrificed to its unity : freedom, tolerance, reason itself. 'My party right or wrong,' said Trotsky. 'I know one cannot be right against the party ... for history has not created other ways for the realisation of what is right.' The only truth, then, was the Party; the Party, increasingly, was Stalin.

Lenin died on January 21, 1924. The body lay in state at the old Nobles' Club in Moscow. An Immortalisation Commission

Alexandra Kollontai, *a general's daughter and energetic feminist, among the delegates of the 2nd International Congress of Communist Women in Moscow in 1921. She advocated free love and said sex should be as natural as drinking a glass of water.*

Stalin, 'Man of Steel', *as it translates, was a man of many aliases – Koba, Nisharadze, Melikyants, Chizhikov. By 1927, the boy born Joseph Djugashvili in a Georgian hovel had emerged as the effective master of Russia, and soon his paranoia was to end any such strolls among the people that he was to terrorise and murder by the million.* [PHOTO: G. PETRUSOV]

was established to preserve the human god. Tutankhamun's tomb had recently been found in Egypt, so Lenin's corpse was embalmed like an Egyptian mummy. A vast mausoleum of red granite was built on Red Square. Petrograd was renamed Leningrad; in the orgy of worship, Sunday was nearly renamed Leninday. Stalin, the boy from the Georgian seminary, grasped the Russian need for liturgy and faith. He urged the Party to collect relics of Lenin. He stood in the guard of honor at the bier. He carried the coffin. Mussolini and Hitler, the fascists who would owe so much to Lenin and Stalin, made themselves the Messiah. Stalin, subtly, was happy to be the Great Disciple. Such public humility acted as a stalking horse behind which he closed in on Trotsky. He continued to attack Trotsky's army power base; a quarter of the staff were Party members, owing preferment to

Stalin and aware that they appeared on the card indexes in his keeping. At the end of 1924, political commissars demanded that Trotsky be dismissed; in January 1925 he resigned from the Red army. Stalin's crony Kliment Voroshilov, an ex-miner and farm worker, an incompetent 'backwoodsman' to Trotsky, became military commander. Stalin had no need of his allies: Zinoviev was thrown out of the Politburo in July 1926, with Stalin's nominee Sergei Kirov inheriting as Leningrad Party boss; Kamenev and Trotsky followed in October.

The top story of the bland Central Committee building was Stalin's eyrie. His rooms were sealed off from the rest of the building; he liked to work alone, puffing Herzegovina cigarette tobacco in his pipe. A special staff combed Tsarist records for material that he then housed there: 'all sorts of documents, accusations, libelous rumors against the prominent leaders without exception.' He liked to keep tabs on his peers.

Stalin completed the rout in 1927. On November 7, the tenth anniversary of the Bolshevik coup, Trotsky and Zinoviev called for street demonstrations in Leningrad and Moscow in protest against Stalinist policies. They were broken up by secret police; a foreign correspondent said that he would 'never forget the bitterness written on Trotsky's face.' Both men were immediately expelled from the Party. Trotsky was still too much the legend to be murdered; he was taken screaming from his apartment by OGPU agents, successors to the Chekists, who dragged him to a train for Alma Ata near the Chinese border in Kazakhstan. He was shipped out to Turkey in February 1929. His friend Yakov Bliumkin visited him on the island of Prinkipo, and carried a

message for supporters home to Moscow. Bliumkin was shot for treason in the summer of 1929. It was the first known death sentence passed on a Party member; the Bolsheviks had shot others with gusto from the start, but not, remembering the self-wounding of the French Jacobins, each other. Soon members were to fall like snowflakes.

His rivals disgraced, Stalin was free to treat Russia as a huge laboratory in which he could experiment, on living flesh, on ways to make her a superpower. 'We are fifty or a hundred years behind the advanced countries,' he said. 'We must catch up this distance in ten years. Either we do it or we go under.' Five years after installing Lenin's mummified corpse in its mausoleum, Stalin visited on Russia a second revolution incomparably more radical and hungry for victims than the first.

The poet Sergei Yesenin with Isadora Duncan *(above)*
*after their Moscow wedding in 1922. The American
dancer founded a school there to teach her fluid style of
dance, inspired by the figures on ancient Greek vases.
The lovers were doomed. Yesenin, seventeen years
younger than his exotic wife, committed suicide in
1925. Isadora Duncan was strangled when her scarf
caught in the wheels of her automobile two years later.*

Vladimir Mayakovsky, *futurist poet, playwright and
satirist (right), with his mistress Lily Brik in Yalta in
1926. Enfant terrible in the last days of Tsarism, he
was one of the few writers to welcome the Bolshevik
takeover. 'Today to the last buttons of our coats life is
being made anew,' he told customers in the Poets' Bar
in Moscow, which he had painted 'cannibal orange'.
During the civil war, he designed propaganda posters to
put in empty store windows. He toed the Party line and
was known for his vicious and petulant attacks on other
artists and writers. But he was increasingly estranged
from Bolshevism, loathing its bureaucracy and
mindlessness, and committed suicide in 1930.*

5
KULAK KILLER

GO NOW TO A RUSSIAN VILLAGE, AND THE CATASTROPHE STILL casts its shadow over the place. Rusting machinery is dumped round slimy yards, weeds flourish in the fields, fenceposts sag; the only splashes of color are in the small private plots on the gray periphery of the collective. The people are listless and wary, the tempo lethargic, the buildings unpainted and cheerless. The animals have a hangdog air. More than sixty years ago, farms and peasant holdings were collectivised. *Kulaks*, peasants who showed vigor and enterprise, were destroyed wholesale. The countryside remains in after-shock. Alexander Solzhenitsyn described the process as an 'ethnic catastrophe' in which Communist volunteers and OGPU agents, like 'raging beasts', rounded up kulaks and their families, and drove them 'stripped of their possessions, naked, into the northern tundra and the taiga.' Boris Pasternak, who made a trip to amass material on collectivisation, found himself silenced with horror. 'What I saw could not be expressed in words … There was such inhuman, unimaginable misery, such a terrible disaster, that it began to seem almost abstract, it would not fit within the bounds of consciousness.'

The terror-famine inflicted as a matter of Socialist policy from the beginning of 1930 probably killed 14 million peasants. The exact figure is not known – as Khrushchev pointed out, 'no one was keeping count'. But the death rate was so horrific that the 1937 census was suppressed; with the black humor that Communism managed so well, members of the census board were arrested for 'treasonably exerting themselves to diminish the population of the USSR'. Whole villages were depopulated. An American labor organiser, Fred Beal, who had gone to Russia to avoid a possible jail sentence in the US, made a random visit to a village two hours by train from Kharkov. He found only one living person, a woman who had gone mad. 'In the houses there were only corpses,' he wrote. He found a note in one cabin: 'My son. We couldn't wait. God be with you.' Beal saw signs on graves: 'I love Stalin. Bury him here as soon as possible.' One social class, the kulaks, was exterminated and a new one, the *bezprizorniye*, the 'homeless ones', was created: orphans and abandoned children, who lived in freight cars and unfinished buildings and scavenged for cats, birds and potato peelings. Of the dead, perhaps four million were children. Arthur Koestler, who found the enormous land 'wrapped in a blanket of silence', said that the wasted young 'looked like embryos out of alcohol bottles'.

Collectivisation was a social and economic disaster. Communist ideology, honed in the reading rooms of western Europe, broke the spirit of the villages and turned the fields barren. Grain production slumped disastrously. Peasants forced to join collectives on pain of deportation to the Siberian wastes

The first tractors arrive. *The scene is a steppe village in 1930. The machines, based on American models, made little impact in a countryside devastated by collectivisation. The breakdown rate of the tractors, often driven by untrained peasants, and maintained by unskilled mechanics, was enormous.*
[PHOTO: A. SHISHKIN]

would sign up in the morning and then in the evening would slaughter their livestock, smash machines and destroy crops rather than let the State have them. They gorged themselves on the slaughtered animals so that 'everyone had a greasy mouth ... everyone blinked like an owl, as if drunk from eating'. Slaughter was protest, even if it also brought starvation. Three years after the start of collectivisation, the number of sheep and goats was reduced by two thirds, of horses by half, of cattle by nearly half. Because Communism is so clearly the handiwork of intellectuals; because its ideology appears, like its language, so complex; because it ruled so much of the earth – it is difficult to dismiss it as one would, say, a quack medicine. But collectivisation was no more than the act of simpletons and sadists.

Grain consumption was less in 1935, after the supposed triumph of collectivisation, than it had been in the 1890s. Crop yields on collective farms in the early 1990s are only marginally better than in pre-mechanisation 1913. Peasants will not work willingly for the State; monster farms are inefficient. Proof was instantly available: in 1938, the small private plots still permitted to peasants grew more than a fifth of total Soviet produce, yet

they accounted for less than one twenty-fifth of cultivated land. Such evidence of the lunacy in the drive to 'Socialist agriculture' was ignored. As to its effect on the Party – it tipped a balance already weighted by Lenin toward inhumanity. 'Pace by pace, as they followed one routine directive after another,' wrote Evgenia Ginzburg of the administrators of Bolshevik terror, 'they climbed down the steps from the human condition into that of beasts.'

Farms recovered under the New Economic Policy in the 1920s. In 1928, more than four fifths of the grain was harvested by private farmers, the vast majority of them peasants with smallholdings; 315 million hectares were in private ownership. If farm production had not yet reached pre-war levels, it was getting there. The Soviet Union was still massively a peasant country; more than 80 per cent of the population lived in its 600,000 hamlets and villages. The Communist attitude to country people, however, was murderous. The Party never enjoyed any rural affection; it was obliged to send in city volunteers when it wished to be heard, for it had no local hold on the villages. Its leaders had no insight into the peasant mass, other than sensing its hostility and its blasphemous urge to own land and livestock. Lenin's brief foray as a landowner had failed; Trotsky had abandoned the family estate; Stalin had been a city agitator. Before them Karl Marx's natural habitat had been the library.

Mixed with the Bolsheviks' lethal hatred of farmers was, to be sure, the characteristic dream of eventual rural Utopia. Lenin said that the future lay in vast Marxist factory farms. The peasant on these huge collectives – Stalin spoke of 'grain factories' of a quarter of a million acres – would be indistinguishable from the factory worker. The villages would be swallowed into 'Socialist agrotowns', where individual wooden cabins and vegetable plots would make way for apartment blocks, restaurants, reading rooms and gymnasiums. Mechanisation in the fields would also help to convert the farmhand into the more malleable proletarian; Lenin claimed that a hundred thousand tractors would turn the Russian muzhik into a Communist. Machinery would be held in Machine Tractor Stations, MTS, which would also serve as political education centers. But malice rode with the seeming benevolence. Rural areas were largely outside Party control. Collectivise the farms and, like the cities, the very countryside would become State property. So would its inhabitants. The peasants realised they were being enslaved. They referred to VKP, the mnemonic for the All-Union Communist Party, as *Vtoroe Krepostnoe Pravo*, the Second Serfdom. With collectivisation, every ear of corn became socialist property; and to snip so much as one merited a ten-year sentence, under a well-used law passed on the seventh day of an eighth month, on August 7, 1932, and known to the thousands sent to camps under it as the 'Law of Seven-eighths.'

Lenin's contempt for rural people had a peculiar quality to it. He had reveled in a famine that hit the Volga region in 1892, and railed against relief efforts. 'Psychologically,' he wrote, 'this talk of feeding the starving is nothing but an expression of the saccharine-sweet sentimentality so characteristic of our intelligentsia.' In the civil war, he wrote with gusto of the 'beautiful plan' by which the Party, under peasant guise, would 'hang the kulaks, priests and landowners'. As for the peasants, they would not escape: 'we will pin it on them later,' he wrote. The NEP had never been more than a forced concession, a 'breathing space' as Lenin put it, 'a strategic retreat that will allow us to advance on a broad front in the very near future.'

The revolution had seen a massive leveling down in farming. The great estates and the farms of the smaller landlords had been seized by peasants, who controlled nine-tenths of plowland. The number of landless peasants halved; while that of farmers with more than twenty-seven acres fell more. The larger farms which had supplied the cities disappeared. The bulk of grain was produced – and consumed – by smallholders. By 1928, there was little incentive for them to part with their grain. There were few city goods for them to buy, and the State price for grain did not cover costs. Grain was hoarded, or eaten, on the farms. The towns were becoming hungry. Quotas were set and requisitioning squads sent out to seize grain. Peasants hid it, or sold it illegally to private traders. An ideological assault was prepared. It was necessary to excite class hatred in the villages. Peasants were duly

Tractors arranged for a propaganda shot *(opposite)*, *at the 'Lenin Kolkhoz', a collective farm, in 1933. Lenin despised peasants as 'petty bourgeois' with an urge to own the land they worked. The collective farm sealed their fate. Take their property, herd them into agrotowns, make them dependent on Machine Tractor Stations for machinery and political enlightenment, and Party control over them became complete.*
[PHOTO: G. PETRUSOV]

Peasants vote to join a collective farm *(right)*, *knowing that a vote against could lead to a ten-year sentence in Siberia. Terror was re-established as standard administrative procedure.*
[PHOTO: A. SHAIKHET]

categorised: poor, middle and *kulak*. The word meant 'fist' in Russian and had been tagged to village moneylenders before the revolution. 'Kulak', though in theory defining a peasant rich enough to hire the labor of others, swiftly became a catchall; where a peasant was clearly too beggared for it to apply, he could, neatly, be dealt with as a *podkulachnik*, a kulak sympathiser. Molotov spoke of dealing the kulaks 'such a blow' that the middle peasants would 'snap to attention before us.'

By 1929, meat was also being requisitioned and rationing was introduced in towns. There was press talk of a 'wholesale' collectivisation campaign; by mid-1929, only about three per cent of peasants were on collective or State farms. On December 27, 1929, six days after celebrating his 50th birthday in what Louis Fischer of *The Nation* called an 'orgy of personal glorification', Stalin formally unleashed a new revolution. The country's grain-producing areas were to be collectivised at once; all kulaks were to be liquidated. 'We must smash the kulaks, eliminate them as a class,' he said. On January 30, 1930, the Politburo approved a resolution 'On Measures for the Elimination of Kulak Households in Districts of Comprehensive Collectivisation'. This document

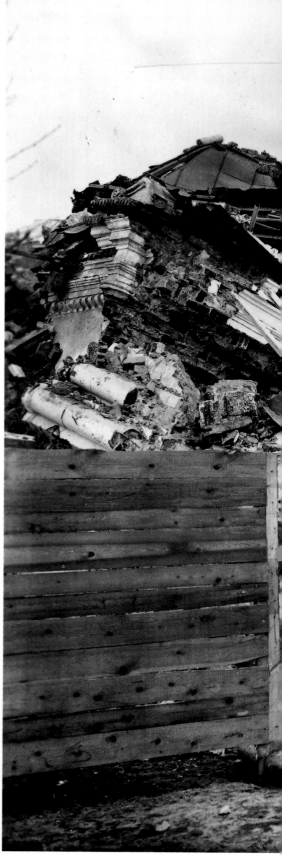

Ikonoclasts. *Party workers remove ikon-covers (above) from ikons taken out of Moscow churches to be melted down for their silver content. The ikons themselves were often burnt as firewood. Jewels and precious metals from churches were used to fund imports of machinery, mostly from the US and Germany. The huge new tractor plants were partly funded by church spoils.*

Licensed looting. *Red army men (right) remove ornaments and valuables from a church.*

Demolition gang. *A group of explosives workers pose with their handiwork (above), the ruins of the Giorgievsky Church in Gorky, the trading city now known once more as Nizhny Novgorod. The* *Bolsheviks closed or destroyed more than 50,000 churches across the country in a campaign which slackened during the war but regained its intensity under Khrushchev.*
[PHOTO: M. DMITRIEV]

has not achieved the notoriety of the Final Solution though it yields nothing to it in terms of scale and malice. It divided the kulaks into three categories. Those in the first were to be shot or imprisoned; the second, including families of the first, faced deportation; the third were to be expelled from the *kolkhoz*, the collective farm, and settled on marginal marsh or forest land. In practice, those in the third category could not meet the State grain procurement from poor land, and so they were deported too. The 'most hostile and reactionary' kulaks were to be sent to concentration camps in 'distant areas' of the far North.

The first arrests took place at the end of 1929. These were carried out by OGPU officers and normally involved the execution of former White soldiers, who had believed themselves amnestied. Mass action began at the start of 1930. It involved hundreds of thousands of families on a scale too large for OGPU, so that Party activists were drafted in from the towns. The novelist Vasil Bykov lived in a Belorussian village too poor to have any recognisable kulaks. But 'dekulakisation' was compulsory; top-secret letters sent out in February 1930 gave 'orientation numbers' of kulaks to be deported by region. 'There shall be no oscillation, no concessions to rightist-deviationist attitudes and no pacifism,' the directive warned in socialist babblespeak. Kulaks had to be found. So one family was deported because it owned a cow and calf; another because its mare had a foal; another because a woman relative helped with the harvest. A peasant with eight acres was forced to clear railroad tracks of snow. On his return, he found all his property seized apart from a kettle, a saucer and a spoon. He was then sent lumbering in the far North. In some villages, a Party activist would arrive from the city, produce a pistol and say that any peasant who refused to join the kolkhoz would be sent immediately to Siberia.

Sometimes the policy of exciting class hatred worked. 'The poor peasants of the village get together in a meeting and decide: "So-and-so has six horses; we couldn't get along without those in the collective farm; besides he hired a man last year to help on the harvest,"' a kulak told John Scott, an American volunteer in Magnitogorsk, the vast new industrial complex. 'They notify the OGPU, and there you are. So-and-so gets five years. They confiscate his property and give it to the new collective farm. Sometimes they ship the whole family out. When they came to ship us out, my brother got a rifle and fired several shots at the OGPU officers. They fired back. My brother was killed.'

Informing, a Russian tradition, flourished. 'It was so easy to do a man in,' a villager recalled. 'You wrote a denunciation; you did not even have to sign it. All you had to say was that he'd paid people to work for him as hired hands, or that he owned three cows.' Peasants were encouraged to denounce neighbors; a 14-year-old role model, Pavlik Morozov, was found. Morozov's father was said to have secretly aided kulaks. Pavlik denounced his father in court; when he later denounced other kulaks for grain hoarding, they ambushed and murdered him in the woods. This was not the truth. The father, a poor peasant who became chairman of a village soviet in the Urals, was convicted on Pavlik's

A Party activist, *in dark shirt, supervises the meeting of a rural committee in the Chuvash republic. Activists would create a state of hysteria against the kulaks, the better-off peasants. 'They'd threaten people with guns, as if they were under a spell, calling small children "kulak bastards", screaming "bloodsuckers",' an eyewitness wrote. 'They looked on the so-called kulaks as cattle, swine, loathsome, repulsive; they had no souls; they stank; they all had venereal disease; they were enemies of the people.'*

A Party organiser reports *(top)*
*in Uzbekistan in 1934. Activists,
like the woman with the
briefcase, would arrive in
villages with banners reading:
'We demand collectivisation and
the liquidisation of the kulaks as
a class.' A kulak was any
successful peasant who might
raise the envy of his fellows; as
Alexander Solzhenitsyn wrote,
'all strong peasants in general
were being so called – all
peasants strong in management,
strong in work, or even merely
strong in convictions.' The best
were destroyed.*

**Suspected 'wreckers and
hoarders'** *on trial at a kolkhoz
(left) in one of the Central
Asian republics in 1931. The
guilty were stripped of their
possessions and driven off with
their families. 'It was terrible to
watch them,' admitted a Party
activist. 'They marched along in
a column and looked back at
their huts, and their bodies still
held the warmth from their own
stoves … We drove them off like
geese.'*

A schoolgirl informer *(above) writes
down the names of her classmates who
attend church services at Baz-
Karabulak in the Saratov region.
Informing on friends and neighbors
was a civic duty in the Bolshevik state.
One 'hero', Pronya Kolobin, a thirteen-
year-old, informed on his mother for
stealing grain.*

evidence of seizing kulak property rather than handing it in to the new collective farm. Pavlik was then stabbed by his infuriated grandfather whilst out cranberrying. But the story that he had been killed by kulaks was more convenient, and it was on that basis that the father-betrayer was held up as a Communist martyr, with the Palace of Young Pioneers in Moscow named for him.

Collectivisation attracted only the poorest peasants, who had no land or livestock to lose. Even so, many of those were opposed to dekulakisation. The Party had to use '25-thousanders', Communist volunteers from the cities. They were given a two-week course and sent off to run villages and manage the new collectives. A farm revolution in the world's largest country was being supervised by factory workers with two weeks' 'training', most of it in propaganda; if these city types could run a farm, the peasants asked, why should a peasant not run a factory? The brutality that the 25-thousanders witnessed and inflicted was enough to break even an OGPU officer. The biographer Isaac Deutscher, on a train trip from Moscow to Kharkov, met an OGPU colonel who was 'almost sobbing' as he said: 'I am an old Bolshevik. I worked in the underground against the Tsar and then fought in the civil war. Did I do all that in order that I should now surround villages with machineguns and order my men to fire indiscriminately into crowds of peasants? Oh, no, no!'

A hunger-ridden waif called Katya was found wandering near a railroad station in the Ukraine. She had got out of the cattle car transporting her and many other kulak families to find water;

Rollcall at the 'New Life' collective, *a farm in the Moscow region. Propaganda claimed collectives were scientifically run and highly mechanised but in reality they relied on the brute strength of exploited peasant women.*

A peasant woman, *one of the many wandering through Russia in search of food as the economy broke down. Tsar Alexander II, 'the Liberator', had freed the serfs in 1861. Seventy years later, a new form of serfdom was introduced by Stalin, and the traditional fate of the Russian countrywoman was re-established: 'thrice a slave; daughter of a slave, mother of a slave, and to her husband a slave.'*

when she returned to the line, the train had gone. Kulaks sometimes spent weeks in the cars as they rolled slowly toward their place of deportation, stacked into cattle wagons or 'Stolypin cars', windowless prison transports. The legs of some did not touch the floor for days, because they were so tightly packed that they hung suspended between each other. They were fed salt herring or dried carp, sometimes Sea of Azov anchovies, and then left for hours without water. 'And thus we set out,' wrote Solzhenitsyn of his own experience in a Stolypin car, 'and, entangled in other bodies, fall asleep to the clacking of the wheels without knowing whether we will see forest or steppe tomorrow.' Sometimes they could judge from a snatch of sun whether they were being taken east or north. They were en route for use as slave labor in a vast new system of camps, controlled by an OGPU agency, the Chief Executive of Corrective Labor Camps. Its Russian acronym was Gulag. The camps had some 30,000 inmates in 1928. By 1931 the figure was above two million and climbing daily as the 'white coal', as the OGPU guards called the kulaks,

was delivered. 'In sheer size this nonrecurring tidal wave (it was an ocean) swelled beyond the bounds of anything the penal system of even an immense state can permit itself,' said Solzhenitsyn. Nobody bothered simply with the head of the family. 'They burned out whole nests, whole families, from the start,' he noted; 'and they watched jealously to be sure that none of the children – fourteen, ten, even six years old – got away: to the last scrapings, all had to go down the same road, to the same common destruction.' Children could not escape their origins; it

Sergei Eisenstein, a film giant *(above). He served in the Red army during the civil war and trained as a theatrical scene painter. His skill in cutting and recutting to achieve an impressionistic climax was seen in the famous Odessa Steps sequence in the propaganda epic* The Battleship Potemkin; *his later classics* Alexander Nevsky *and* Ivan the Terrible *confirmed him as one of the world's greatest directors. Here (left) he is on location shooting* The Old and the New *on the steppe in 1930. The movie starred one of the earliest tractors to be built in the Soviet Union. Such was the growth of Stalin's paranoia in the 1930s that even Eisenstein, who had been happy to lend his talents to the campaign to sell Communism, was not allowed to make another film until* Alexander Nevsky *in 1938.*

[Top Photo: D. Debabov]

was written in their IDs, opening them to a whole world of discrimination, in which they were ineligible for rations, for clothing vouchers, for education.

Some kulaks toiled on the White Sea-Baltic Sea canal, hacking at rock with hammers and chisels, carting the spoil on their backs. Half-clad, they faced the winter in flimsy barracks; perhaps 100,000 died. Stalin cruised through their handiwork on its completion, his 160-foot portrait decorating its banks. Too shallow for the naval vessels for which it was designed, it was soon idle and unrepaired. Stalin had a passion for gold as well as canals. He read Bret Harte's *Sutter's Gold* and other books on the California gold rush. A fresh OGPU agency, Dalstroy, was set up with a headquarters in Magadan to develop gold mining by forced labor in Kolyma in north-east Siberia, one of the coldest regions on earth. Entire camps perished, including guards and their dogs. In a camp on the Yenisei river, kulaks lived in dug-outs. At camp no. 205 in the Siberian taiga north of Severnoe, they worked in the mine on rations of a pint of soup and five ounces of bread a day.

Two million kulaks were dumped in 'special settlements' on the 400-mile stretch between Gryazovets and Archangel. Strings of carts rolled through the villages, flanked by convoy troops, vanishing into the snowy steppe. At Yemetsk, there was a vast camp of families that had become separated from their fathers. Thirty-two thousand lived in ninety-seven barracks, with no medical care. In Kazakhstan, kulaks found pegs stuck in the raw ground with little notices saying settlement no. 5, no. 6, and so on; 'they dug themselves holes in the ground. A great many died of cold and hunger.' Anything between a quarter and a third of the deportees died, many of them children. A saying was that 'Moscow does not believe in tears.' Any sadism could be visited

The chorus line: *a propaganda team take the Party line to the villages in Turkmenistan in 1936. The Party maintained a stream of propaganda, unavoidable, constant, a background to all activity, as ceaseless as the hum of the engine on a ship at sea. No harvest was reaped, no sowing completed without banners and slogans.*

Young Pioneers *are awarded badges for being 'excellent fighters for the kolkhoz harvest'. The Party, like the church before it, made great efforts to win children's minds at the earliest age.*

on the kulak, for his 'class essence' rendered him a sub-human to be eliminated en masse. 'You do not lament the loss of hair of one who has been beheaded,' said Stalin.

The Party claimed in the spring of 1930 that half of all peasant households had been collectivised. The effects were ruinous. A quarter of the cattle, sheep and goats, and a third of the pigs in the Soviet Union were slaughtered in 1930. The great bulk of them were killed and eaten in February and March by peasants who were determined that they should not be given to the collectives. The most productive peasants were herded off as kulaks; the wastrels and idlers who denounced them flourished; the surviving middle peasants, cowed and sullen, were in no mood to exert themselves for the State. Total collapse threatened at the start of the spring sowing season. On March 2, 1930, Stalin wrote

an article in *Pravda* under the headline 'Dizzy with success'. Collectivisation was a stunning success, Stalin lied, but some local officials were going too fast. The pace should be slowed. Almost half of the new collective farms collapsed in March and April; millions of peasants went back to working for themselves, but they did not escape for long. Once the harvest was gathered, the campaign restarted.

Stalin ended the drive in a secret circular in the spring of 1933. The victory of the collective farm system was now won, he said, 'which makes it possible, as a rule, to stop the use of mass deportations and sharp forms of repression in the countryside.' By that time two-thirds of peasants had been subjected to the second serfdom; in the grain-growing areas, ninety per cent had been stripped of ownership and toiled on collectives.

Farmworkers drafted in *to hew the Central Asian
Fergana irrigation system in 1935. The project,
which watered a huge cotton-growing belt, took
fifteen years to complete with pick and shovel.
Child labor was also widely used. The completed
system was said to be one of the wonders of the
Soviet world. It linked the old oases on the borders
of the depression between the two great mountain
ranges of Tien-Shan and the Pamirs, running
through Uzbekistan, Tadzhikistan and Kirghizstan.*
[PHOTO, LEFT: M. ALPERT]

Special treatment was meted out to regions which Stalin suspected of nourishing nationalism. Worst among them was the Ukraine, which suffered a terrible ordeal by deportation and starvation. Warning of his malice was given in a series of show trials in the Kharkov opera house, in which a string of scholars, priests and lawyers 'confessed' after torture to membership of an underground nationalist movement. The 'plot' had been extended into the villages by 1932. Collectivisation, and resistance to it, were particularly strong in the Ukraine. By the middle of the year, almost three-quarters of Ukrainian peasants had been forced into collectives, far above the norm in Russia. The Ukrainian kolkhoz was bigger and more brutally managed. So was grain requisitioning. In 1931, 7.7 million tons of grain was demanded by the State from a Ukrainian harvest which collectivisation had brought down to 18 million tons. This left the peasants on near-starvation rations. In July 1932, Stalin served a death sentence. He again ordered 7.7 million tons to be delivered to the State. By now, the ravages of collectivisation had reduced the harvest to a mere 14.7 million tons. The demand, even when eventually reduced to 6.6 million tons, condemned millions to death by starvation.

Requisitioning gangs of Communist activists, armed with steel rods up to ten feet long, swarmed over the Ukraine. 'They searched in the house, in the attic, shed and cellar,' a victim recalled. 'Then they went outside and searched in the barn, pig pen, granary and straw pile …' Crude watchtowers were put up in the fields, posts with a hut of wood and straw atop them. Here guards armed with shotguns would look out for snippers; those who were driven by hunger to cut off ears of corn with scissors. Those who were caught got a minimum of ten years under the law of Seven-eighths; some were shot. One Kharkov court issued fifteen hundred death sentences in a month; a woman was given a ten-year sentence for cutting 100 ears of corn from her own plot, two weeks after her husband had died of starvation. The remaining chickens and pigs were eaten in the early winter of 1932. Then the dogs and cats went. 'It was hard to catch them,' wrote Vasily Grossman. 'The animals had become afraid of people and their eyes were wild. People boiled them, but were left with tough veins and muscles. And from their heads they made a meat jelly.' Only 4.7 million tons of grain had been delivered by the end of 1932. A new levy was announced. A further 17,000 activists were drafted into the political departments of Machine Tractor Stations, and 8000 into farm political departments. They made no difference; there was nothing left to take. Scapegoats,

A Party requisitioning squad *removes hidden grain (opposite). Any peasant whose grain cache was found was automatically treated as a kulak, and deported or shot; yet to retain some grain was a matter of survival. 'The peasants lay helpless in their huts with swollen limbs,' an activist wrote. 'And yet we had to get bread out of the villages somehow, and fulfill the plan.'*

A watchtower *(left). These were built in the fields so that Party activists, some of them Young Pioneers, could spot starving peasants who snipped ears of corn to feed their families. The countryside thus resembled an enormous concentration camp, whose inmates spied upon each other.*

agricultural 'wreckers', had to be found to explain the shortfall. Meteorologists were arrested for issuing false weather forecasts to damage the harvest. Veterinarians were shot for sabotaging livestock. Agronomists were accused of being kulaks and deported to Siberia. 'In almost every MTS wrecking in the repairing of tractors was discovered,' wrote Solzhenitsyn. 'And that is how the failures of the first collective farm years were explained!'

Mass starvation started when the snow melted in March 1933. People ate rats, ants and earthworms. They made soup with dandelions and nettles. The *New York Evening Journal* correspondent visited a village twenty miles from Kiev. 'In one hut they were cooking a mess that defied analysis,' he wrote. 'There were bones, pigweed, skin and what looked like a boot top in the pot.' Cannibalism came; children and strangers were ambushed and eaten. 'There were people who cut up and cooked corpses, who killed their own children and ate them,' wrote Vasily Grossman. 'I saw one. She had been brought to the district center under convoy. Her face was human, but her eyes were those of a wolf.' Some were shot, but 325 Ukrainian cannibals labored on canal projects. The famous blind bards of the Ukraine, who kept alive old national ballads, were less useful than cannibals; they made poor slave laborers. So they were asked to a special congress and shot, along with film-makers, artists and newspapermen.

People abandoned their villages. They squatted along rail tracks begging for crusts to be thrown from carriage windows, and inundated railroad stations. They followed troops on maneuvers. They crawled about on all fours in towns. Carts went through the streets of Kiev each morning collecting the corpses of those who had died in the night. The children had thin, elongated faces like dead birds. 'Some of them were still muttering,' wrote Grossman. 'I asked the driver about them, and he just waved his hands and said: "By the time they get where they are being taken they will be silent too."' In Kirovohrad, children were herded into an open encampment, from which people heard 'frightening, inhuman cries.'

Still the activists searched for grain; shot mothers whom they found digging up potatoes; beat those who were not swollen up in the tell-tale sign of starvation to make them reveal their source of food. 'We were realising historical necessity,' wrote the activist Lev Kopolev. 'We were performing our revolutionary duty. We were obtaining grain for the socialist fatherland ... I saw women and children with distended bellies, turning blue, with vacant, lifeless eyes. And corpses – corpses in ragged sheepskin coats and cheap felt boots; corpses in peasant huts, in the melting snow of old Vologda, under the bridges of Kharkov ... I saw all this and did not go out of my mind or commit suicide ... I believed because I wanted to believe.'

In the killing fields of the Ukraine *(above). The men died first, then the children and lastly the women. 'The most terrifying sights were the little children,' wrote a Party activist. 'Starvation had wiped every trace of youth from their faces, turning them into tortured gargoyles: only in their eyes still lingered the remainder of their childhood. Everywhere we found men and women lying prone, their faces and bellies bloated, their eyes utterly expressionless.'*

Cannibals caught with cuts of human flesh *(opposite). They were accused of having killed their victims. The progress of Soviet Russia was marked by cannibalism: in the civil war, during the mass starvation in the Volga in 1921 as shown here, at the height of collectivisation in the Ukraine, in Leningrad under the Nazi siege. The starvation that caused it was then bought off with imports of Western grain; but collectivisation has meant that the largest country on earth remains incapable of feeding itself on a consistent basis.*

This starvation was politically induced. There was food in the Ukraine, the old breadbasket of the Tsarist empire. It was piled, rotting and smoking from spontaneous combustion, in dumps guarded by OGPU machinegunners; it was stacked on groaning sidetables in canteens for Party officials; it was available for hard currency or precious metals in Torgsin stores, so that Roman Catholics in Zhytomyr province, who buried their dead with gold rings and jewelry, now dug up the graves at night and survived; it was exported to earn foreign currency for the industrialisation drive. Almost 2 million tons of grain were exported in 1932; in 'Hungry Thirty-Three' 1.7 million tons were sold on international markets at knockdown, depression prices.

The savagery was not restricted to the Ukraine, where Robert Conquest, in the classic account of collectivisation, *Harvest of Sorrow*, estimates that five million died, between a fifth and a quarter of the Ukrainian rural population. Perhaps a quarter of the Kazakh people died during collectivisation. The Germans of the lower Volga, who had been encouraged to immigrate by Catherine the Great, lost perhaps 200,000 of their number to hunger and the Gulag. Cossack regions of the Don and Kuban suffered grievously through deportation and hunger; a *stanitsa* that had supported 20,000 was reduced to a naked man fighting with cats in the dust over a dead pigeon. The remainder had been deported or killed in one of the many revolts that marked collectivisation. Red army morale slumped, for 'in every unit there was a mass desertion of peasant soldiers, who hastened to their native villages, with or without their rifles, to wreak vengeance on the executives of the collectives.' In parts of the Ukraine and north Caucasus, aircraft were used to put them down. A squadron which refused to machinegun Cossack villages was disbanded and half its personnel executed.

It was an offense, punishable at best by three to five years in a labor camp, to refer to the famine. A doctor who complained that his sister had died of hunger was sentenced to ten years 'without the right of correspondence', the euphemism for a death sentence. The newspapers in the Ukraine, Arthur Koestler found, were full of pictures of smiling children whilst skeletons tottered in the streets. Word of the famine reached the West, through diplomatic reports and foreign correspondents, notably Malcolm Muggeridge of the *Manchester Guardian*, W. H. Chamberlin of the *Christian Science Monitor*, the New York *Herald Tribune* and the New York Jewish paper *Forwaerts*. An international relief committee was set up under the archbishop of Vienna. It could do nothing, however, for the Soviet government denied that any famine was taking place.

The lie was reinforced by Western fellow travelers. George Bernard Shaw, the famous playwright, visited the Soviet Union in 1932. 'I did not see a single under-nourished person in Russia, young or old,' he said after his chauffeur-driven tour. 'Were they padded? Were their hollow checks distended by pieces of india rubber inside?' Collectivisation was supported by Sidney and Beatrice Webb, pioneers of social science and founders of the London School of Economics. Visiting in 1932 and 1933, they

The Fellow Travelers *gave Stalin aid and comfort. The writer George Bernard Shaw, at the height of his fame, was driven through Moscow and to selected country areas during collectivisation. 'Tales of a half-starved population dwelling under the lash of a ruthless tyrant' were nonsense, he wrote in a letter to the London* Times: *'crowds of brightly dressed well-fed happy-looking workers' was nearer the truth. At a time when thousands of priests were being sent to the camps, and cathedrals turned into cinemas and warehouses, 'GBS' added: 'In the USSR, unlike Britain, there is freedom of religion.'*

approved of 'driving out the universally hated kulaks'. The government, they said, 'could hardly have acted otherwise than it did.' If there had been a 'partial failure of crops', this was made worse by individual peasants who, out of spite, sabotaged grain fields, 'even cutting off a whole ear, and carrying it off for individual hoarding.'

When a visit was made by Edouard Herriot, twice French prime minister, shop windows in Kiev were filled with food and starving orphans were cleared off the streets. The distinguished

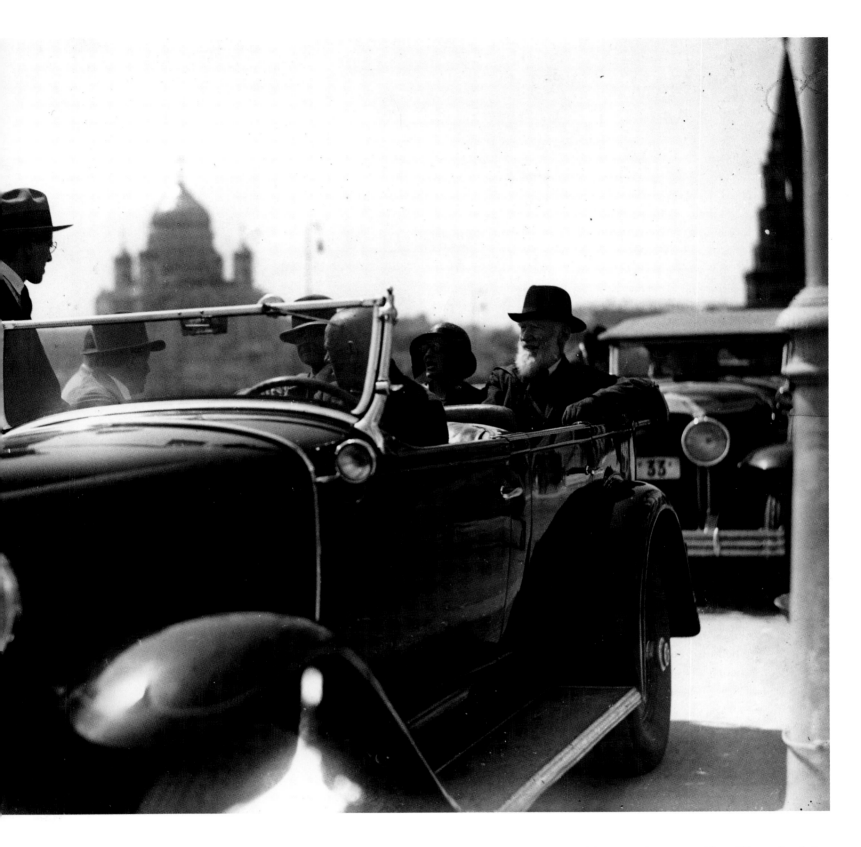

radical was taken to the October Revolution collective farm near Kiev. The buildings had been decorated with furniture from a local theater and with carpets and tablecloths trucked in from Kiev; the peasants were fed hunks of meat washed down with beer. Herriot returned to France, to say with a clear conscience that he had seen no hunger in the Soviet Union.

Walter Duranty of the *New York Times*, whom Muggeridge thought 'the greatest liar of any journalist I have met', wrote in November 1932 that 'there is no famine or actual starvation nor is there likely to be.' The following August, with millions dead, he informed *Times* readers that 'any report of a famine in Russia is today an exaggeration or malignant propaganda.' He would allow no more than a 'food shortage'. Duranty, who won a Pulitzer prize for 'dispassionate, interpretive reporting' of the news from Russia, knew full well what was afoot. He told the British chargé d'affaires in Moscow in private conversation that it was 'quite possible' that as many as ten million had died from starvation. The Soviet Union always had its Western apologists.

6
THE SECOND AMERICA

THE NEW REVOLUTION CHANGED THE COUNTRY'S DEMOGRAPHY, as millions were killed or deported to remote areas of Siberia and Kazakhstan and others were enslaved in the forced labor camps of Solzhenitsyn's Gulag archipelago. It almost finished off the church; the Chapel of the Iberian Virgin at the entrance to Red Square disappeared one night, and the great gold-domed Church of Christ the Savior, built by the Moscow river to celebrate the defeat of Napoleon in 1812, was blown up to make way for a Palace of Soviets. Topped with a statue of Lenin, this was to have been higher than any skyscraper in New York, but the ground was too soggy and the site became an open-air swimming pool. The second revolution changed art and literature, with the new cult of 'Socialist realism' in which clean-limbed workers performed heroic deeds to a backdrop of Red flags. It even, for a time, changed the calendar; the seven-day week was abolished in favor of the unbroken five-day workweek. The days lost their names; they were simply numbered from one to five.

What collectivisation was to agriculture, Stalin's Five Year Plans were to industry. The first Five Year Plan started in October 1928, overseen by the State planning commission, Gosplan; its aim was to create 'the second America'. Stalin, who had sneered at Trotsky and Zinoviev as 'super-industrialisers', who shelved plans for a vast hydro-electric station on the grounds that it was like a muzhik buying a gramophone instead of a cow, now set unrealistic and then fantasy targets for industry. The country suffered from *Piatiletka*, 'Five-year' hysteria. Pig iron production was first slated to increase threefold in five years; then fivefold; and finally seven times. Buildings were covered with Stalin's portrait and the slogan of his obsessive belief: 'There are no fortresses that Bolsheviks cannot storm'. The original plan was based on 20 per cent annual industrial growth for five straight years. The US had never achieved better than 8.7 per cent; Russia's best, in the Stolypin years before the First War, had been 8 per cent. Valerian Kuibyshev, the regime's chief economist, worked late into the night trying to fix the statistics to reflect the fantasy targets. 'This is what's been troubling me,' he scribbled in a note to his wife. 'I can't balance it out ...'

A workforce that labored to exhaustion and premature death could not cope with the demands. Stalin refused any respite. 'No, comrades, it is not possible,' he told managers in 1931. 'The pace must not be slackened! On the contrary, we must quicken it ... We are fifty or a hundred years behind the advanced countries. We must make good this distance in ten years. Either we do so, or we shall go under.' A new slogan blossomed on factory walls: 'The Five Year Plan in Four!'

Giant bearings *serve as propaganda at a May Day celebration in 1935, bringing the promise of 'the technological independence of the USSR' amidst 'fast technical growth and progress.' The building in the background is the Bolshoi Theater in Moscow. Stalin subjected the cities to an industrial drive as intense but more successful than the revolution foisted on the countryside. The first Five Year Plan created an urban hysteria as workers toiled to fill impossible quotas; but slowly the industrial foundations of the coming superpower were laid.*
[PHOTO: B. IGNATOVICH]

The fight for fitness. *The regime promoted physical culture with propaganda parades and photographs, like the Germans' 'Strength through Joy' movement. As in most areas of Soviet life, stress was laid on the 'combat' element in gymnastics and sport. This was another facet of the struggle against the encircling capitalist countries; exercise helped keep people alert to the 'wreckers' and 'spies' in their midst. The girls are marching in Red Square, Moscow. Mayakovsky wrote, 'There are no better clothes in the world than bronzed muscles and freshness of skin.'*
[Photo Above: A. Shaikhet]
[Photo Opposite: I. Shagin]

The cost was compared with a war. One and a half billion rubles was spent in foreign currency during the plan to buy equipment and import foreign managers and workers. This colossal sum was raised by exporting food, at a time of mass starvation, and by the plunder of gold and jewelry from those who still possessed some. Labor was drafted in from the villages, with collective farms later signing contracts to supply set numbers of workers for the factories; more than fifteen million peasants were shifted from the land to become dispossessed proles in the towns,

ill-treated by the new elite. Those who tried to move could not; internal passports were introduced in 1930, and no one living in one town could go to another without police permission. John Scott, the American volunteer at Magnitogorsk, likened it to the front line. 'Tens of thousands of people were enduring the most intense hardships to build blast furnaces … I would wager that Russia's battle of ferrous metallurgy alone involved more casualties than the battle of the Marne.' A young University of Wisconsin graduate, Scott found depression America 'sadly

Soviet skyscraper. *The Council of Ministers building in Moscow (left) reflected Party monumentalism; but efforts to match New York's were in vain, although a beautiful eighteenth-century church was destroyed to make way for the building. The Moscow subway, its construction overseen by Nikita Khrushchev and Lazar Kaganovich, its stations glowing with marble and mosaics, was superior to any in the West. Above ground, the Soviets lagged.* [PHOTO: N. GRANOVSKII]

The first train on the Turkestan-Siberia Railroad *(below). The country was, and remains, ill-served by roads. The railroads, with their broad-gauge tracks, and the slow-moving, swaying cars were of immense importance to industrialisation. Accidents were common, with overladen trains and exhausted drivers negotiating flimsily-laid track. They were invariably blamed on 'capitalist wrecking'.* [PHOTO: M.ALPERT]

dislocated'. After training as a welder with General Electric in Schenectady, he went off to Russia to build 'a society which seemed to be at least one step ahead of the American'. Magnitogorsk was a larger-scale version of Gary, Indiana raised on a virgin site in the Urals; the Arthur G. Mackee Corp of Cleveland, Ohio supervised its construction in an 800-million ruble deal described as 'the contract of the century.' On arrival, Scott worked on iced-up scaffolding that swung in the wind, whilst bodies fell past from the top of the blast furnace he was welding. 'The riggers were mostly plowboys who had no idea of being careful,' he wrote. 'At thirty-five below without any breakfast in you, you didn't pay as much attention as you should.' He toiled with Ukrainians, Mongols, Jews and a Tartar called Shaimat Khaibulin who had never seen a staircase, locomotive or electric light before – 'his life had changed more in a year than that of his ancestors since Tamerlane.'

On the railroads, a report on engine-drivers involved in collisions found that 80 per cent had tuberculosis and that all were exhausted and undernourished. Workers were treated as cannon fodder, flung into the 'Red offensive' to outproduce the West. 'The fifty thousand tractors you are going to give the country each year,' Stalin told workers at the tractor plant in the Volga city renamed Stalingrad, 'are fifty thousand shells blowing

Anna Akhmatova *(above). With Blok,
Mayakovsky and Mandelstam, she had been a
member of the 'Stray Dog' circle of poets in pre-
revolutionary Petrograd. Wearing black silk,
she read her famous call to decadence:*
We are all winners, we are all whores
How sad we are together.
*She was silenced from 1922 until 1940. Her
estranged husband was shot as a counter-
revolutionary and her only son was arrested
during the purges. She wrote a moving cycle of
poems on the victims published in 1963,*
Requiem, *shortly before her death.*
[Photo: M. Nappelbaum]

up the old bourgeois world.' Vladimir Mayakovsky, the Futurist
poet who had painted his face white in pre-revolutionary St
Petersburg, wrote 'The March of the Shock Brigades' in 1930:
'Fight today, revolutionary, on the barricades of production ...'
But he was depressed, tired of the hack propaganda work he was
expected to serve up – the painter poet had turned out scores of
propaganda posters to put in shopfronts to conceal the empty
shelves. A few months later, he shot himself through the heart.
'Love's boat has smashed against the daily grind,' he wrote. Safely
dead, Pasternak wrote, Mayakovsky 'began to be introduced
forcibly, like potatoes under Catherine the Great. This was his
second death. He had no hand in it.' It was Stalin who decreed
that museums, squares and a Moscow subway station should be
named for him; the standard question in final school exams reads
'For what do I love Mayakovsky?' His plays – *The Bedbug* and
The Bath House with their savage satires on Bolshevik
bureaucrats – were quietly suppressed.

Stalin, describing equal wages as 'petty bourgeois prejudice',
brought in the 'Party envelope' which gave Party members higher
pay and perks, special rations and dining rooms, apartments,
Black Sea holidays, visits to health spas. An eleven-story block on
the Moscow river embankment provided five hundred big
apartments, well furnished, with central heating, stores, a clinic,
theater and cinema, and a branch of the Kremlin restaurant. This
'Government House' was copied in the big provincial cities. The
concept of the 'shock-worker' centered on Alexei Stakhanov, a
Ukrainian miner who cut 102 tons of coal in a shift in place of the
norm of seven tons. The performance was a fraud – other workers
had done all the support work necessary before actual coalcutting
that a faceworker usually did himself – but the 'Stakhanovite' was
now invented, the superworker who set new production targets
and was rewarded with a big salary and a smart apartment. Fellow
workers did not appreciate these highly paid colleagues; they
drove up production norms, and were often rewarded for acting as
informers and stool-pigeons. Would-be Stakhanovites were
sometimes lynched. As to liberty, strikes were illegal, trade
unions were party mouthpieces – and a Stalin aide, Lazar
Kaganovich, said that a factory should quake when the director
walked through it.

The huge steel complex at Magnitogorsk had 250,000 workers,
yet it had no church. John Scott thought that it was probably the
only place of such size on earth which had no building devoted to
a religion. In other ways, though the brand-new product of an
experimental creed, it was more conventional. It had four distinct
societies. A quarter of the men were forced laborers, 'specials'
and common criminals serving five or ten-year sentences, living
in tents on the freezing earth and fed half the meager rations of
free men. They toiled under the eyes of OGPU guards at the most
brutal work, digging foundations by hand, shoveling slag and
wheeling concrete. Many were condemned kulaks. 'Very
frequently the "specials" worked better than average,' Scott
noted, 'since they were usually the most energetic elements of the
village.' For this was a remarkable aspect of the Bolshevik slave

Ménage à trois. *Osip and Lily Brik, and Lily's lover Vladimir Mayakovsky (left). Increasingly disillusioned with the Bolshevik regime he had once supported with passion, Mayakovsky fell foul of the Party hacks in the Association of Russian Writers. His last play, The Bath House, a savage lampoon of Stalinist bureaucrats, was soon suppressed. After Mayakovsky shot himself, Lily Brik wrote to Stalin to complain that no museum had been set up to commemorate her lover. Dead poets were no threat to Stalin. 'Mayakovsky was and remains the best and most talented poet of our Soviet epoch,' the dictator replied.*

The Bedbug, *a performance of Mayakovsky's play at the Meyerhold Theater (above). Vsevolod Meyerhold had directed the first Soviet play, Mayakovsky's Mystery-Bouffe, in 1918. His theater was the brilliant heart of the Soviet stage until Socialist Realism was introduced in the Thirties. Meyerhold's theater was closed in 1938; he was arrested and disappeared to die in the Gulag at a date unknown.*

In the Baku oilfields.
*In 1933, as now, little
heed was paid to the
environment. Stalin
had been a Bolshevik
agitator in Baku
before the First War,
when foreign oil
companies had
exploited the
concessions. The
huge oil and mineral
wealth of the country
now served the Party;
the Soviet Union
would later become
the world's largest oil
and gas producer.*

state; that it was amongst the condemned underclass that the most vigorous, the best educated and the most independently minded were to be found. The criminals, known as *Itekovtsi*, or 'ITKs', these being the initials for Corrective Labor Camps, were sullen and had to be driven to work with blows. Among the political 'specials' was a brigade of forty or fifty priests and bishops, in 'dirty, ragged black robes and black miter-like hats.' They wore their hair long, falling to their waists in some cases. They were hard at work with pick and shovel, digging away at a little hill, whilst a 'pugnosed plowboy', an OGPU man, watched over them with a rifle.

Ordinary workers lived in barracks, eating one rationed meal with 200 grammes of bread a day. Pay was reasonable in theory. A welder could make 300 rubles a month, well enough to raise a family when the rent for a barrack room was ten rubles a month and the official price of bread was 0.15 rubles a pound. But there was no bread to be bought at that price. The main store in Magnitogorsk, to which ordinary workers were restricted, had in the winter of 1932-3 nothing to sell beyond a little pile of silk handkerchiefs and some summer shirts.

'The size of the pay envelope, the number of bank notes under the mattress, no longer determined living standards,' said Scott. 'What one ate or wore depended almost exclusively on what there was in the particular store to which one was attached.' That, in turn, depended on one's class. Those at middle level – engineers, brigade leaders, foremen, doctors – lived on a third more food a day in a section called Sotsgorod or 'socialist city' with stone apartment buildings. Its store ran to a few winter clothes, meat and bread. The elite – managers, political personnel, the local Party and OGPU bosses, and some prisoner specialists – lived in a suburb known as 'American city'. Around 400 German and American engineers supervised construction of the giant plant. The Americans were paid in gold. They, and the privileged Russians, shopped at the Insnad foreigners' store. It stocked 'caviar, Caucasian wines, imported cloth and materials, shoes, suits, books and food at a tenth of Russian prices.' The individual houses in 'American city' had running water and heating, their designs copied from American architectural catalogs. The result was 'something very much approaching Mount Vernon, New York'. The works director, Abraham Zavenyagin, in whose presence the city quaked, built himself a 14-room mansion with billiard and music rooms, and a deer park.

The secret police were so numerous that they sometimes qualified for their own suburbs. The big industrial center at Chelyabinsk had a 'gorodok OGPU', an 'OGPU city' of six-story apartment blocks with nurseries, laundries, dining rooms and kindergartens. From this redoubt, they took 'an abnormal interest in other people's business', encouraging the rest of the city to report to them on any spying or sabotage, real or merely anticipated, and on any 'counter-revolutionary' remark made by a neighbor – a classification so wide that it could, and did, include complaints if there was a power outage or a train was late.

Failure to meet production targets, caused by shortages,

A group of shock workers *look at the 'Socialist competition board' (top) in the new steel town of Magnitogorsk in 1931. Workers who outperformed their production quotas, 'Stakhanovites', were given extra rations and comfortable apartments and starred in movie newsreels. Their achievements were often fraudulent.*

An American drilling rig *at the Magnitogorsk site in 1930 (above). Much of the machinery that made the industrial effort possible came from the United States; so did technicians and engineers.*

M'accuse. *Andrei Vyshinsky, the presiding judge, reads the eleven death sentences at the end of the first of Stalin's great show trials in 1928. The secret police extracted confessions, before the trial began, in front of an audience of foreign correspondents and handpicked Russians. Vyshinsky's bullying technique was not yet perfect. The wife of one of the accused was allowed into court. 'Kolya darling, don't lie!' she screamed as he admitted to signing a confession. 'Don't! You know you are innocent.'*

ignorance and lack of experience, by physical exhaustion and by the absurdity of the target 'norms', was ascribed to 'wrecking'. Lathe operators measured 'precision' grinding with their fingers because they had no instruments. Tractors suffered cracked blocks and stripped gears because the peasants who drove them 'knew no more than that when you pushed the pedal the tractor moved – matters such as lubrication and timing were completely beyond them.' The overloaded railroad system almost collapsed in 1933; locomotives were derailed by inadequate track or broke down for lack of spares; an acute fuel shortage developed because of the shortfall in oil and coal transport. It was convenient to blame wreckers; 'class enemies', as the house journal of Gosplan put it, 'white-guardists, kulaks, have the chance to creep into "modest" and "insignificant" jobs, like those of greasers, and silently sapping, they carry on their wrecking, becoming organisers of crashes and accidents ...' Real wrecking did exist; John Scott came across a turbine filled with ground glass by deported kulaks. But it was rare; Scott saw no other cases in three years. The country drifted into a madness: a Magnitogorsk foreman, who fainted when overcome by blast furnace fumes, was sentenced to two years; 7000 of the country's 35,000 trained engineers were in prison by 1931. They were so scarce a resource that 'technical bureaux' were set up in prisons and camps where they could labor on design projects under the eye of OGPU guards.

The imperialists, having failed in the civil war, were now trying to kill off Bolshevism by sabotaging its industry. This the workers were told every day, in newspapers, on radio, in theaters where special plays on sabotage were performed. Joseph Barnes of the New York *Herald Tribune* saw one in a big industrial city. It was called *The Confrontation*, and its villains were foreign agents who had been trained to infiltrate and wreck Soviet factories. As he left the theater and its hyped-up audience, Barnes said: 'It will take a generation to live down the fear and suspicion that is being created.' Yet American expertise was widely copied; the Stalinets 8 tractor was a clone of the Caterpillar D7; the Taylor system of scientific management was adopted as gospel by Soviet managers. Russian engineers were trained in the Ford works at Dearborn before building Ford-designed cars in a 'new model Communist town' at Gorky designed by the Austin Company of Ohio and New York. The Soviet asbestos industry was created by the American A. Ruckeyser, who was taken to a secret place called Asbest in the Urals, which existed on no maps, and given a large dollar contract to exploit its asbestos deposits. Help from Ford enabled the Russians to build 140,000 cars in 1932; in 1929, at a time when there were already 26 million automobiles in the US, the Soviet Union had just 30,000. Most were assigned to Party bigwigs and to OGPU men.

Payments were not always forthcoming. 'Although their tractors follow very closely the lines of the machines produced by Caterpillar, no arrangements have been made to pay to use the patents,' wrote the American journalist H. R. Knickerbocker when he visited the Chelyabinsk works. 'Freedom from "bourgeois" inhibitions as to private property places Soviet

The accused. *They listen to their sentences. Fifty-three engineers were accused of being part of a foreign-based conspiracy to wreck the Soviet coalmining industry. The Shakty trial served Stalin by deflecting blame for shortfalls and poor living conditions, and for equipment broken by unskilled peasant laborers. The 'conspirators' were said to have worked for the French, German and Polish intelligence services. Eleven were sentenced to death; the others were imprisoned. Although six of the condemned were reprieved, five entirely innocent men were shot.*

industry in a singularly advantageous position.' Nevertheless, it was the Americans who were attacked as 'bloodsuckers'. The villain of Valentin Kataev's bestselling novel *Time, Forward!* was an American consulting engineer working on a Russian tractor project; he thinks only of the money he is making, whilst the visiting tycoon Roy Roop cries out 'Babylon! Babylon!' in fear at the new Bolshevik world being built in the Urals wilderness.

When the Donbass coal mines fell behind target, a huge 'conspiracy' of managers and engineers with the former capitalist owners of the Shakhty pits was uncovered. The trial was held in the Hall of Columns in Moscow. 'Death to the Wreckers' yelled the press headlines. The Shakhty trial, with its 'confessions', its defendants driven insane or to suicide, was, like the Five Year Plans themselves, a blueprint for the future. One of those clamoring for the death sentence was the 12-year-old son of one of the accused. More victims were found as more production norms went unmet. In the 'Industrial Party' trial of 1930, a colossal 'wrecking center' was invented whose tentacles spread into shipbuilding, engineering, chemicals, gold mining, oil and munitions. Some of the accused 'died during investigation', so that the OGPU could use their 'evidence' to extract confessions from the living. Two thousand engineer-wreckers were said to be bankrolled by three big foreign companies – Royal Dutch Shell oil, Vickers engineering and Nobel explosives – by Lawrence of Arabia and by the French General Staff.

'Scientific-theoretical wrecking' was said to infect high tension technology, microbiology, even ichthyology where 'wreckers' said

that the natural laws of fish reproduction made the fisheries' targets of the Five Year Plan impossible. Ecologists were attacked for criticising the plowing of woodland on huge new state farms, on the grounds that birds and predators were being killed off, so increasing pest levels. To conserve nature was to frustrate socialism, and thus to wreck. The 'cultural revolution' demanded 'proletarian class belligerency' on the 'cultural front'. Historians were accused of belonging to 'historiographical counter-revolutionary wrecking centers', and were deported to Siberia. Novels went unpublished unless they satisfied the scrutiny of the Russian Association of Proletarian Writers, RAPP, to show a sound 'dialectical materialist method'.

Industry was already showing signs of the over-centralisation and bureaucracy that would ultimately wreck it more effectively that any imagined capitalist agent. Overmanning was rife. Where an American steel hearth had fifty men, a Russian one had more than double that – brigadiers, under-brigadiers, foremen, general foremen, shift foremen, technical observers, 'all getting in each other's way and most of them doing nothing productive'. Vast numbers were absorbed into office work. The People's Commissariat of Heavy Industry in Moscow decreed the setting up of new departments in distant factories at the stroke of a pen, regardless of actual need. The All-Union Academy of Agricultural Sciences had a staff of 11,000 'researchers'. Many worked on identical projects, due to obsessive secrecy. In any event, Stalin swallowed the bogus ideas of Trofim Lysenko, a plant breeder and charlatan; those who saw through Lysenko and upheld genetic science disappeared into the camps. The colossal new State organisations were proudly compared with American conglomerates. 'You call it General Electric,' a powerful figure in State industry told a visiting American. 'We call it the Ministry of the Communications Equipment Industry.' Real power, stripped from the republics, settled in Moscow. The Ukraine, producing four fifths of the country's sugar, had no say whatever in its own administration; all decisions were made in Moscow. Politics and class origin were more important to promotion than ability. 'Social purges' of non-proletarians were carried out in government offices.

Stalin's portrait was on every shop floor, his slogans on every lip. His books – he had weekly lessons in dialectics and wrote jargon-heavy political philosophy – were on every shelf. In 1932, almost seventeen million were published; Stalin's *Problems of Leninism* was translated into fifty-two languages and remains, if rarely read, one of the century's bestsellers. The normally sycophantic American journalist Louis Fischer complained in *The Nation* of the 'orgy of personal glorification'. Stalin had the article translated. '*Svoloch!*' he spat. 'The bastard!' His sensitivity extended to animals. He had a caged parrot in his Kremlin apartment; it would watch him as he paced the room, smoking his pipe, occasionally spitting on the floor. One day, his daughter Svetlana recalled, the parrot aped him by spitting. Stalin reached into the cage with his pipe and killed the bird with a blow to the head. He was, the poet Osip Mandelstam wrote in 1933, the 'Kremlin mountaineer':

His fingers are fat as grubs
And the words, final as lead weights, fall from his lips
His cockroach whiskers leer
And his boot tops gleam.
Around him a rabble of thin-necked leaders – fawning
half-men for him to play with.

They whinny, purr or whine
As he prates and points a finger.
One by one forging his laws, to be flung
Like horseshoes at the head, the eye and the groin.

But there was a fierce pride in achievement. Scott felt it. 'Men froze, hungered and suffered,' he wrote, 'but the construction work went on with a disregard for individuals and a mass heroism seldom paralleled in history.' Every evening, the streets of Magnitogorsk were filled with adult students hurrying with books and notebooks under their arms, Russians 'making up for several centuries of lost time'. After a ten-hour day, the worker went to night school and, sitting with empty stomach on a backless wooden bench, in a room so cold 'you could see your breath a yard in front of you', learnt mathematics and mechanics. He did not have much, Scott said, but 'he felt he would have more next year. His children were going to school. He was secure against sickness,

as were his children. Unemployment had been forgotten.' Among those adult students was Leonid Brezhnev, then in his twenties attending a metallurgical institute in the Ukraine.

In Germany, six million were unemployed and Hitler was beginning to triumph. America was paralysed by the Great Depression. The human price was grotesque, but huge plants were built in Magnitogorsk, Chelyabinsk, Stalingrad; the giant hydroelectric scheme on the Dnieper, which quintupled Soviet electric power output when it came on stream, was for two years the world's largest single construction site under the supervision of Colonel Hugh Cooper, creator of the Wilson Dam at Muscle Shoals, Tennessee; new mines opened in Kazakhstan; heavy industry reached into Georgia. Moscow's cobbled winding lanes were replaced by broad avenues and concrete buildings, beneath which ran a subway system with marbled stations. Russia was growing; so, at a time when many thought capitalism done for, was socialism.

The blast furnaces at
Magnitogorsk *(opposite
page) were to be vital in
the coming war. John
Scott, a University of
Wisconsin graduate who
volunteered to work in the
steel town, described how
riggers with frozen hands
and clumsy feet slipped
from the crude
scaffolding high on the
furnaces and fell past
him. Unskilled peasants
and forced laborers were
killed by the score.*
[PHOTO: I. SHAGIN]

Horsepower: *foundations
being dug by hand
(above) in the new steel
town at Magnitogorsk in
1934. Peasants and
horses were drafted in to
build the huge complex,
the world's largest, on the
bare grassland. The
heaviest work was done
by convicted* kulaks *and
others who had shown
enough initiative to be
sentenced to hard labor as
'speculators' and
'parasites'. The site's
chief engineer was a
convict.*

**The means of
production.** *Imported
equipment (left), here
from Germany, was
essential to the
industrialisation effort.
It was paid for in gold
and jewels extracted from
those who still owned
them, and by exported
grain and lumber. The
sale abroad of millions of
tons of grain, at
Depression prices,
combined with 'class
struggle' against the
more prosperous peasants
to produce mass
starvation.*

7

TERROR

Crocodile tears. *Stalin attends the funeral of Sergei Kirov, the Leningrad Party boss whose assassination at the end of 1934 was the excuse for letting loose the horror of the purges. The murder was almost certainly carried out at Stalin's orders. Kirov was killed at the Smolny Institute in Leningrad, Party headquarters since 1917. The Smolny security men were inexplicably absent on the day of the murder. Kirov's own bodyguard died in a mysterious road accident before he could give evidence. The killing was as convenient for Stalin as the Reichstag Fire had been for Adolf Hitler the year before.*

A HOMEWARD-BOUND CARGO SHIP PASSED KRONSTADT ON A HOT fall day in October 1937. On it Colonel Ilya Starinov was coming home to Leningrad from Barcelona after a year training Spanish Republicans in mine warfare. He checked into a hotel and saddled the telephone to get in touch with his friends. Every number he called was answered by a stranger. Eventually he got through to the assistant military commandant's office at the main railroad station. A familiar voice answered, usually 'loud and cheerful', now timid. 'Good morning, Comrade Cherniugov,' he said. 'This is Starinov.' He chatted about Spain and then asked how he could get in touch with an old mutual friend, Boris Ivanovich Filippov. There was a silence, and Cherniugov said: 'He is now at a health resort.' Then he rang off. Starinov hoped his friend had gone south on vacation. He got through to an acquaintance in army transport. Where was Filippov? He heard the 'short, terrible words' of the reply: 'They took him!' Rumors of purges, liquidations, of people being 'taken' had reached Spain. Starinov roamed Leningrad until late; then took a train to Moscow where he went to find his former commander, Ivan Georgievich Zakharov: 'I could tell him all my fears; he would clear up my doubts.' Zakharov's wife was dressed in black. Her husband had been in a nervous state for weeks. Two of his immediate superiors had been arrested, then there had been a hurried and persistent knock at the door one dawn. Zakharov collapsed as he tried to get up, dying of heart failure. The man at the door was merely the duty officer from his unit with a message.

Starinov wandered the Moscow streets until he found himself outside the apartment of another friend who had served eight years in the same regiment with him. He climbed the stairs and rang the bell. His friend opened the door nervously. 'Why are you wearing foreign-made clothes?' he asked suspiciously. 'Because I was abroad,' Starinov replied. 'I haven't had time to change them yet.' To have been abroad was dangerous. Starinov's friend examined the toes of his slippers. 'Pardon me, Ilya ... but you know, at a time like this ... By the way, some of our regimental pals were arrested recently. Iukov and Lermontov were taken. And they didn't belong to any opposition groups ...' he said, bending his head so far that his chin touched his chest.

Starinov left. The night turned cold and the streets were emptying. The only crowds were round the cinemas and restaurants in the center. The film star Liubov Orlova smiled down on him from a poster. *Volga-Volga* was playing at the Metropole. It was showing at the Kremlin, too. Stalin, pushing his daughter in front of him, calling her by her pet name, 'Housekeeper', allowed her to guide him to the cinema he had had built on the site of the Tsars' winter gardens. His bodyguards and two armored cars crawled at snail's pace behind father and daughter to protect them.

After the kulaks, it had been time for others. On a gray December afternoon in 1934, Sergei Kirov was shot dead by an assassin in Leningrad, where he was Party leader. Stalin took the night train to the city; he struck the city police chief in the face when he met him on the platform at the Moscow Station. Stalin was establishing his grief; he carried Kirov's coffin, named the Ballet for him, supervised the interrogation of his murderer. The last was done without witnesses; it was almost certainly on Stalin's orders that the killing had been carried out, ridding him of a popular rival. At the Party Congress earlier in the year, a group had tried to draft Kirov to stand against Stalin as General Secretary. His murder established the atmosphere of fear and mistrust in which to launch a witchhunt against all opponents, real and, more often, imagined. The Congress had been attended by 1966 delegates. Perhaps a dozen had approached Kirov; by the time the next Congress was held five years later, 1108 of the delegates had been shot. Such was the scale of terror; and such – Party members – were most of its victims. A purge joke had an arrest squad knocking on a door. 'You've made a mistake,' says the man who answers it. 'The Communists live upstairs.' In the spring of 1935, thousands of Party members were sent from Leningrad to the Arctic and Siberian camps as accessories to Kirov's murder. Stalin raised his sights. Grigori Zinoviev and Lev Kamenev had been co-rulers with Stalin a decade before. Their prestige as senior Old Bolsheviks, intimates of Lenin, no longer protected them. They were accused of terrorism, Trotskyism and the Kirov murder. The trial opened in August 1936, in the former ballroom of the Nobles' Club in Moscow, to a hysterical press campaign. The cream of purge victims were executed after such open trials, in which they sweated in the heat of arclights as their confessions were filmed for the widest possible distribution on newsreels. Painstaking skill was needed to awake and sustain spy-mania in the population.

All pleaded guilty, though their 'confessions' were nakedly absurd; one defendant admitted meeting Trotsky's son in a Danish hotel that had been demolished twenty years before. Confessions were a characteristic of the purge. They satisfied Stalin's paranoia – 'everywhere and in everything he saw "enemies", "two-facers" and "spies"', said Nikita Khrushchev – and he insisted on them. They were filed in NKVD folders, stamped 'To be preserved forever'. The confessional process was helped by rubber truncheons, the 'conveyor' of continuous interrogation, the 'swan dive' where toweling was put between the jaws and feet and tightened, arching and breaking the back. But often it was voluntary; because the Party demanded it, as one survivor recalled, and 'serving the Party was, for old Communists, not just a goal in life but also an inner need.' Facing the death sentence as a 'mad dog of capitalism', knowing the charges to be false, Kamenev still said from the dock: 'No matter what my sentence will be, I in advance consider it just.' The sentence was death.

Among the thugs. *Stalin with his henchmen in Moscow in 1936. Khrushchev, who sits at the extreme left of the front row, would later denounce the Stalinist killings. But he knew full well they were taking place – as did the other cronies. On Khrushchev's left sit the censor Andrei Zhdanov, the collectiviser Lazar Kaganovich, the third-rate defense commissar Kliment Voroshilov, while the hack bureaucrat Vyacheslav Molotov and the cipher Mikhail Kalinin sit on Stalin's left. Two other survivors, Georgy Malenkov and Nikolai Bulganin, sit second and fifth from left in the second row. So servile were Molotov and Kaganovich that they continued to fawn on Stalin, though the former's wife was sent to the camps and the latter's brother was executed. On the far right of the front row is Marshal Mikhail Tukhachevsky, hero of the civil war, of whom it was said that he could do a pull-up in the saddle, horse and all. Stalin was in the business of destroying rival heroes. In 1937, Tukhachevsky was tried and shot.*

A second great show trial was held in January 1937. A group of seventeen, including the former industry minister Gregory Piatakov, parroted admissions of wrecking, sabotage and conspiring with Trotsky and the Germans. 'I stand before you in filth, crushed by my own crimes,' Piatakov told the court, 'a man who has lost his Party, ... who has lost his very self.' A crowd of 200,000 packed Red Square in 27 degrees of frost to hear Nikita Khrushchev read out the death sentences. Nadezhda Mandelstam, widow of the poet Osip, who was arrested in 1938 and died a few months later in a camp near the Kolyma river, thought that terror had made ordinary Russians 'slightly unbalanced mentally – not exactly ill, but not normal either.' The hysteria was unceasing,

inescapable. 'We were told every day, in newspapers, over the radio, and in meetings, to cooperate with the NKVD and to report any suspicious fact immediately,' John Scott said of the purge years in Magnitogorsk. The terror convinced him that 'Westerners have no place in Russia. I survived black bread, rotten salt fish, the cold and hard work. I did not survive the purge. I could not live with it.'

Only the famous could orchestrate their confessions at public trials. Most victims simply disappeared. They were taken quietly and without fuss, from lecture rooms, off sidewalks, at the fancy food counter of the Gastronom store, between acts of *Swan Lake* at the Bolshoi, in the sleeping car of a train heading for the gentle

Boris Pasternak, *who received a bizarre midnight telephone call from Stalin after the arrest of the poet Osip Mandelstam. Stalin had been told that Pasternak was upset by the arrest, and he assured the novelist that all would be well for Mandelstam. The dictator then asked why Pasternak had not interceded for the poet, saying: 'If I were a poet and a friend of mine was in trouble, I'd do anything to help him ... He is a genius, isn't he?' Despite Stalin's assurance, Mandelstam died in the camps. 'One would have to write about it in a way to make the heart stop beating and the hair stand on end,' Pasternak wrote of the period of purges.*

shores of the Black Sea. They included heroes of long-distance aviation, recalled diplomats, catering chiefs, sportsmen, the conductor of an army band. Nobody in the country was safe from that 'frightful moment', as one victim, the Cossack Filipp Mironov, put it, when 'finally they say to you, "your pit is ready".' The man who had stormed the Winter Palace, Vladimir Antonov-Ovseenko, was taken from his cell in the Butyrka Prison in Moscow and shot. The director of the Lenin Library was executed. Victims were hunted down abroad; the civil war hero Fedor Raskolnikov was murdered in the south of France, Leon Trotsky died with an icepick embedded in his brain by an NKVD agent in Mexico.

NKVD officers with purple identity cards carried out the arrests. They drove black sedans that were called 'ravens'. Their favorite calling hours were between 11 pm and 3 am. People kept a small bag packed in case the knock came. They slept badly; Russia was full of insomniacs. A Moscow girl who had been out partying late rang the doorbell when she came back in the early hours. Her father answered the door fully dressed, bag in hand, and slapped her face when he saw who it was.

Stalin moved his office from Staraya Square into the Kremlin for greater isolation. He kept late hours; the lights in thousands of ministry windows would go out at 5 pm, and then burn again from 10 pm as bureaucrats returned to sit in their offices on the offchance of a call from the Kremlin. He made no major speech in public for two years from March 1937. Many thought that he knew nothing of the arrests, and would stop them if he did. 'If only someone would tell Stalin about it,' Boris Pasternak told an acquaintance as he walked his dog one night. 'Life has become better,' said the Stalinist slogan in every workplace. 'Life has become more joyful.' The saying that was on all lips gave this the lie; 'Nowadays it is a good thing to be a telegraph pole.' Stalin did know; indeed, he spent three or four hours most days closeted with Nikolai Yezhov, a little man, just five feet tall, an orphan who had been thought a kindly soul as a deputy commissar of agriculture. The two would work their way through a thick list of potential victims with suggested sentences. Stalin is known to have approved 383 lists containing 44,000 names. Only the most senior figures reached the discussion stage between Stalin and the NKVD head; millions of other cases were disposed of by juniors. Stalin is thought to have spared a few names; he told Yezhov that 'we won't touch the wife of Mayakovsky', saving Lily Brik; he may have scribbled 'Don't touch this cloud-dweller' against Boris Pasternak. But most he destroyed, taking a particular pleasure in embracing acquaintances shortly before they were taken. With an affectionate pat, he assured the historian Yuri Steklov that he was safe; the NKVD came for Steklov that night. The scribbled initials SMP, Supreme Measure of Punishment, filled the margins of his lists. The public used the expression 'eight grams', that being the weight of the bullet from a TT eight-shot automatic pistol in the back of the head that constituted the SMP.

Pasternak was fortunate to remain untouched. About a thousand writers were killed; the same number survived the camps. So many disappeared that those left were half paralysed with fear of the news of fresh arrests, 'news that reached one by phone, that overtook one on the street, that came crashing into one's home, that ripped off the door of every refuge,' wrote Pasternak's cousin, Olga Friedenberg. She herself was attacked in an article in *Izvestiya*; people then avoided her on the street, friends no longer telephoned, at lectures she was isolated in a circle of empty chairs. Musicians, artists and movie directors were also vulnerable. Stalin liked simple tunes and folk music so he loathed Dmitri Shostakovich's score for *Lady Macbeth of Mtsensk* when he heard it in 1936; a vicious criticism in *Pravda* lambasted it as 'muddle in place of music'. It was not social realism; its success in the West was due to the 'perverted bourgeois taste for the neurotic'. A State Jazz Orchestra was permitted, but its lead singer, the beauty Nina Donskaya, was fired for singing authentic and complex jazz at a Kremlin evening attended by Stalin. The dictator's test for painting, too, was that it should be easily understood and reflect heroic Bolshevik themes; artists who strayed were attacked as 'leftist daubers'.

Master film-makers had dominated the Twenties; Sergei Eisenstein with his *Battleship Potemkin*, Vsevolod Pudovkin's *The End of St Petersburg*, Alexander Dovzhenko's *Earth*. They fell on hard times in the Thirties; Eisenstein made no new film between *Old and New*, his collectivisation saga of 1929 whose title came from Stalin, and *Alexander Nevsky* in 1938. Stalin acted as personal cinema and theater censor; he insisted on the 'cast-iron scenario' where every detail of the script had to be cleared by himself or by the State Committee for Cinematography, then he previewed the movies in his own projection room in the Kremlin. He had a taste for sentimental musicals by the director Grigori Aleksandrov. One, *Circus*, was an attack on American racism. A circus performer is forced to flee her native America because she has a black child. She travels to Moscow where she falls in love with a circus director, who sings to her the smash hit of terror-ridden 1936:

I know of no other country
Where a man so freely breathes.

Aleksandrov directed *Volga-Volga*, Stalin's favorite; a light romance of two competing amateur folksong groups who race in boats along the Volga to Moscow, where they join forces to sing the 'Song of the Volga' and win first prize in the folk festival as the song's pretty composer falls in love with the conductor. Stalin watched it so compulsively in the great Terror year of 1938 that he knew the lines by heart.

Denunciation was the engine of purge. The NKVD had a vast network of secret informers; they ran into millions, in every workplace. They had to unmask traitors, or themselves stand accused. Among the victims were a 70-year-old schoolteacher using an old textbook which still had a picture of Trotsky, a man who took down a portrait of Stalin whilst painting a wall, a woman who made the sign of the Cross when a funeral passed, a philatelist whose stamp of Queen Victoria had a higher face value than that of Stalin. All organised philatelic activity in the country

Vsevolod Meyerhold, *brilliant actor and director who had had his own theater in Moscow since 1920. He was in mortal danger after the play he wished to produce for the twentieth anniversary of the Revolution in 1937 was rejected by Party hacks, and the theater was closed. He was protected by the great Stanislavsky until his death in 1938. Meyerhold was arrested in 1939 and tortured by the bestial interrogator Boris Rodos. In January 1940, having at last 'confessed' to treason, he wrote a letter to Andrei Vyshinsky, the degenerate chief prosecutor, detailing the treatment given him. Having forced him to drink his own urine, his interrogator then broke his left arm whilst forcing him to sign his confession with his right.*

A watchtower at a Gulag camp *in Chukotka. Zeks, prisoners, in their millions peopled the vast network of forced labor camps that Alexander Solzhenitsyn called 'the Gulag archipelago'. There were so many zeks that in order to hold them all before their trials, the exhibits of wax figures kept in old Tsarist cells, to remind people of capitalist oppression, were removed and replaced with living prisoners.*
[Photo: Y. Raskopov]

ceased in 1937, as stamp collecting was unmasked as a cloak for treason. A woman in Kiev is believed to have denounced 8000 people, most of whom died; Nikita Khrushchev recalled that the sidewalks emptied as she walked through the city. People sought to avoid her gaze. Inside prison, denunciation had yet more impetus behind it. The first question at interrogation was: 'Who recruited you?' The second was: 'And whom did you recruit?' Sleep deprivation, beatings and solitary confinement in a hutch almost invariably produced the needed names. A rare exception was I. I. Rubin. Another man was brought in to the interrogation room. Rubin was told that the man, a stranger to him, would be shot if he did not confess. After the murder of two strangers in front of him, Rubin broke. By mid-1937, there were so many denunciations that the system was breaking under the volume of flesh fed into it. Monasteries and bathhouses were pressed into use as prisons. The Lubyanka, in central Moscow, had a reception 'kennel' where three prisoners were stuffed into each square yard of space.

The military joined politicians as prey. On June 11, 1937, the cream of the Red army, stripped of medals and insignia, were ushered into a courtroom. They included Marshal Tukhachevsky, 'victor of Kronstadt', the most brilliant soldier of his generation, a pioneer of armored and airborne warfare; and Ion Yakir, the pioneer of tank manufacture, seized the night before in his berth when his private sleeping car was uncoupled by NKVD officers. They were accused of spying for the Germans, found guilty, shot and dumped in a trench on a construction site, all within eighteen hours. Six of the eight officers who condemned them were themselves soon shot. All those commanding military districts were shot; 57 out of 85 corps commanders disappeared within a year; 3 out of 4 naval fleet commanders were shot. Of the 100,000 Red army officers on active duty in 1937, perhaps 50,000 were purged. Stalin murdered more of his own officers of the rank of colonel and above than the Germans were to kill in the war; as to Hitler's army 'purge', he merely dismissed sixteen generals, neither imprisoning nor shooting them.

Those who were not sentenced to death were sent to work in the camps of the Gulag empire first settled by the kulaks. The gold mines of Kolyma were a 'pole of cold and cruelty'; they were more truly a 'supreme penalty' than execution. After Stalin criticised the 'coddling' of prisoners, felt boots were replaced by canvas shoes and many froze to death. Others died of pneumonia, their lungs destroyed by the use of ammonal explosive in blasting, or from exhaustion caused by hauling frozen earth and rock. A *zek*, a convict, would sink to the ground, blood would gush from his mouth, and it was over. Starvation added to cold. General Karpunich-Braven described fellow officers 'on all fours, growling and rooting about, they had become semi-idiots whom no amount of beating could drive from the refuse heaps.' Those too sick and weak to work were killed by NKVD guards in mass shootings, whilst tractor engines were run to hide the screams. Some Old Bolsheviks in the camps felt that they were expiating the guilt of having helped to inflict Communism on Russia.

A canal worker, *T. Byelikova. This is a rare portrait of one of the countless women who labored, in terrible conditions, on the White Sea Canal project that turned out to be useless. It was too shallow for the ships of the Baltic Fleet for which it was designed.*

Zeks toil *to the strains of a prisoner orchestra in a propaganda picture taken during the building of the White Sea Canal. To lull foreign opinion, a book with a reassuring description of working conditions by Maxim Gorky was published about the canal. In reality, 100,000 prisoners may have died on the project.* [PHOTO: A. RODCHENKO]

Stalin the family man, *with his son Vasili and daughter Svetlana (above). The dictator's private life was harsh and tragic. During a banquet in 1932 Stalin snapped at his wife Nadezhda: 'Hey, you, have a drink.' She screamed, 'Don't you dare talk to me like that' and ran from the table to her Kremlin apartment. Stalin's outburst was the final straw for her and so she shot herself. When his other son Iakov was taken prisoner by the Germans in 1941, Stalin refused to exchange him for German officers in Russian hands. The German treatment of Russian prisoners made this a death sentence. By the time she was a young woman, Svetlana thought Stalin had 'reached the point of being pathological, of persecution mania.'*

Svetlana Stalin sits on the knee of Lavrenti Beria *(right) whilst her father works on papers at his country dacha in 1936. Beria was to become head of the NKVD secret police in 1938. The scene is tranquil, ordinary. But Russia was undergoing a terror insane in its scope. In 1991 the KGB, shortly before its demise, claimed forty-two million Soviet citizens died between 1928 and 1952 as a result of the forced collectivisations and the purges.*

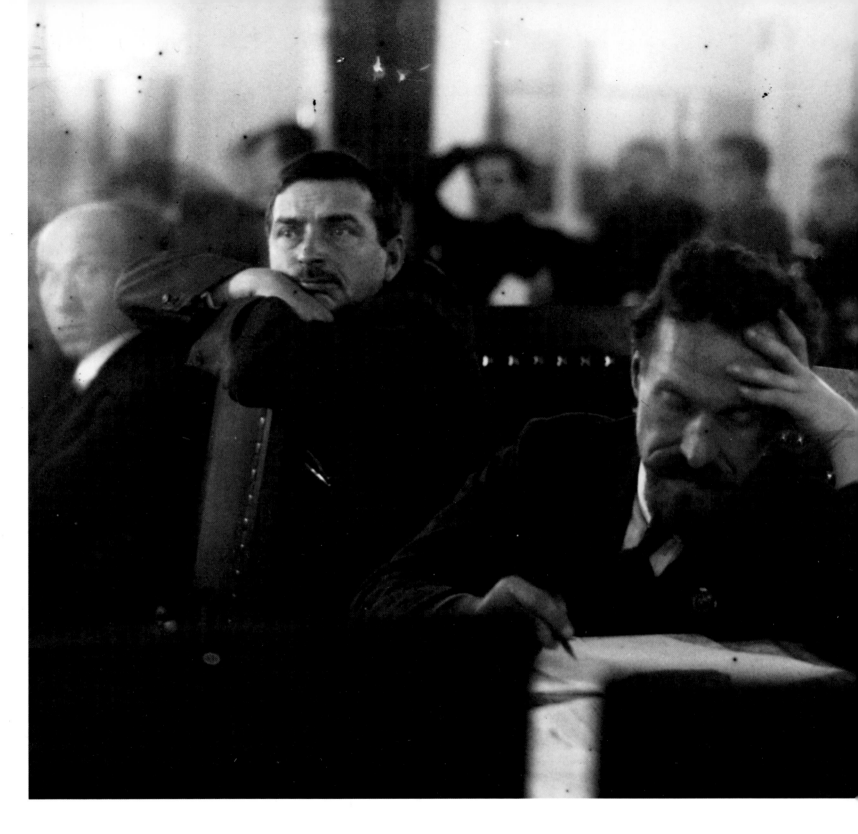

The last major show trial took place in March 1938. Its victims included Nikolai Bukharin, Rykov and Yagoda, the head of the NKVD before Yezhov; amongst other crimes, they admitted to poisoning 30,000 horses. (Stalin had little Yezhov shot; Lavrenty Beria, 'plump, greenish and pale, with soft damp hands ... and bulging eyes behind his pince-nez', a Georgian, replaced him.) By the end of that year, the pace could no longer be maintained. The NKVD had files on perhaps half the adult urban population; files were compiled on children, too, as well as by them, for they were encouraged to inform on their parents and friends. Industries were running down for the shortage of skilled men. Prison laboratories and testing grounds were established. Here 'prisoner specialists' perfected the designs for military and civilian equipment; in a small forest clearing, surrounded by a double barbed-wire fence, the convict V. M. Petliakov designed the Pe-2 dive bomber, the Red answer to the Nazi Stuka. Fitfully, the Terror began to abate.

The average number of zeks in the camps under Stalin has been estimated at eight million. In 1938 there were more prisoners in Kolyma, perhaps twice as many, as the maximum number held in Tsarist prisons of all types in all Russia. Kolyma was one of many Gulag colonies. More prisoners were killed in a single death camp, Serpantinka, in 1938 than were executed in the last century of Romanov rule. Stalinism may have killed

Alexei Rykov and Nikolai Bukharin under guard *before the last big show trial in 1938 (above). Stalin played cat and mouse with Bukharin before his arrest, insisting that he join him in the place of honor above Lenin's Tomb during Red Square parades. Bukharin agreed to 'confess' to treason after he was assured that his young wife and baby son would not be harmed. In fact, she was sent to a Siberian camp. Stalin had the trial transmitted to his quarters by special microphones. Once, a spotlight in the hall where the trial was taking place focused accidentally on a darkened room at the rear, revealing Stalin as a ghoulish secret spectator. After he had been condemned to death on March 13, 1938, Bukharin wrote Stalin a note referring to him by an old nick-name: 'Koba, why do you need me to die?' His wife claims that Bukharin also wrote a final letter to her – 'I am afraid for you, and for our friends, but most of all I am afraid for you … How madly, how deeply I love you' – which she says was discovered in secret police files and finally delivered to her in 1992 when she was 78. Bukharin was shot with Rykov, two days after sentence was passed.*

Alexei Rykov takes notes whilst Mikhail Tomsky looks on *at a meeting in Moscow in 1930 (left). Along with Lev Kamenev, Leon Trotsky and Grigori Zinoviev, all of whom were killed on Stalin's orders, they made up with Stalin the six full members of Lenin's 1923 Politburo. Stalin had a lethal dislike for old colleagues. Tomsky committed suicide in 1936. Rykov was dissuaded from doing so by his family, who bitterly regretted this when he was arrested, tortured and shot in 1938.*

anything between 20 million and 40 million; the mass graves are too dispersed, the records too incomplete, to be sure.

It was not Stalin alone. Lenin had created the Cheka; though the name changed, the dynasty remained through OGPU (1922-34), NKVD (1934-43), NKGB (1943-6), MGB (1946-53), MVD (1953), KGB (1953-91). Lenin was the philosopher of 'Red Terror'; and he found its technician in Felix Dzerzhinsky, whose statue dominated the square named for him outside the Lubyanka until it was toppled and smashed in 1991. Lenin approved the Gulag; 'the Soviet republic should be made secure against class enemies by isolating them in concentration camps,' his Red Terror decree of September 1918 read. He had urged

'merciless war' against the kulak, the 'flea-crook and the bedbug rich'. He wanted them to be given yellow tickets after they had done their time in penal servitude – they would be 'put to cleaning latrines in prison … so that all the people shall have them under surveillance … One out of every ten idlers will be shot on the spot.' Such yellow tickets were little different from the yellow stars the Nazis sewed upon the Jews. Lenin's contempt for kulaks and bourgeois sounds like Hitler's later racial hatreds: 'these dregs of humanity, these hopelessly decayed and atrophied limbs, this contagion, this plague, this ulcer that socialism has inherited from capitalism.' The grisly waxwork on Red Square played his part in The Terror, too.

The NKVD file of the poet Osip Mandelstam *(above), discovered in the Gulag archives in Magadan in 1993. Magadan was built by Stalin to administer the Arctic labor camps and mines of Kolyma, which Solzhenitsyn describes as 'the pole of cold and cruelty'. Mandelstam was sentenced to five years for 'counter-revolutionary activity'. He arrived in Kolyma from Moscow in October 1938. He died, in the concentration camp SVITL of the NKVD, on December 26, 1938. No details of his death were known until a British writer visited Magadan in 1993, and was allowed fleeting access to rooms packed with prisoners' files in the archive of the Arctic city. Mandelstam's wife Nadezhda wrote in* Hope Against Hope, *'As I constantly tell myself: the sooner he died the better.' Many believed he was the finest poet of his day.*

Alexander Solzhenitsyn *(above right), the chronicler of the Gulag Archipelago, as a zek in 1946. Arrested for anti-Stalin remarks whilst serving as a wartime artillery officer, he was sentenced without trial to eight years in the camps for 'malicious slander'. One of the century's greatest writers, the Nobel laureate was forced aboard a Swiss-bound airliner in handcuffs in 1974, the first person to be expelled from the Soviet Union since Trotsky. He settled in Vermont, whose long, cold winters reminded him of Russia.*

Skulls of purge victims *(right) excavated from a mass grave near Chelyabinsk. Like millions of others, they were killed with a single shot to the head. NKVD executioners worked in shifts, wearing leather aprons, gloves and hats to protect them from the gore their handiwork produced.*
[Photo: D. Grafov]

8
ONSLAUGHT

WHILST COMMUNISM UNDERWENT ITS TERROR, ITS SISTER CREED was destroying the post-1918 settlement in Europe. Poland, Czechoslovakia, Finland and the Baltic states had not existed as independent states before the war. Neither Russian Communists nor German Fascists wished them to survive. Czechoslovakia became a Nazi 'protectorate' in 1938. Adolf Hitler next turned on Poland. In August 1939 his foreign minister, Joachim von Ribbentrop, arrived in Moscow, greeted by swastika banners that had been hastily rounded up from film sets where they were in use in anti-Nazi films.

Stalin personally welcomed Ribbentrop and the Nazi-Soviet pact was signed on August 23; mortal enemies before, they now agreed to mutual non-aggression. The world was stunned. A British cartoon showed the two dictators bowing deeply to one another. 'The scum of the earth, I believe?' said Hitler, whilst Stalin smilingly replied 'The bloody assassin of the workers, I presume?' In a week, Hitler invaded Poland. The Kremlin's reward for remaining neutral was hidden in a secret protocol allowing it the return of territory lost after the revolution. As the Germans crushed Polish resistance in the west of the country, the Red army advanced in the east to the pre-arranged demarcation line. The NKVD came with it, deporting thousands of Poles in cattle trucks to the Gulag. Captured Polish officers were never seen again; they were massacred on Stalin's orders in the forests of Katyn.

Finland was harder to break. The Russians attacked in November 1939, but suffered terrible casualties as poorly led units floundered in snowdrifts. Many froze to death as Finnish ski troops concentrated on destroying Russian field kitchens and tents. The command was affected by the trauma of the purges; infantry were flung in doomed frontal assaults on Finnish machinegunners. Overwhelming Russian superiority in men and armor forced the Finns to sue for peace in March 1940; by then German intelligence, observing the incompetence, had concluded that the Red army would be easy meat.

In June 1940, the day after France fell to the Nazis, the Red army occupied Lithuania, Latvia and Estonia. The NKVD was hard on its heels. The better-off farmers, the pastors, Jews, hoteliers, shopkeepers, diplomats, bank staff, even people who spoke Esperanto, were shot or shipped to the Gulag. On the single night of June 14, the NKVD rounded up 10,000 Estonians for deportation to Siberia; in all, 1.2 million people were torn from the newly occupied lands and sent to Siberia, where most died. The Rumanian province of Bessarabia suffered the same fate a few days later. The land promised under the protocol was taken. Hitler had kept his word; the Russians kept theirs with tankers

Relatives identify the dead *after the Germans had massacred all the men in a village. The Germans torched hundreds of villages; in the towns, they tried to exterminate the Jews as a whole; Russian POWs suffered terribly. Germans captured by Russian partisans were found with their heads tied inside the stomachs of dead comrades, or stripped naked with their feet strapped in drinking troughs where the water froze solid.*
[PHOTO: D. BALTERMANTS]

Refugees try to escape from Kiev *in September 1941. The speed of the German advance stunned the purge-weakened Russian officer corps. Red units were left floundering in the rear of hard-* *driving German armor. The Germans captured almost 900 tanks in Kiev, and the Russian rifles they took were piled 18 feet high. Russian civilians in German-occupied territory were* *shipped to the Reich as slave labor, or fled the ruined and half-starved cities for the villages.*

and freight cars of oil, rubber, copper and grain that rolled westward on the Moscow-Berlin rail line to feed the German campaign against the stubborn British. The pact appeared in perfect order.

Stalin had warnings in plenty that it was not. Hitler held Bolshevism to be Jewish-inspired, and thus to be eradicated; he was equally obsessed with the immense *Lebensraum*, living space, of Russia, which could be settled by colonies of German soldier-farmers with 'such indigenous inhabitants as remained to do the menial work'. The master spy Richard Sorge gave Russian military intelligence details of the German invasion plan in April 1941; Winston Churchill sent an urgent warning on June 13. The German ambassador in Moscow, who opposed war with Russia, gave the day; a German deserter supplied the hour. Russian observation posts on the frontier picked up the sounds of tank

engines at night; by day, German aircraft overflew them on reconnaissance missions. Rabbit to the stoat, Stalin ignored the intelligence, instructing his armies not to react to any provocation. He ordered the deserter to be shot.

For the Russians, June 21, 1941 was a normal day. In the border fortress at Brest, where Trotsky had signed the peace with Germany in 1918, the hot afternoon was passed in drilling to a military band. A packed house at the officers' club watched an evening performance of the popular comedy *The Wedding at Malinkovka* while German infantrymen were moving up to their start lines through cabbage plots and cornfields. Shortly after midnight, Soviet frontier guards passed the Moscow-Berlin express through the railroad station. Three hours later the German guns opened fire; the guards, rushing half-dressed from their barracks, were the first casualties of Operation Barbarossa.

The Nazi invasion was the largest offensive in history, involving 3.2 million German troops deployed against 170 Red divisions along a front that stretched, in American terms, from New York to Minneapolis.

The tanks of the leading German panzer group had forded the Bug river at Brest by 0445 on Sunday, June 22. Their radio operators picked up repeated appeals for orders from Moscow; the reply was: 'Comrade Stalin has forbidden opening artillery fire on the Germans.' Moscow Radio woke the capital at 0600 with keep-fit exercises and the weather forecast; the invasion was not mentioned until midday. By evening, two Soviet fronts had been broken and German tanks were moving at speed deep in the Russian rear. Their advance was marked by plumes of dust that hung in the still air like contrails. Motorcyclists scrawled direction arrows on the wings of crashed Russian aircraft –

Luftwaffe pilots said they were wreaking 'infanticide' on their poorly-trained opponents. Minsk was taken on the ninth day, June 30. The Red western army group fell into two gigantic German encirclements at Bialystok and Minsk; it lost 3785 tanks, more than the Germans possessed, and 440,000 men. On July 16, German armor captured Smolensk, within 200 miles of Moscow, in an encirclement that yielded a further 300,000 prisoners.

The Baltic states were overrun. Pealing church bells, and flowers thrown by girls in national dress, welcomed the German columns. Men in the green caps of the NKVD called on senior officers who escaped the Germans; commanders of fronts, armies and divisions were shot by firing squads as the rout continued. Where possible, the NKVD evacuated its prisoners and slave laborers; the roads and railways were clogged with eastbound Polish, Ukrainian and Balt prisoners. Where time did not permit,

Architect of victory. *Georgy Zhukov (left) at the forward edge of the combat zone, an ill-mannered, ruthless personality, prepared to use penal battalions to clear minefields without mine detectors. His winning streak started with the battle for Moscow.*

A wounded Red fights on *(far right). The Germans, used to softer fighting in western Europe, were amazed at the fortitude of Russian infantry, 'indifferent to weather, hunger and thirst and almost as indifferent to life and losses, pestilence and famine'. A German colonel thought that the Nazis in Russia were like an elephant attacking a host of ants: 'In the end their numbers will overcome him and he will be eaten to the bone.'*
[Photo: I. Shagin]

Red Square, November 1941. *These troops (below right), taking part in the annual November 7 parade to commemorate the Bolshevik takeover, marched straight on to the front. The snowstorm and icy wind that blew through the parade caused the first severe cases of frostbite among German troops. General Winter, the traditional Russian ally, had arrived.* [Photo: A. Ustinov]

the NKVD massacred its prisoners. Several thousand Ukrainian nationalists were held in three prisons in Lvov. When the Germans broke into the city on June 29, they found scores of grieving relatives round prisons which smelled like charnel houses. Maria Spiridonova was being held in Orel prison. As a tiny delicate teenager, she had assassinated a Tsarist police chief on a railroad platform in 1906. Her death sentence had been commuted to life imprisonment in Siberia; freed, she was a hero figure to young revolutionaries until the Bolsheviks re-imprisoned her. Orel fell so swiftly that the trams were still running when the lead German tanks appeared, but her NKVD guards had time to kill her in her cell.

The Germans had hatreds in plenty to tap: fresh memories of purge and collectivisation, nationalist yearning, old Christian loyalty. Country women greeted them with the sign of the Cross and gifts of salt and bread. But they came as slavemakers, not liberators. As the NKVD shadowed the Red army, so the murder squads of Heinrich Himmler's *Einsatzgruppen* followed the Wehrmacht. The 'Bolshevik bosses and commissars', and the 'Jewish-Bolshevik intelligentsia', were killed out of hand. The rest were shipped west to work in German labor camps, or were treated as sub-human *Untermenschen* in their own land. Pacification, Hitler said, 'can best be achieved by shooting anybody who shows a wry face.' Such treatment soon led to the counter-horrors of partisan warfare.

Kiev saw the greatest encirclement battle of the war. The Germans surrounded an intact Red army group on September 17. The city fell two days later. SS men in black uniforms and death's head cap badges ordered 'Commissars, Communists and Jews –

Forward!' These were stripped to the waist and marched off to be shot. The booty was immense; 665,000 prisoners joined the dun-uniformed tide that was flowing back to die in German camps and factories. But the German troops did not feel that they were in a defeated nation: 'Instead there was resistance, always resistance, however hopeless. A single gun, a group of men with rifles …' At Kiev, a speech by Stalin was played over loudspeakers in the Russian trenches. The Germans found something 'diabolical and naive' about the 'stubborn, violent gestures of these men who died so terrible a lonely death on this battlefield, amid the deafening roar of the cannon and the ceaseless braying of the loudspeakers'. Trapped Russians with a few rifle rounds attacked German artillery that killed them over open sights. The horizon was a miasma, never reached; the Germans felt they were marching 'into a dark hole, the landscape pale and bare'. Overrun one unit and another was identified. Estimates of 200 Red divisions were replaced by 360 on intelligence sheets.

The German armored commander, General Heinz Guderian, began his drive on Moscow on October 2, 1941. Almost three million soldiers fought in the battle for the capital. It seemed to Hitler, and the watching world, that one final lunge would finish it. German staff officers estimated that the Red army had lost just under half of its total strength. Before noon on October 5, Soviet fighter pilots were reporting that a fifteen-mile long column of German tanks and trucks was advancing on the town of Yukhnov, 130 miles from Moscow. The Kremlin refused to believe it, accusing the men of 'panic-mongering'. A further 600,000 Russians were surrounded, now in front of Moscow, undergoing the grim process of shelling and air strikes that preceded captivity. In Berlin, Goebbels told a conference of the foreign press that the war had 'definitely been brought to a close.'

On October 14, Panzers broke into Kalinin, 100 miles north of Moscow. The Germans found signs of rare prosperity, asphalt roads, restaurants with fancy names like 'Culinaria' and 'Lucullus' amidst the mix of modern blocks and wooden shacks. The capital itself was seized by the *bolshoi drap*, the big scram. Government offices and the diplomatic corps were shifted east to Kuibyshev. Stalin's daughter Svetlana was packed off to the Kuibyshev museum, smelling of paint and mice, equipped with cooks, waitresses and bodyguards, that had been made ready for his retinue. By October 18, the Germans were in Mozhaisk; in 1812 it had taken Napoleon three days to get from Mozhaisk to Moscow on horseback. But the panic was transitory. Though the Germans were driving ever east into the sunrise, each day broke over Red units that were still fighting. Groups of German graves, tripods of birch branches topped with helmets, punctuated the yellow autumn grass.

The first snow fell. General Georgy Zhukov was transferred from Leningrad, which had been cut off by the Germans, to command the Moscow front. Tough and self-willed, a remarkable strategist, Zhukov had grown up in the countryside west of the city where the battle was centering. He brooked no meddling

Zoya's story. *A photograph (above) found on a dead German showed a girl after she had been taken prisoner by the Germans. Survivors said that she was an eighteen-year-old partisan called Tanya who had been caught trying to set fire to some stables. The Germans tortured, then hanged her. Her body (left) was found on a gallows during the first successful counter-attack of the war, in front of Moscow in December 1941. Her story was published in* Pravda *in January 1942. Her real name was Zoya Kosmodemyanskaya and she came to personify German atrocity and Russian resistance. She had been carrying out the scorched-earth tactics of the partisans under which youths were sent in to burn everything that might be of service to the Germans. Later, rumors circulated that the Russian villagers themselves handed her over to the Germans. But the immediate effect was that the 'swamp animals', as Hitler called the Russians, fought with new anger and desperation on the Moscow front. 'They bellow like bulls when they attack,' wrote a German infantryman near Petrishchevo. 'No more prisoners are being taken in the front line.'*

from Stalin, speaking to his Supreme Commander in Chief in a 'sharp, commanding tone'. He showed a timing and self-restraint that had been lacking in the earlier Soviet profligacy. The Germans were approaching exhaustion. Assault groups were strung along forest trails, mined by Russian horsemen. German tanks were outmaneuvered in the ice by the broad-tracked Soviet T-34s. The Panzer crews were losing confidence: 'Better machines, that's terrible … You race the motor, but she responds too slowly. The Russian tanks are so agile, at close range they will climb a slope or cross a piece of swamp faster than you can traverse the turret. And through the noise and the vibration you keep hearing the clangor of shot against armor … There is so often a deep, long explosion, a roar as the fuel burns, a roar too loud, thank God, to let us hear the cries of the crew.'

Each evening, the Germans saw clouds building above the distant steppe and over the forests, dark masses that 'carried in the stratosphere the rain, the ice and snow of the coming winter'. Moscow women dragged sacks of sand to build tank traps, the volunteers voting to excuse only breast-feeding girls from this work. Autumn mud reduced the German advance to a crawl at the end of October. Guderian noted that the exhaustion now beginning to affect even his best officers was 'less physical than spiritual'. An NCO complained that 'the Russians attack all night. The trees drip in the fog and the crows shake their feathers … We talk about what is to become of us, of Russia and of Germany.' The parade to celebrate the twenty-fourth anniversary of the Bolshevik seizure of power was held in a snowstorm on Red Square on November 7. The tanks were fully armed and some of the troops marched straight on from the parade to the front.

Red cavalry *attacks German positions in January 1942. Each squadron of a hundred men had its own field gun and mortars. They rode small Steppe horses, agile in the snowy, ravine-filled landscape, and could move sixty miles in a night. They charged with drawn sabers, shouting the Russian battlecry: 'Ourrah!'* [PHOTO: A. USTINOV]

A frozen corpse *lies in front of a Russian trench in the fighting round Moscow. The wounded were dead in ten to fifteen minutes unless stretcher bearers reached them with heavy blankets and a drink of vodka laced with morphine against the shock. Food had to be cut with saws. It could take two hours to start a tank engine and another half-hour to thaw the gearbox. Russian troops, in fur hats, gloves and mittens, their feet wrapped in bands of cloth, were better protected than the Germans, who still got close enough to see the Kremlin towers through their field glasses.*
[PHOTO: A. USTINOV]

Stalin spoke to the troops of their 'great ancestors', Alexander Nevsky, who had beaten the Teutonic knights in 1242, Dmitri Donskoi who routed the Tartars in 1380, Suvorov and Kutuzov who had battled against Napoleon. The impact of associating the Communist regime with the old patriotism of Holy Russia was deepened by the nearness of the Panzers. The speech built a sense of common purpose and intimacy.

The wind that blew the grit and sand off Red Square brought the first severe cases of frostbite for the Germans. The temperature fell to minus 20 deg F in brilliant pink and violet clarity on December 7, snapping photographic film, boot soles, steel cranes and the bark of trees. Flesh exposed for more than a few seconds was frostbitten. The dead were rigid within an hour. Engine and gearbox oil became first a paste and then a glue. The killing range of a mortar was reduced to a radius of a yard by the snow. Only grenades and flamethrowers kept their reliability. The Russians had padded jackets, *valenki* felt boots and fur hats with earflaps. The Germans, with only issue denims and overcoats, stripped Russian prisoners and the dead of their clothes. 'Only the national emblem showed that they were Germans,' wrote Guderian.

The final stage of the battle began on November 16. On November 28 the Germans reached Krasnaya-Poliana, fourteen miles north of Moscow. The towers and domes of the Kremlin

Leningraders among the ruins *of their bombed and shelled city (top). They sold silver (above) to buy food, but it was soon without price. Cannibalism made its grisly appearance. 'One often saw corpses with the buttocks carved out,' recalled one* blokadnik, *a survivor of the siege. Meanwhile Andrei Zhdanov, Leningrad Party boss, was receiving his personal supply of orange juice by plane.* [Photo, top: D.Trachtenberg]

could be seen from its high-rise apartment blocks. They were approaching the limits of endurance. They had suffered almost 750,000 casualties; 200,000 had been killed, seven times the figure for all the campaigns of 1940. Battalions were led by lieutenants. Russian aircraft bombed villages and isolated huts to deny the Germans shelter, forcing them to live in bivouacs of poles pitched like tepees under a roof of pine boughs, urinating into their hands, so easing their chilblains and worsening their sores, burning beams from destroyed houses by their gun pits. Abandoned horses trotted through the snow 'hanging their heads, appearing and disappearing in the solitude'. At 5 am on December 1, the German 4th Army launched a final attack along the Smolensk road to Moscow. By midday, it had broken through the Red defenses to a depth of two miles. Zhukov ordered every available reserve into the breach and, where the forests bleed into the western suburbs of Moscow, the 4th Army was stopped. 'We only needed another eight miles to get Moscow within artillery range,' said a German lieutenant. 'We just could not make it.'

On December 5, the Russian counter-offensive began. Three days later, the Japanese attacked Pearl Harbor. Stalin had feared an assault on the Soviet Far East where Russian troops had earlier clashed with the Japanese in Manchuria. Japanese involvement with the US reduced this risk and Zhukov was free to transfer more troops west. Understrength German divisions, riddled with dysentery and frostbite, their automatic weapons jamming in the cold, sometimes panicked when they were attacked by warmly clad Siberian troops backed by T-34s. 'It's so very cold my soul is freezing,' a German infantryman wrote in his last letter to his wife. 'I beg of you – stop writing about the silks and rubber boots I'm supposed to bring you from Moscow. Can't you understand I'm dying? I'll die for sure. I feel it.' At night, cavalry on agile Steppe horses attacked stragglers on the German flanks with drawn sabers.

The Russians were now liberating territory. What they found drove them on. 'All that remained of the villages was stove chimneys and the charred skeletons of houses,' wrote the novelist Konstantin Simenov. 'Twice I saw gallows in liberated villages, and by one of them lay the bodies of peasants hung by the Germans.' Slowly Zhukov's Far Eastern divisions wore themselves out, their bodies lying in piles round the German gunpits, 'twisted on top of one another, frozen green and brown in their poor nakedness.' By mid-March 1942, the front was stabilised forty miles west of Moscow.

Leningrad did not escape. Rather than storm it in costly streetfighting, Hitler decided to strangle the birthplace of Bolshevism by siege. Three million people were trapped in the city. By December 1941, the official ration of bread, heavily cut with cellulose and cotton-seed oilcake, was nine ounces a day for manual workers and troops, and 4.5 ounces for the rest. But the ice road across Lake Ladoga, the only lifeline, was tenuous and rations were rare. Pharmacies had been emptied of cough drops, bad breath tablets, peach stone oil, castor oil, hair oil and glycerine. In January and February 1942, 200,000 Leningraders

Water drawn from the frozen canals *led to epidemics. Leningrad was full of corpses. 'People were dying in the streets; for days the bodies would lie where they had fallen,' wrote the opera star Galina Vishnevskaya. 'When someone in a family died, the survivors would try to hold off burying him and reporting his death for as long as possible, so that they could use his ration book. Mothers lay in bed with dead children for a few extra crumbs of bread. Frozen corpses were left in apartments until spring.'*

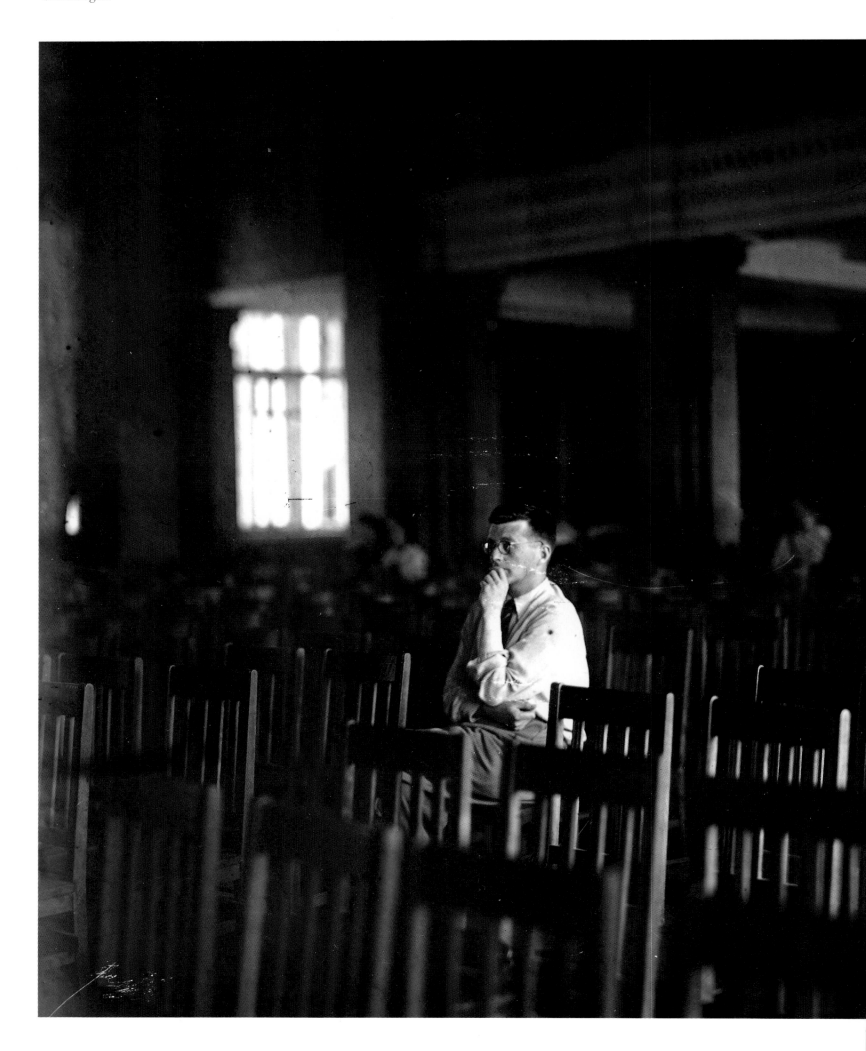

Dmitri Shostakovich *(left) rehearses in Leningrad in 1942, with the Germans a few miles away. He wrote his famous seventh symphony, the Leningrad Symphony, in the city. 'If it turns out to be good and if I manage to complete the third and fourth movements, I will call it the seventh symphony,' he told a radio audience. 'I am saying all this so that those who are listening to me will now know that the situation in our city is normal. We are all at our battle stations …' The British correspondent Alexander Werth said that the first movement, depicting the German invasion, conveyed 'the naked evil in all its stupendous arrogant inhumanity, a terrifying power overrunning Russia – there is almost nothing to equal it.'*

At the Hermitage depository *in Leningrad (above right) after a German air raid. One of the museum's classical sculptures has been decapitated by the bombing.* [PHOTO: S. SUKHANOV]

Dancers of the Musical Comedy Theater *shiver on stage (below right) during the rehearsal of Kalman's operetta* Countess Maritsa *during the siege of Leningrad in 1942. 'We went to shows and concerts, tried to keep our dignity,' said Ludmila Barteyenetseva, a schoolteacher. Another survivor, Arturovich Gausman, who conducted an army orchestra, recalled that he played Beethoven overtures at concerts in the city. 'It was the best thing we could think to do,' he recalled. 'We wanted to show the enemy that we loved life so much that we could play German music and still draw some strength from it. I remember how we tried to broadcast it over their radios. I was very proud to be Russian then.'*

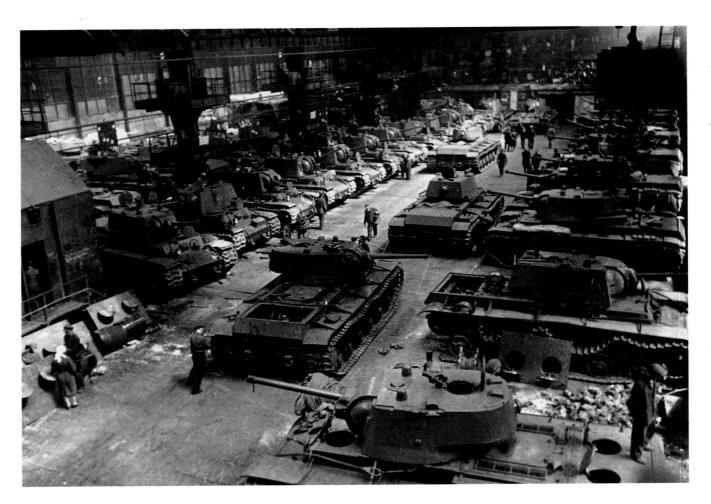

Tanks roll off a production line *at a plant in Nizhny Tagil in the Urals. The Germans overran most of the great factories in European Russia, but machines and workers were moved east, where no buildings awaited them, just frozen earth.*
[PHOTO: G. ZELMA]

Women and children *supplied most of the labor on the farms. They took the place of tractors, too, hauling plows. Forty-two per cent of the pre-war area under cultivation fell to the Germans. With it were lost half the country's cattle and horses.*
[PHOTO: M. SAVIN]

died of cold and hunger. They fell in the street and at work; an actor, dying on stage at the Pushkin Theater, was pulled into the wings and the performance continued. Alcoholics died very fast. So did misers, who had been hoarding money and food for years; 'all too often their greed got the better of them, even on the brink of death.' People pulled relatives to the cemeteries on sledges, but often became exhausted themselves and abandoned the corpses on the street. Horses were eaten early, and a dog or cat was worth a month's salary on the black market. Soup was made from glue and boiled book bindings; jellied calfskin was mixed with cloves; the city's crows and rooks fled or were eaten. So were people. Gangs of cannibals dismembered fresh corpses in the recesses of unlit apartment houses. Water was dragged from holes cut in the Neva, and filtered through gauze; it tasted terrible. Fuel was exhausted; the trams stopped running and there was no light.

Leningrad Radio was run from the generator of a ship trapped in the frozen Neva. Between programs the sound of a metronome was broadcast to remind people that the city was still alive, and years later, survivors shuddered at the sound. The city was under constant German shellfire; the front line was in the suburbs. Women and children were evacuated over the lake; as the numbers in the city fell, and the volume of food that could be carried through the lifeline increased, conditions in the city gradually improved. Yet when the siege was finally lifted after 900 days, on 27 January 1944, 900,000 people had died in the city.

At the time of the Moscow battles, the Soviet Union had lost a quarter of European Russia, the richest slice of the nation where

45 per cent of its population lived. The coal mines and chemical industries of the Donbass had fallen, and the eastern Ukrainian steel plants. A third of the wheatfields were gone, and half of the country's cattle and horses. The losses were equivalent in American terms to the Midwest grain states, and the great industrial belt from Chicago to Buffalo and as far south as Indianapolis and the West Virginia coalfields, with Washington under siege and New York threatened.

Huge 'evacuation bases' in the east had been planned before the war. Within a fortnight of the outbreak of war, the vulnerable Zaporozhie steel mills in the Ukraine were being loaded onto 8000 railroad trucks for relocation in Magnitogorsk. The tube-rolling mill at Dniepropetrovsk was stacked onto nine groups of freight trains in September, which steamed eastward for 1150 miles to Pervouralsk in the Urals. It was in production again on Christmas Eve. A forty-wagon train left the Iakovlev fighter aircraft plant every eight to ten hours carrying people and machines. In this vast migration, 1360 large war plants and 17 million people were moved east over four months. They went to the Urals, Kazakhstan and Central Asia, Siberia. More than half a million head of cattle were herded east from Belorussia.

No buildings awaited workers and machines in the east, only 'the earth ... like stone, frozen hard by our fierce Siberian frost' as was said of a plant moved to Sverdlovsk from the Ukraine in November. 'Axes and pickaxes could not break the stony soil. In the light of arc lamps people hacked at the earth all night. They blew up the stones and the frozen earth, and they laid the foundations … Over the charts and blueprints, laid out on packing cases, the blizzard was raging … ' Pits were hacked in the ground and wood laid in them at an evacuated aircraft plant in Kuibyshev. This was drenched with fuel oil and lit to provide the only heating; there were no windows or roofs and snow covered the shop floor where the workers slept. Machines were carried from the railway cars by hand. Food, 'something resembling soup', was served in the open. On December 29, the roar of a motor filled the site. The evacuees searched the sky for an enemy aircraft and then realised : 'They have begun testing!'

The workers rebuilding the evacuated Kharkov tractor plant lived in dugouts, setting up the first machines on the earth. *Voskresniks*, voluntary labor Sundays, meant that many worked seven days a week. In the Karaganda coalfields of Kazakhstan, most of the new miners were women and adolescents. On the farms, only women, teenagers and old people were left to work. Cattle were used as draft animals. In some cases, women drew the plows. The effort paid off. The average plant was working within three months of arrival in the east. By June 1942, most restarts had been completed. A huge new power station was built at Chelyabinsk to supply dozens of armaments plants. New coal pits were sunk in the Urals, Kuzbass and Karaganda; molybdenum mines were developed in the waterless steppe near Lake Balkhash in central Asia. By July 1942, monthly aircraft production was greater than in 1941. Tank production doubled in 1942; diesel engine output was up fourfold; mortars three times. The 'swamp animals', as Hitler called them, were outbuilding the Germans.

It was as well. There was a desperate edge to the campaigning of 1942. The Germans wanted a conclusion at any price; they were depressed by a 'landscape always the same … One can't bear to see it any more, the rain, the ankle-deep mud, the eternal sameness of the villages. One doesn't even want to know their names.' Before troops returned from Germany on leave, taking the long train ride to the front through country devastated by burning, deportation and mass murder, their families would look at them 'with a certain look in their eyes, that animal curiosity

when you gaze on something condemned … And deep down so many of us believed it. Some slit-eyed Mongol sniper was waiting for each one of us.' Casualties were constant and numbing. 'You say: "Damn it, he was a good lad,"' wrote a German. 'And next day you see the wreath the boys have made, with bunches of red fir cones, like the blossoming of a wound. You see his face again, just as it was when he went outside. Then it gets blurred.'

STALINGRAD

Hitler decided to attack in the south, aiming to cripple the Soviet economy by seizing the Donets industrial belt, Stalingrad and the Caucasian oilfields. The offensive slammed into four Red armies on June 28, 1942. Tracked by German aircraft in the clear heat of high summer, isolated Red units wandered until their fuel or strength ran out and clustered round an isolated building or a streambed to await the end. By July 5, German combat teams were assaulting the western suburbs of Voronezh and Panzers had reached the Don on both sides of the city. 'The Russian is finished,' Hitler told his Chief of Staff on July 20. 'I must admit, it looks like it,' replied the cautious general. Shortly before midnight on August 23, a Panzer unit of General von Paulus' 6th Army radioed that it had penetrated the northern suburbs of Stalingrad and had reached the river that flows on to the Caspian. The Germans were on the Volga.

The city stretched for over twenty-five miles in a long and thin industrial clutter on the high western bank of the Volga. Three huge industrial complexes, the Tractor, Barricades and Red October Factories, showpieces of 1930s industrialisation with their surrounding garden cities of schools and apartment blocks, dominated the north of the city. The Volga, between two and two and a half miles wide, was the lifeline for small boats and ferries taking supplies to the Russian defenders of 62nd Army on the west bank. To cut it, the Germans had to reach the east bank. The Germans were equipped and attuned for open space and grand maneuver. Now the war shifted, a German general said, into 'the jagged gullies of the Volga hills with their copses and ravines, into the factory area … spread out over uneven, pitted, rugged country, covered with iron, concrete and stone buildings. The mile, as a measure of distance, was replaced by the yard …' German infantry and tanks burst into the central sector of the city to chop the Russians into reducible pockets. 'The Germans obviously thought that the fate of the town had been settled,' wrote Vasily Chuikov, the Russian commander. 'We saw drunken Germans jumping down from their trucks, playing mouth organs, shouting like madmen and dancing on the pavements.' They penetrated to within two hundred yards of his command post. The war diary of 62nd Army recorded the struggle for the platforms and halls of Stalingrad-1, the Central Station, the next morning: '0800 Station in enemy hands. 0840 Station recaptured. 0940 Station retaken by enemy. 1040 Enemy … 600 meters from Army command post … 1320 Station in our hands.' The station

Russian infantry attacking on the Stalingrad perimeter.
The Germans reached the Volga close to the city on August 23, 1942. The last fighting in the city was recorded on February 2, 1943. Two million casualties resulted between these dates in the elemental struggle between Fascism and Communism.

[Photo: D. Baltermants]

A Red assault squad
*advances through the
ruins of Stalingrad. The
fighting in the city was
constant and so violent
that individual buildings
often changed hands
several times in a day.
But troops were rarely
seen in the open. They
made rat runs through the
rubble and dug
themselves deep into
ruined sewers.*
[PHOTO: G. ZELMA]

changed hands fifteen times. Above the city and the river wheeled the Luftwaffe aircraft, their screamer sirens blaring, flying up to 3000 sorties a day.

Fighting imploded from blocks to buildings, then to rooms. At the Central Station, a battalion of Soviet Guardsmen dug in behind smashed railroad cars and platforms. Bombed and shelled, 'the station buildings were on fire, the walls burst apart, the iron buckled'. The survivors moved to a nearby ruin where, tormented by thirst, they fired at drainpipes to see if any water would drip out. During the night, German sappers blew up the wall separating the room holding the Russians from the German-held part of the building and threw in grenades. An attack cut the battalion in two and the headquarters staff was trapped inside the Univermag department store where the battalion commander was killed in hand-to-hand fighting. The last forty men of the

battalion pulled back to a building on the Volga. They set up a heavy machinegun in the basement and broke down the walls at the top of the building to prepare lumps of stone and wood to hurl at the Germans. They had no water and only a few pounds of scorched grain to eat. After five days, a survivor wrote, 'the basement was full of wounded; only twelve men were still able to fight'. The battalion nurse was dying of a chest wound. A German tank ground forward and a Russian slipped out with the last anti-tank rifle rounds to deal with it. He was captured by German tommygunners. Apparently, he persuaded his captors that the Russians had run out of ammunition, because the Germans 'came impudently out of their shelter, standing up and shouting'. The last belt of machinegun cartridges was fired into them and 'an hour later they led our anti-tank rifleman on to a heap of ruins and shot him in front of our eyes'. More squat German tanks appeared and reduced the building with point-blank fire. At night, six survivors of the battalion freed themselves from the rubble and struggled to the Volga.

The stakes were constantly increased as both sides fed in new troops, Hitler dangerously from the defensive screen of the 200-mile front stretching back to the west, Chuikov more happily from the reserves on the east bank. Paulus launched a further offensive on September 27. Under the harsh magnesium light of parachute flares, Chuikov's guardsmen counter-attacked on the raddled heights of the Mamayev Kurgan in the center of the city. Men driven beyond exhaustion slid into depression or, fueled with benzedrine, schnapps and vodka, rallied in half-mad exhilaration. The Germans were slowly grinding their divisions to pieces in a desperate attempt to end it before winter came. Already the nights were drawing cooler and cloud-banks were building. The

German flanks were highly vulnerable, with large sectors held by satellite Rumanians and Italians who had little stomach for the Eastern Front. Hitler refused to give up 'a single yard'. Paulus attacked toward the Tractor and Barricades factories again on October 14. Individual shots and explosions could not be heard above the general bombardment. By midnight, the Germans had surrounded the Tractor factory on three sides and were fighting in small, savage spasms through the machine shops and assembly halls. Reaching the Volga on a front of more than a mile, the Germans cut 62nd Army in two. The factory fell the following day. The Germans moved on to the Barricades and Red October plants.

From burrows made of collapsed girders and concrete shards, the war of knives and tommyguns and grenades progressed. 'We have fought during fifteen days for a single house,' wrote a Panzer

Cut off in November 1942, *the German 6th Army knew it was dying.*
'I read my boys the Christmas story according to the Gospel of Luke,' a
chaplain wrote. 'The men sat on footstools and looked up to me from large
eyes in their starved faces.' Of the 93,000 Germans marched into captivity
in February 1943, only 6000 survived the war.

officer. 'The front is a corridor between burnt-out rooms; it is the thin ceiling between two floors ... From story to story, faces black with sweat, we bombard each other with grenades in the middle of explosions, clouds of dust and smoke, heaps of mortar, floods of blood, fragments of furniture and human beings ... The street is no longer measured by meters but by corpses ... Stalingrad is no longer a town. By day it is an enormous cloud of burning, blinding smoke; it is a vast furnace lit by the reflection of the flames. And when night arrives, one of those scorching howling bleeding nights, the dogs plunge into the Volga and swim desperately to gain the other bank. The nights of Stalingrad are a terror for them. Animals flee this hell; the hardest stones cannot bear it for long; only men endure.'

Early on the morning of November 19, the Germans heard heavy guns to the far northwest. The front here was held by poorly equipped Rumanians who were overwhelmed in a Russian counter-offensive. Russian tank crews steered by compass across the wastes of the Don steppe, linking up with others advancing from the south. The German 6th Army, 250,000 men, was trapped in a pocket 35 miles wide and 20 miles from north to

Friedrich von Paulus, *the German commander of 6th Army, surrenders. On January 31, 1943, Hitler promoted Paulus Field Marshal. Later in the day, 6th Army sent its last radio message before surrendering. Two Russian lieutenants with some tommygunners broke into a bunker beneath a ruined department store. They found Paulus lying on a cot, unshaven. '"Well, that finishes it", I remarked to him,' said one of them. 'He gave me a sort of miserable look and nodded.' Paulus became a convert to Communism during his captivity, and served the post-war regime in East Germany.*

south. A Panzer division, advancing across a frozen steppe strewn with dead horses and wrecked tanks and guns to open a line of retreat, got close enough for the men to see the flares hanging above the Stalingrad perimeter. Hitler forbade a break-out. The division pulled back on Christmas Day, 1942; 6th Army knew it was doomed. A chaplain read the Christmas story according to the Gospel of Luke. A soldier played Beethoven's Appassionata on a grand piano dragged from a wrecked building into the street. Temperatures fell to minus 40 degrees. Frostbite was induced as an anesthetic for the wounded. A meteorologist continued to make reports on cloud ceilings for aircraft that rarely came. 'Around me,' he wrote, 'everything is collapsing, a whole army is dying, day and night are on fire.' On January 31, Hitler promoted Paulus to Field Marshal. Later that day, 6th Army sent its last message: 'The Russians are in front of our bunker. We are destroying the station.' Paulus came out of the basement of the Univermag store to surrender. With him, 23 generals, 2500 other officers and 90,000 men went east into captivity. The Red army, in trucks, horse carts and sleighs drawn by camels, began to move west.

9
SPINE SNAP

THE SOVIET UNION NOT ONLY BOUGHT ITS SURVIVAL AT STALINGRAD but set out from there on the road toward global power. The liberation of the country's fourth largest city was marked with a surge in confidence among the Party leadership, with Stalin making himself Marshal of the Soviet Union. Politics had wisely kept a low profile during the defeats of 1941 and 1942. Now the Party and its ideological baggage came out of the closet. 'Party organisation is the real backbone of the Army,' *Red Star* crowed three days after Kharkov was retaken. 'All the magnificent achievements of our Army are due to the fact that the Red army's military doctrine is based on the well-tested principles of the wisest doctrine in the world – that of Marx, Engels and Stalin.'

Kharkov provided grim evidence of the fate of great cities that fell to the Nazis. The population when the Germans had taken it late in 1941 was about 700,000. Only half that number was left in February 1943. Of the missing, some 120,000 had been transported to Germany as slave labor. A further 80,000 had died of starvation. The Germans had fared well enough; the Red army men found stocks of Hungarian and French wine, Portuguese sardines, Austrian chocolate and Italian pickled lemons. Thirty thousand inhabitants, half of them Jews, had been murdered. The Gestapo had thrown people off the balconies of their headquarters with ropes tied to their necks. The Jews had been herded into a brickworks on the outskirts of the city and killed. Whilst the Germans had amused themselves watching Viennese operettas at the theaters and in Armenian-run night clubs, every secondary school in the city had been closed. Kharkov was a human wasteland. Some survivors had little reason to cheer. The NKVD was back within hours of liberation.

The Germans were not finished yet. They recaptured Kharkov in a brilliant counter-attack that persuaded them into a final summer offensive. When the front stabilised in mid-March 1943, the Russians held a large salient west of Kursk. To the north, the Germans held Orel and to the south Kharkov. Between them, the Kursk salient was less than a hundred miles in width and bulged some eighty miles deep into the German line. The Germans planned to bite it off and the Russians were well aware of their intentions. Now a Marshal, Georgy Zhukov was able to persuade Stalin to wait for the German offensive rather than risking a premature Soviet lunge. The concentrations of armor built up around Kursk have no parallel. The salient was rolling plain covered by wheatfields and tree stands, and cut by streams and valleys. Into it were poured almost 7000 tanks and self-propelled guns. There was one machine to every thirty-five yards of front in the north while in the south nine of the finest divisions in the German army stood shoulder to shoulder. In all, the Germans

Motherland, a T-34 tank, *so christened, goes into action against the Germans. The T-34 was to the Russians what the Spitfire was to the British: an essential element in national survival. Its wide tracks kept it going in snow and mud that robbed German machines of maneuver-ability, and its 500hp engine was full of heart.*
[PHOTO: G. ZELMA]

Russian tank spearhead *breaks through German defence lines (left). The Soviet Army that pursued the Germans was the largest land force in history. Millions of troops were on the move, with watering eyes and hoarfrost on their lips. After Stalingrad, they were 'cheerful and strangely happy, and they kept shouting about the job they had done. Westward! Westward! ... They were going west. How much better it felt than going east!'*
[Photo: M. Savin]

Signal flares illuminate the steppe *during a night attack by Red tanks (right). The Russians, aided by US-built trucks and jeeps, were more mobile than the Germans after 1942. They were better fed, too, with American Spam. The front was colossal, stretching in American terms from New York to Mexico City, or from London to Timbuktu. There was no continuous line. Groups of Germans and Russians fought each other where they met in the gigantic landscape, rather like battle fleets at sea.*
[Photo: D. Baltermants]

had amassed almost a million men for 'Citadel', the Kursk offensive. As they waited on their start lines, they received a personal message from Hitler: 'This day you are to take part in an offensive of such importance that the whole future of the war may depend on its outcome.'

The primeval battle between Fascism and Communism was joined on the morning of July 5, 1943. The Russians knew the hour of the attack from a deserter: Kursk was one of the best-advertised battles of the war. The Russians watching the Germans moving up saw the 'dark, stooped figures of weary men ... in a straggling line melting away into the darkness.' Mines disabled many German tanks in the first 750 yards; their crews, forbidden to abandon them, were at the mercy of roaming Russians with explosive charges and incendiaries. Smoke from burning fields and machines drifted across the brilliant sun as the Germans were bled by the mines and guns of the first Russian defense zones. The Russian communiqué on the first day claimed that 586 enemy tanks had been destroyed or crippled. The figure caught the country's imagination: there had never been anything like it.

Reserves were thrown in the next day. The Germans attacked in armored flails of a hundred and more machines, a 'huge black rhombus, like a piece of the forest that had broken away from the main mass,' advancing across the buckwheat fields. A Russian infantryman was transfixed by the camouflage of a tank advancing on his trench, seeing it as 'a map, with dark lowlands, yellow deserts and the brown zigzags of mountain chains, and on those chains the swastika, its spidery legs reaching down into the valleys ...' As it crossed the trench, he 'lay in total darkness, like in a cellar with the hatch closed' until it passed. Then he could see 'the dark figures of the submachine-gunners in their angular helmets' following behind. The armored contact was so intimate that German and Soviet tanks rammed each other, whilst the Germans hosed their comrades' armor with machinegun fire to dislodge Soviet infantry who had clambered on their decks to pump flamethrowers through the air intakes. Medical staffs were unable to cope with the wounded, even when they could be extricated from a battlefield seething with snipers and tommy-gunners.

July 8 was the critical day, as the Germans came close to overwhelming the Russian anti-tank defenses. The wreckage of the aerial battle slammed burning into the stands of wheat. 'Tragic, unbelievable visions,' wrote a soldier with *Gross Deutschland* on the ground, 'tightly riveted machines ripped like the belly of a cow that has just been sliced open, flaming and groaning; trees broken into tiny fragments ... the cries of officers and noncoms, trying to shout across the cataclysm to regroup their sections and companies.' The Russians held. The weather deteriorated, with cold winds and rain driving across the sky.

The cream of German strength was concentrated in the south to achieve a decisive breakthrough in the area of the small village and collective farm at Prokhorovka. The Germans had the black-uniformed SS men of *Totenkopf, Adolf Hitler* and *Das Reich,* five Panzer divisions, *Gross Deutschland* and three infantry divisions. A reserve Soviet tank army, 5th Guards, made a 210-mile forced march to meet them. Zhukov gave Stalin hourly reports of the battle. There was rough parity in tank strength. The killing ground was an area three miles by four, where the Russian T-34s closed to point-blank range to offset the heavier armor of the Tigers. Gouts of steel and flesh were flung in the air as the tanks engaged in individual combat. The Germans had never experienced 'such an overwhelming impression of Russian strength and numbers as on that day', the T-34s 'streaming like rats.' They fought for eighteen hours. When the *Prokhorovka poboishche,* the slaughter at Prokhorovka, was over, 5th Guards Tank was half-destroyed. But it was the Germans who withdrew from the darkened battlefield, leaving behind them more than 300 wrecked tanks. They had lost almost twice as many men in not much more than a week as the Americans lost in the years of the Vietnam War. There was not to be another major German offensive in the east.

Russian tank strength was by now growing at the rate of 2000 new machines a month. The manpower pool was increased as men in the liberated territories were impressed into the Red army. A Russian nationalism intense enough for the *New York Times* to refer to 'a return to Tsarism' was being bred. Stalin scrapped the symbol of world revolution, the Comintern. Guards regiments and divisions were created. Army regulations dating back to Peter the Great were revived. 'Suvorov schools', closely modeled on the Tsarist cadet corps, were set up. Stalin personally ordered the production of Sergei Eisenstein's film *Ivan the Terrible.* In September, the Patriarch of Moscow was crowned and the Holy Synod was restored. An *ofitser* could once more wear *pogon* shoulder boards, which would have been hammered into his flesh if he had fallen into Bolshevik hands twenty years before; he ate in a separate mess; he was taught fine manners and the waltz as a cadet; he could be buried beneath a Christian cross. Confidence bred Red respectability.

Though Leningrad remained under German shellfire, the front from Orel to the Black Sea was driven westward. On August 23, Kharkov was recaptured for good. A few days later, the Red army broke through to the Sea of Azov. The Germans were rapidly retreating from the smashed plants and mines of the Donbass. On September 22, the Red army won a bridgehead on

Kursk, the greatest tank battle in history. *Almost 7000 tanks and self-propelled guns joined in the battle for the salient on the morning of July 5, 1943. The density reached 160 tanks to a mile of front in places. That night, as German infantry fought hand-to-hand battles to protect vulnerable armor from Russian anti-tank squads, the Russians were claiming to have inflicted record losses on the Nazis.*
[PHOTO: M.SAVIN]

There were deep veins of hatred for Stalinism in the Soviet Union *which the Germans could have mined. Anger at collective farms, and outrage at the suppression of Christianity, ran through the country districts. In the villages of the Ukraine and western Russia, peasants stroked the black crosses on Nazi tanks, thinking the Panzer crews their allies in Christ. But Hitler's 'Commissar Order' made clear that no moral restraints would apply in Russia and behind the German combat troops came the Reich commissars, who let loose the SS in an orgy of public whippings, hangings and shootings. At first, they targeted Communists and Jews, but soon the population in general was involved. Their brutality, the Panzer general Heinz Guderian noted, 'soon managed to alienate all sympathy from the Germans and so prepared the ground for the horrors of partisan warfare.' The partisan campaigns led to a horrific cycle of atrocity and counter-atrocity. Advancing Russian units moving into liberated cities would find 'gallows with bodies swinging in the wind, the charred corpses of people burnt alive in their own homes and the emaciated corpses of those who had starved.'*

Not much is known about the photographs on these pages, but they stand here as examples of Nazi handiwork.

212

One in four *of the people in Belorussia died in the war; shelled, shot, hanged, starved or worked to death as slave labor in the Reich. Villages were burned to the ground in their entirety, the villagers shot or locked in their burning houses and churches.*

On the brink of a lonely death *against the wall, their hands tied together, Red stars sewn on their jacket sleeves, two youths are marched off with a girl by German troops. The girl is bandaged; the boys have been beaten. Such bestial treatment encouraged more resistance; the vicious circle of atrocity eventually weakened the Germans by forcing them to take troops from the front to protect the rear.*

the west bank of the Dnieper south-east of Kiev. Three days later, Smolensk was retaken in heavy fighting. The days were getting shorter and colder, the sun 'like a reflection of brass'. German morale sank with it. They added utter ruin to a country that had suffered Great War, civil war, collectivisation and purge within a generation. Few villages survived two summers after Barbarossa; only brick fireplaces showed where they had stood. Gardens were abandoned to wild carrots, lupins and wormwood. 'Now the smoke is going up from the last ruins,' wrote a retreating German, Helmut Pabst. 'Soon there will only be the tracks of the woodmen through the wilderness.' In the suburbs of Bryansk, the sun was red long before evening as the Germans fired the city. 'It hung sick and thirsty above the march of destruction,' Pabst wrote. 'We raced through the white heat of dying streets ... through a forest of chimney stacks which, rigid and angular, revolved before our gaze.'

The human ruination was as great. Three million Russians, Belorussians and especially Ukrainians had been deported to the Reich as slave labor. Attempts had been made to exterminate the Jews in their entirety. The massacre at Babyi Yar, near Kiev, where about one hundred thousand men, women and children were killed, was but the largest of many. The treatment of

Russian PoWs was little better. 'We were stationed at Rovno (in the Western Ukraine),' a Hungarian tank officer wrote. 'I woke one morning and heard thousands of dogs howling in the distance ... I called my orderly and said: "Sandor, what is all this moaning and howling?" "Not far from here," he said, "there's a huge mass of Russian prisoners in the open air. There must be eighty thousand of them. They're moaning because they are starving."' It is possible that the sum of PoWs who died in captivity reached three million.

Traumatised German units fell back on the Dnieper east of Kiev. Thousands of men packed its sandy eastern bank, wrote Guy Sajer of *Gross Deutschland*, 'in a state of indescribable panic.' When Russian tanks appeared on their way to Kiev, officers tried to stop the mob drowning itself in the water, 'like shepherds trying to control a herd of crazed sheep'. On November 5, Soviet troops broke into burning Kiev to find only 80,000 people left alive, a fifth of the pre-war figure, in a city that within a quarter of a century had been taken by Austro-German armies, Denikin's Whites, the Poles, the Reds, the Nazis.

On January 27, 1944, as a mass of red, white and blue rockets were fired over Leningrad to celebrate the lifting of the siege, one Belgian SS and eight German divisions were caught in a pocket at

Korsun south of Kiev. They prepared to break out. They slaughtered the cattle in the village and made a last meal of them with a barrel of pickled cabbage; then they killed their wounded to prevent them from falling into Russian hands. 'They shot them,' said a Russian officer, Boris Kampov, 'as they usually shoot Russians and Jews, through the back of the head.' Two columns of 14,000 men each then stumbled down two ravines to the west. Clearing the ravines, they thought they had escaped and 'burst into frantic jubilant screaming, firing their pistols and tommy-guns into the air.' Then Russian tanks and cavalry fell on them. 'Hundreds and hundreds of cavalry were hacking at them with their sabers,' wrote Kampov. 'They massacred the Fritzes as no one has ever been massacred by cavalry before ... It was a kind of slaughter that nothing could stop until it was over.' Belgian SS men threw themselves into the icy currents of the Tikich river to escape west, and froze or drowned. Twenty thousand were killed, with the residue taken prisoner over the following days in the ravines and woods where they had hidden. The Russians thought Korsun a psychological victory of great importance: it was a reminder to the Germans of Stalingrad.

Spearheads of T-34s and Studebakers rolled west at up to thirty miles a day. Two thirds of Red army trucks were American; Studebaker and Dodge with a few Macks. Aid had started even before the US entered the war; the agreement was celebrated with thirty-one vodka and champagne toasts in the marble and gold Catherine Room of the Kremlin in October 1941. Arctic convoys ran a gauntlet of U-boats and bombers amid ice floes, drifting fog and heavy seas. The Russians provided no naval or air support. In the summer of 1942, the outbound convoy PQ 16 lost a quarter of its tonnage and an American freighter, *City of Joliet*, was attacked eight times by torpedo and eighteen times by dive bombers in a day. The crews were not welcome; the dock laborers were prisoners under NKVD guard. The effort was immense. The Americans largely clothed, shod, fed and transported the Red army. Enough cloth was sent for 54 million uniforms, together with $1.5 million-worth of buttons to do them up. Red soldiers marched on 14.5 million pairs of US boots. They ate a quarter million tons of Tushonka canned pork produced to a Russian formula by Midwestern packers. Red army cooks used Ford corn oil from Cedar Rapids and Pilsbury flour from Minneapolis. As well as the trucks – 409,526 of them – the Russians were supplied with tens of thousands of Willys jeeps, which they called *villises*. Freighters supplied enough railroad equipment for a new trans-Siberian. Russian mobility, which so terrified increasingly horsebound German units, was American-engined.

There was little Soviet gratitude. The Americans, so the Russians had it, bought the German defeat with Russian blood and paid in Spam; before the Normandy landings, Red army men referred sarcastically to canned meat as 'Second Front.' 'The Russian authorities seem to want to cover the fact that they are receiving outside help,' US Ambassador Standley, an admiral, said bitterly at a Moscow press conference. 'Apparently they want their people to believe that the Red army is fighting this war alone.' Molotov retorted: 'Every man in the street knows we are getting lend-lease supplies from our Allies.' 'That may be so, Mr Molotov,' said Standley. 'But we have no contact with the

A youngster, Tolya Frolov, *next to the burnt family house (left) in a village in the Orlov region in July 1943. Hundreds of thousands of children were orphaned during the war, or lost contact with their parents. Families were still advertising to try to re-establish contact twenty years after the war ended. The Germans devastated the country as they retreated. On the railroads, a trolley would make a final journey down the track with two men sitting on it throwing out explosives.*
[Photo: M. Savin]

It's over. *A German (right) whose gun has been put out of action waits to be taken prisoner by the Reds in the Kursk salient. Hitler called off the Kursk offensive on July 13. By then, the Russians were claiming to have killed 90,000 Germans and to have destroyed 2952 tanks.*

man in the street. The man in the street does not dare talk to us.'

The Ukraine was cleared of Germans. Hitler ordered that the Crimea should be held. It was said that he intended to retire one day to the Livadia Palace, the white limestone retreat where Nicholas II and his family had exchanged Fabergé eggs at Easter. The Germans were driven back to Sevastopol. As the city fell on May 9, they fled across bleak moors to a promontory. Rescue ships were driven off by aircraft. At the lighthouse on the tip of the spit, 750 SS men fought to the last. A terrible vengeance was visited on those the NKVD suspected of collaboration with the Germans. Hundreds were hanged from trees and telephone poles in Simferopol; on May 18 every Crimean Tartar, man, woman and child, was herded onto cattle wagons and sent on four-month rail journeys across the dusty steppe to permanent exile in Central Asia. Kalmyks, Karachai-Balkar, Chechen-Ingush, other southern minorities, were similarly deported; the Volga Germans, loyal farmers since immigrating two centuries before, were banished to Kazakhstan.

The Germans felt themselves pursued by a medieval host. 'The advance of a Russian army is something that Westerners cannot imagine,' said General Manteuffel. 'Behind the tank spearheads rolls on a vast horde, largely mounted on horses. The soldier carries a sack on his back, with dry crusts of bread and raw vegetables collected on the march ... You can't stop them, like an ordinary army, by cutting their communications, for you rarely find any supply columns to strike.' They fought without home leave. Discharge involved death or severe wounds. Discipline was enforced with penal battalions that cleared minefields with their feet or advanced on winter positions without camouflage to draw enemy fire. A Russian assault coming out of a dawn sun was a terrifying spectacle. 'The long gray waves come pounding on, uttering fierce cries, and the defending troops require nerves of steel,' wrote the German general, von Mellenthin. 'Divisions decimated by our fire were withdrawn and fresh formations thrown into the battle. Again, wave after wave attacked, and wave after wave was thrown back, suffering appalling losses.' They could be held only if German units stayed intact; but Russian superiority in tanks and aircraft was blossoming, and behind their lines the Germans were engaged in a spiral of atrocity and counter-atrocity with partisans. Wounded Germans were found with their heads tied inside the stomachs of dead comrades; villages were massacred in their entirety by Germans. Perhaps a million people were killed in Belorussia during the Nazi occupation. The partisans retained control of swathes of forest and marsh. For two nights from June 19, they destroyed the railroad tracks west of Minsk with demolition charges to prevent the Germans moving up reinforcements for Zhukov's great offensive, Bagration.

It started on June 22, 1944, exactly three years after Barbarossa. Zhukov amassed 1.6 million men in 166 divisions against 32 German divisions. His artillery density in breakthrough sectors reached 3209 guns a mile. A fleet of 12,000 trucks, most of them American-supplied, ferried 25,000 tons of

On the heels of the Gestapo.
A Russian suspected of collaborating with the Nazis is interrogated in public in a liberated area near Leningrad in late 1943. The secret police followed hard on the heels of the advancing Red armies. NKVD men set up large letter-boxes in newly liberated zones and encouraged people to drop denunciations into them. In Kharkov, the NKVD took over the building vacated a few days before by the Gestapo.
[PHOTO: V. KAPUSTIN]

supplies a journey. Within three days, Zhukov had trapped four German divisions in the ruins of Vitebsk. On June 27, the Russians retook Orsha and the Germans abandoned Mogilev, Nicholas II's headquarters twenty-seven years before. To the south, like Napoleon's *Grande Armée* before them, the Germans were caught on the Beresina. 'The Nazis ran out of the forests, rushed about in the clearings, many attempted to swim across the Beresina but even this did not save them,' said the Soviet general Konstantin Rokossovsky. The Russians broke into Minsk on July 3; 57,000 German prisoners were taken, to be marched through the streets of Moscow a fortnight later. The following day the Russians broke into Poland. The inhabitants of Warsaw soon heard Russian guns firing on the east bank of the Vistula and the Polish Home Army rose against the Germans. The Russians could clearly see the progress of the doomed rising from their forward observation posts; they had no political motive to cross the Vistula and help non-Communist Polish patriots to fight the SS men, released criminals and partisan hunters who were tracking them down in the cellars and sewers of Warsaw. The Red army stayed put. Every dead patriot was one less around to resist the post-war renewal of Russian domination over Poland.

The impetus switched to the Balkans. By August 26, as Paris fell to American and Free French units, the Germans in Rumania were fleeing through the Carpathians, drawn irresistibly west 'as the north attracts the needle of a compass', the now familiar wreckage of a once proud army, 'on foot, in rags, their faces livid after so much suffering, dragging along with them nauseatingly wounded men on litters made of branches, like the litters of the

Sioux.' At the end of the month, Soviet tanks clattered into Bucharest. It was the first large capitalist city to fall, and the crews marveled at the canary-yellow water fountains and the art nouveau villas of the rich. Local Communists greeted them. Bulgaria was next; and then a joint offensive with Marshal Tito's Yugoslavs in Belgrade. Following the mass burial of Yugoslav and Russian soldiers in communal graves, Tito held a victory parade. The Russian T-34s swept past him for the Danube bridges and the drive into Hungary.

Seven hundred miles to the north, the Red army then broke through onto German soil in East Prussia. The men went berserk. German paratroops who retook the village of Nemmersdorf came upon a cart with four naked women nailed to it through their hands. Moving on, they came to the village

A woman sniper, *Maria Kulshinova, pictured at the front. The huge losses of men in the opening months of the war made it possible for women to volunteer for specialist training as snipers. They were relatively rare, but many medical staff in the front line were women who advanced with their units to Berlin. Another woman sniper, sent on a tour of Britain in 1942, claimed a tally of 309 Germans to her rifle.*

[Photo: M. Savin]

Women night bomber pilots *relaxing at a forward airfield. All volunteers, the women crewed the slow and vulnerable aircraft that could be used for bombing missions only in the relative safety of darkness. Russian women made their most decisive impact on the war in the munitions plants and on the farms, where they and teenagers supplied the great bulk of the labor.*

[Photo: Y. Khaldei]

inn. On each of its two barn doors a naked woman had been crucified. A German lieutenant who took part in the counter-attack stated: 'I did not find a single living German civilian.' Only local counter-attacks were now feasible in the east; the final German offensive of the war went in against the Americans in the Ardennes forests of Belgium on December 16. On the approaches to Berlin, the Russians had a superiority of twenty to one in artillery and aircraft, eleven to one in infantry and seven to one in tanks. The end in the east, as the Ardennes offensive ran out of thrust and collapsed in the west, was close.

The Soviet assault in the east opened on January 12, 1945, with an artillery storm so furious that, the Soviet Marshal Koniev reported, 'those Germans who survived it could no longer control themselves.' Threatened with encirclement, the German garrison began evacuating Warsaw in the night of January 17. At midday, after final hours of looting and demolition, martyred Warsaw was finally free of German troops. The incoming Russians found 'gallows with bodies swinging in the wind, the charred corpses of people burnt alive in their own homes and the emaciated corpses of those who had starved.' Poland's freedom, in the dawning age of Soviet domination, would prove as bleak and vulnerable as its capital's ruins.

East Prussia was cut off from the rest of the Reich. Its invasion had a terrible finality, for it ceased to exist, divided between Russia and Poland. 'In certain sectors of the Russian zone there were practically no Germans left,' the British Field Marshal Bernard Montgomery wrote. 'They had all fled before the onward march of the barbarians', whose behavior 'especially in their treatment of women was abhorrent to us.' Between four and five million people fled from the eastern German territories: East Prussia, Pomerania, Silesia and eastern Brandenburg. Rape awaited those who did not flee. 'Red soldiers during the first weeks of their occupation raped every woman and girl between the ages of 12 and 60,' said a British prisoner whose camp had been in Pomerania. 'That sounds exaggerated but it is the simple truth.' Alexander Solzhenitsyn wrote of the entry of his regiment into East Prussia: 'All of us knew very well that if the girls were German they could be raped and then shot. This was almost a combat distinction.'

Stalin took a train in February to Nicholas II's Livadia Palace in Yalta where he did not bargain over Russia's post-war influence with his guests, the British aristocrat Winston Churchill, the dying American grandee Franklin Roosevelt. It was won for him by the men massing in the Oder bridgeheads, descendants of serfs, like himself, and of Mongols, *Untermenschen* whose tank assaults, barrages and air strikes had snapped the spine of the Wehrmacht. Two days after Yalta, Budapest fell. The sound of Russian guns was heard in Berlin throughout March. On April 1, Marshals Koniev and Zhukov, both former sergeants in the imperial army, entered the Kremlin. Stalin asked: 'The soyuznicki (the 'little allies') intend to get to Berlin before the Red army. Well, who is going to take Berlin, we or the allies?' The Americans and British were advancing at up to thirty-five miles a

Advancing Russian troops *substitute their own signs, written in Cyrillic script, for German road signs. The names seem to be of the soldiers' home towns and villages and the top one is Yasnaya Polana, where Tolstoy lived. With Studebaker and Mack trucks, and Willys jeeps, the Russian infantrymen enjoyed a mobility the Germans had long lost. At times, they swept forward at thirty miles a day.* [PHOTO: G. ZELMA]

day from the Rhine against minimal resistance. The Germans were taking thirteen times more casualties on the eastern front than on the western, whilst ten times as many were surrendering in the west. It was clear to whom the Germans preferred their country to fall. Koniev was the first to reply. 'We will, and before the Anglo-Americans,' he said.

On April 11, the American 2nd Armored Division reached the Elbe. The Americans were as close to Berlin as Koniev. On April 12, the day that Roosevelt died to be succeeded by Truman, three American battalions crossed the river. But the Russians crammed in the Oder bridgeheads were 'like horses trembling before the hunt.' The final assault started at 5 am on April 16, dumping 1,236,000 artillery and mortar shells on German positions in a firestorm so intense that it raised its own wind. The Germans slowly gave ground. April 20 was Hitler's 56th birthday. He received Goebbels, Bormann, Ribbentrop and Himmler in his bunker. Pale and shaking, he emerged briefly from underground, like 'a submarine commander coming up for air'. Zhukov's troops were fifteen miles away. On April 25, the Russians encircled the city. It was dying, ravaged by Soviet assault squads.

Shortly after midnight on April 29, the Bunker sour with the fumes of Russian shellbursts, Hitler married his mistress Eva Braun. The bridegroom was hunched, his head sunken into his shoulders like a turtle, his eyes 'like wet pale-blue porcelain, glazed … his face puckered now like a mask, all yellow and gray.' The bride wore black taffeta. As he dictated his political 'testament', the Russians were firing from the hippopotamus house in the zoo and riflemen were attacking the SS men in the Reichstag. In the great monkey house, a gorilla and a large chimpanzee lay dead in their cages with two SS men. At 1 pm on April 30, as Hitler sat down to a final lunch of spaghetti and tossed salad, the assault on the Reichstag began. At 2.15 pm,

Russians climb atop the Reichstag (*right*) *to fly the Red flag over Berlin in the early afternoon of April 30, 1945. At almost the same time, Adolf Hitler and Eva Braun committed suicide a few hundred yards away in the shattered city. Their bodies were burnt on waste ground to a cannonade of Russian katyusha rockets. Germans were still fighting in the basement of the Reichstag as this picture was taken; they held out until dawn on May 2. The Russian guns fell silent at 3pm that day.* [PHOTO: Y. KHALDEI]

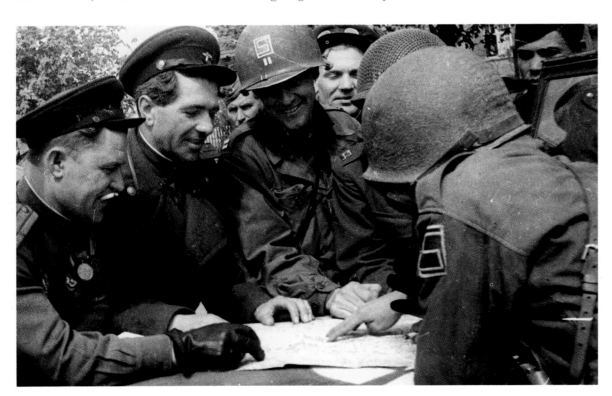

Meeting on the Elbe. *Men of the Soviet 5th Guards Army join up with American infantrymen in April 1945 (below). This took place, according to the Russians, on 'green sunlit banks amid the sweet aroma of fresh leaves and tuneful birdsong.' The sweetness between the new superpowers would not last long, but the linkup sliced the Third Reich in two and left Berlin surrounded.* [PHOTO: A. USTINOV]

Red tommygunners *pose in a Berlin tramcar (right) at the end of the great battle for the city. The final Russian push through Germany cost them 304,887 casualties. The Red army was a harsh taskmaster. These troops had no home leave; they rarely received mail; they lost contact with their families. If they were captured, they expected to die since the Soviet Union was not a signatory of the Geneva Convention. They went into combat with NKVD troops behind them; those who retreated without orders were shot, or sent to a penal battalion where life expectancy was a few weeks. The only means of discharge before victory was death or severe wounds.* [PHOTO: I. SHAGIN]

The creation of a superpower:
Russian troops at the Brandenburg Gate in the heart of Berlin. Their guns had ceased firing a few moments before, at 3pm on May 2, 1945. This historic shot was taken by Yevgeny Khaldei, front-line photo correspondent for Tass *and* Pravda *all through the war. He is seen (above) in front of the statuary on top of the Gate. He also took the picture of the Red flag being raised on the Reichstag on page 223, one of the most famous photographs ever.*
[PHOTO: Y. KHALDEI]

General Andrei Vlasov in 1944 (top) with German officers at the editorial offices of the collaborationist newspaper Za Rodina, For the Motherland. Vlasov had been one of the heroes of the Red army in 1941. He was trapped with the 2nd Shock Army in swamps near Leningrad in 1942. He refused to be flown out of the pocket, urging his men to break out in small groups. The Germans caught him hiding in a farmer's hut. Disillusioned by Stalin's abandonment of his men, he turned collaborator. Touring prison cages, Vlasov raised the Russian Liberation Army of ex-prisoners willing to fight on the German side. The Nazis had little faith in it, however, and it saw little combat.

A secret trial: Vlasov (above), uniformed and bespectacled, and fellow collaborators in front of the Soviet Military Court in Moscow in July 1946. Vlasov and his men ended the war in Prague. Made desperate by the approach of the Red army, they turned on the German SS in the city in an attempt to make a deal with the Czech resistance. The Czechs would have none of it. Fueled by a common desire to avoid capture by the Reds, mixed Vlasov-SS groups fled Prague for the American lines. The turncoats, however, were handed over to the Russians. Vlasov was flown back to the Lubyanka in Moscow for more than a year of interrogation before the secret trial was held.

Vlasov and his comrades hanging in the Lubyanka on August 1, 1946. He is on the extreme right; eleven others were hanged with him. This and the preceding photograph were taken specifically for Stalin and the high command. This is the only known picture of a *hanging in the Lubyanka, and comes from Vlasov's KGB file. Thousands of collaborators were returned to the Soviet Union after the war, and shot. Only Vlasov, the ex-hero of the 1941 Kiev encirclement and the battle for Moscow, commanded Stalin's personal interest.*

Hats outside the Conference room at Potsdam. *The Conference settled the details of the occupation of Germany and opened on July 17, 1945, the day after the first explosion of an atom bomb at Alamogordo in New Mexico. The coming Cold War was already in the air. President Truman made only the vaguest reference about the bomb to his Soviet allies: 'I casually mentioned to Stalin that we had a new weapon of special destructive force.' As to Winston Churchill, he was 'already seeing himself capable of eliminating all the Russian centers of industry and population.'* [Photo: Y. Khaldei]

Victors: *Stalin with Truman and Churchill at Potsdam (far right). The first was the son of Georgian serfs, brought up in a hut; the second came from a Missouri farming community; while Churchill, grandson of the Duke of Marlborough, was born at Blenheim Palace. Stalin's withered left hand can be seen. Allied control in Germany, reparations, and a new German-Polish frontier line, involving the expulsion of 6 million Germans, were discussed. By the end of the Conference Churchill had lost office to Clement Attlee, seen here over his right shoulder.* [Photo: Y. Khaldei]

Sergeants Yegorov and Kantariya of the 150th Division waved a Red banner from the second floor. Three-quarters of an hour later, Hitler bit into a capsule of potassium cyanide and shot himself through the right temple. Eva Braun poisoned herself. In the early hours of May 1, May Day, a German general told the Russians that Hitler was dead. Zhukov contacted Moscow where the late-retiring Stalin had just gone to bed. Zhukov ordered that he be woken and told him of Hitler's death. '*Doigralsya, podlets!*', said Stalin. 'So, that's the end of the bastard.'

Whilst the May Day parade rolled through Red Square in Moscow, T-34s prowled the Unter den Linden and Russian troops roasted an ox in the Pariserplatz between the ruins of the American and French embassies. That night, the last occupants of the Bunker attempted a break-out, listening to wild screams from a hospital where Russian troops had been drinking ether. The Russians received a radio message shortly after 1 am on May 2 asking for a ceasefire. At dawn, the streets began to fill with German prisoners. The Russian guns stopped firing at 3 pm.

The prisoners being marched out of the city to their captivity in the east saw column after column of Red army support units. The horsecarts had soldiers perched atop them on bales of straw, singing and dressed in weird mixtures of looted civilian clothes. When they spotted the Germans, they fired angry volleys into the air. 'There were Circassians, Kalmuks, Uzbeks, Azerbaijani, Mongols,' said the captured General Mohnke. They had with them poster beds, toilets, umbrellas, quilts, rugs, bicycles, sinks, ladders and cages with live chickens and ducks. The speechless Germans recognised that what was happening on the streets of Berlin was 'something out of the great vastness of Russia beyond the Urals … Asia on this day was moving into the middle of Europe.'

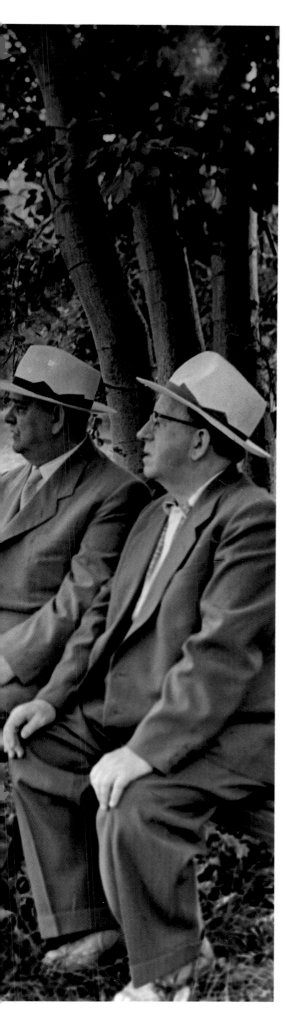

Nikita Khrushchev *sits in the grounds of his dacha in 1963, flanked by members of the Politburo. Emotional and at times humane, Khrushchev had launched a violent attack on Stalinism in 1956. Millions were released from Gulag camps, or had their honor posthumously restored. But Khrushchev had no doubts about the Soviet beliefs and dealt brutally with the Hungarians when they tried to rid themselves of Communism in the uprising of 1956.*
[Photo: V. Sobolyev]

10
CURTAIN FALL

IN GERMANY, A PIG WAS A MARK OF WEALTH, A DOG-DRAWN cart a luxury. France, weakened and demoralised, a quarter of its people voting Communist, was being sucked into war in Indochina, while Britain was preparing to abandon India. Might was now divided between Russia and the United States.

No relaxation came with triumph. The post-war years were a desperate time. Great cities had been smashed: over half the buildings in Kiev had been destroyed and three in four of its citizens had been killed or deported to Germany. The population was a fifth of the pre-war figure. Minsk was worse. Eighty per cent of its buildings had been blasted away. Village Russia was devastated, too. In the forests of Belorussia where the Germans had exterminated communities wholesale, tracts of land, so vast that the scale could only be grasped from an aircraft, were stripped of cabins, crops and people. One in five of all Belorussians had been killed or had toiled at slave labor. Families across western Russia lived in caves, in drained water tanks and pits covered with tarpaulins. Millions of evacuees roomed in earth-floored barracks in the Urals or further east, forbidden to return to their old homes in the west.

The United States, honoring its GIs with university courses, meeting its returning PoWs with marching bands at flag-decked railroad depots, was starting the greatest consumer boom in history. In Russia, rations stayed at near-starvation levels: cabbage, potatoes, the skins made into thin soups, and beets. Ten years after the war, the city ration was half a pound of meat and under four ounces of fat a week; the equivalent of two hamburger patties. State food prices rose; the cost of black bread tripled, but many lost their savings when large-denomination ruble notes were declared illegal tender overnight in an anti-black market move. Work norms were unaltered at ten to twelve hours a day, six days a week. Heavy industry and weapons remained an absolute priority; under continuing wartime labor discipline, absenteeism and drunkenness earned ten years in a Gulag.

Those prisoners who survived the German camps were thought traitors, contaminated by foreign influence. They passed without pause from the Reich to the Gulags, like 'shoals of herring', in long trains with machinegunners squatting above cattlecars sealed with barbed wire. 'Who are you?' locals asked the inmates through the cracks when they stopped in sidings. 'Prisoners of war,' they replied. 'Where do you go?' 'To Siberia,' they said. The Allies were pressured to return collaborators, Cossacks and Ukrainians who had fought with the Germans; when British ships returned some of them to Odessa, they were taken behind sheds and shot on the very quayside.

Newspapers were now censored twice, before and after typesetting. Marshals and generals dropped from sight. By 1948, *Pravda* commemorated the fall of Berlin in a lengthy article without once mentioning Zhukov. Andrei Zhdanov, the 'savior of Leningrad' as Party boss in the city during the siege, now savaged its survivors. Shostakovich and Prokofiev were pilloried for writing 'bourgeois' music with tunes too complicated for proletarians to whistle. Anna Akhmatova fell foul of Zhdanov for the 'decadence' of writing love poems. Boris Pasternak returned to writing *Doctor Zhivago* once, he said, he 'observed the thwarting of our hopes for postwar change.' He read parts of it, with damning sequences on the Revolution, to a Moscow audience; his lover, Olga Ivinskaya, pregnant with his child, was interrogated in the Lubyanka and sent to the Gulag. She lost the child; Pasternak continued the novel basing its heroine, Lara, on her. 'A grown man must grit his teeth and share his country's destiny,' said Zhivago.

Beria, pale and unhealthy looking, with bulging eyes behind his pince-nez, laid his 'soft damp hands' upon the Leningrad Party. It was thought too independent and, after Zhdanov's sudden death in 1948, it was purged. No longer was it a hero city; the Defense of Leningrad Museum was closed, its director arrested. Svetlana Stalin thought her father had now 'reached the point of being pathological, of persecution mania ... He saw enemies everywhere.' Some were imagined; others, the Americans, the British, were not. The warmth of the wartime meeting on the Elbe did not survive ten months. 'Unless Russia is faced with an iron fist and strong language, war is in the making,' Harry S. Truman wrote in January 1946. 'Only one language do they understand – "How many divisions have you?"' That March, Winston Churchill made his speech in Fulton, Missouri, warning of the 'Iron Curtain' that was falling across Europe. The formal onset of the Cold War followed in March 1947; the President outlined a policy of US commitment against Communist expansion, to become the 'Truman Doctrine' and to dominate world politics for four decades. Four months later, the National Security Act was passed, establishing the CIA. In the western half of Europe, the Marshall Plan rebuilt shattered countries. The flow of thirteen billion dollars helped drown the powerful Italian and French Communist parties. Across eastern Europe, where the old order of compromised kings and churchmen and nationalist politicians had been swept into limbo, the Red army was the power in being. East Germany was looted of machines and men. German military specialists in the Soviet zone, 6000 of them, were rounded up on the night of October 22, 1946 and sent on 92 special trains to Russia. The Zeiss optical works at Jena were shipped to Monino, near Moscow; the Opel auto works at Brandenburg were freighted to Moscow where they produced the Moskvich, a copy of the Opel Cadet. The Soviet Union had still been the world's only Communist nation at the end of the war. It was joined now by Poland, East Germany, Rumania, Bulgaria, Czechoslovakia; those places where a simple process of deportations, intimidations, popular fronts, bannings, 'suicides'

A tent village for workers *building a plant in Kazakhstan in 1956. The poverty of the post-war years was savage. Rationing was kept to bare essentials. Housing was desperately short. These workers are lucky: some families in western Russia lived in holes in the ground.*

Night-shift workers *in a recreation center at a Tashkent textile plant in 1960. The factory remained named for Stalin, despite the de-Stalinisation being carried out in the country as a whole, and a huge bust of him looms in the corner of the room. Lenin is above the doorway.*

Naval cadets *at the Nakhimov military school, many of them war orphans, are put through a dancing lesson. The Red army in its infancy had abolished all distinctions of rank. Victorious, the Soviet armed forces revived epaulettes, saluting, officers' clubs, Guards regiments. The post-war cadet schools were much like their Tsarist antecedents. Bolsheviks or not, the young cadets were taught English, fine manners, the waltz and the mazurka.*

and rigged elections could be carried out under the protection of the Red army. The last to go was Czechoslovakia. On March 10, 1948, the foreign minister Jan Masaryk was found dead on the pavement below his official apartment; a democrat whose ideal was 'to be able at any time I like to ride in a tramcar down to Wenceslas Square in Prague and say "I don't think much of our present government."' Suicide, the inquest found, brought on by 'depression increased by Western recriminations'. The doorman had seen strangers enter the building; cigarette butts were found in his room; his underclothes were soiled, as if he had been in fear of his life. On June 7, 1948, the legitimately elected President Benes resigned.

A few days later, the Russians blockaded West Berlin. Stalin ordered road, rail and river links to the city to be cut. It was a foolhardy move since, while Stalin had the brute strength of the Red army, the Americans had a nuclear monopoly. Had the blockade degenerated into fighting, General Lucius Clay said that he would not hesitate to use the atomic bomb and would 'hit Moscow and Leningrad first'. Berlin was kept alive by an Anglo-American airlift, and Stalin lifted the blockade in May 1949.

East Europeans were put to work in Russian mines and lumber camps. Four hundred thousand Lithuanians, Letts and Estonians were deported to Siberia; by 1950, fifteen per cent of the Baltic population had disappeared. A German worker mining a coal seam beneath the barren tundra in Vorkuta in 1951 said that in his camp, Pit No. 29, there were thirty different nationalities. 'Women of many nationalities were driven out to work day after day in 30 or 40 degrees of frost to work on road-building in Vorkuta,' reported another German who survived a five-year stint there.

Though the Russian industrial effort in the war had made a deep impression, the West felt it had little to fear from Soviet science and technology. It was infected with Party paranoia; its boasts – that Russians had invented the incandescent lamp before Edison, the telegraph before Morse, radio before Marconi, penicillin before Fleming – seemed proof of inferiority. The Americans thought it would take the Russians between ten and twenty years to produce an atomic bomb 'by normal effort'. The Soviet effort was abnormal. It involved the intense use of spies – Nunn May, Pontecorvo, Fuchs, the Rosenbergs – and of transported German scientists. Much of the research in the Soviet Union was carried out in prison laboratories and as secret police chief, Beria was responsible for the nuclear project, codenamed Borodino. Slave labor extracted uranium from mines in Altai and Turkestan in Soviet Central Asia that were no more than open, unprotected pits. Life expectancy in some of them was little more than a month. Borodino commanded a vast conglomeration of mines, factories, testing grounds and airfields, all under wartime security. American aircraft were on constant patrol off the Soviet borders to take air samples for analysis and in September 1949 an aircraft over the north Pacific sucked in one which proved radioactive. President Truman, advised that it was more likely to come from a laboratory accident than from a bomb, announced

Siberian uranium mines *at Butuguchak (left). This was part of Beria's empire in Operation Borodino, the Soviet nuclear project; and the uranium ore used in Russia's first atomic bombs was mined here. The area is still highly radioactive. Most inmates died of radiation sickness within three months; few survived a year. They were buried in adjoining valleys; the only marker was a pole, with a tin can on it bearing their prisoner number and no name. Some of the skulls have been found to have been sawn in half. Nobody knows why. The work in the mine pits was so bad that the zeks preferred to serve in the ore treatment plant, although radiation levels were so high there that few survived more than thirty shifts.*
[PHOTO: A. KOTLYAROV]

Inside the Gulag: *the photographs on the right were taken at No. 7 prison camp attached to Mine No. 25 in the Vorkuta-Pechora Gulag system in Siberia, where coal was mined in Arctic conditions. They come from an album compiled by Ministry of Interior officials to show 'humane' conditions in the camps. Neither Lenin, who started the camps, nor Stalin, who hugely expanded them, ever visited one.*
   Solitary confinement block *(top right);* **Sleeping quarters** *(upper right). When the camps filled with a new intake, zeks slept two to a wooden bunk or in shifts. A group of army officers, sentenced for momentary criticisms of Stalin despite having fought the Germans, killed their guards in a camp near here in 1948. Paratroopers and aircraft were used to stop them marching on Vorkuta town.* **Inmates** *of Vorkuta's No. 7 camp (lower right). At another Vorkuta camp, in July 1953, women zeks from the Ukraine rebelled. Tanks were called in. The women linked hands and walked towards them. 'The tanks drove straight over the live bodies', an eyewitness said. 'There were no cries. All we heard was a horrible sound of bodies being crushed and cracking bones. Meanwhile soldiers went round the barracks shooting down everyone they came across.'* **The camp steam bath** *(bottom right). 'There's absolutely no difference between the German Fascists and Stalin, except that Stalin was worse,' commented Yevgenia Vryublyovskaya, a veteran of the Arctic camps.*

235

simply that an 'atomic explosion' had occurred in the Soviet Union. The Russians retorted that it was a bomb; it had been detonated in Kazakhstan at 4 am on August 29, 1949.

Both superpowers now had their superbombs. The US moved on to fusion weapons with the hydrogen bomb. The Russians followed. 'I found myself caught up in the rotation of a special world of military designers and inventors, special institutes, pilot plants and proving grounds,' wrote Andrei Sakharov, the dissident physicist who was father of the Russian H-bomb. 'Every day I saw the huge material, intellectual and nervous resources of thousands of people being poured into the means of total destruction …' The cost of the H-bomb was prodigious, even for wealthy America; whilst in Russia, the burden of it distorted the whole way of life.

Stalin's own life was twisted. His daughter thought him a prisoner of his own system, 'stifling from loneliness, emptiness and lack of human companionship'. He was everywhere – his gigantic portrait was suspended above Red Square from a balloon to mark his 70th birthday in 1949; he celebrated at the Bolshoi seated between the newly victorious Mao Tse-tung, and a rising Politburo star, Nikita Khrushchev; that day's copy of *Pravda* devoted every line of its twelve pages, save two column-inches on women's chess, to him. A light was kept burning in a Kremlin window each night, so that anyone walking on Red Square could look up and know that the 'pillar of peace' was working endlessly for the proletarian cause. But when he traveled by curtained car the roads were emptied; when he took a train, no passengers were allowed in any station he passed, and he walked alone on the platform with his daughter. After the autumn of 1951, he went no further from Moscow than his dacha. Here, surrounded by two walls with dog-runs between them, his private rooms were

protected by armor-plate doors. They had sliding panels, through which trays of salted salmon, cucumbers, soups, bear meat, Georgian wines, brandy and vodka were passed when he caroused with his cronies – Beria, Malenkov, Bulganin, and the new man, Khrushchev. He would not eat a crumb until the others had tasted it. He enjoyed watching them get drunk and would goad them into dancing for him. He liked making Khrushchev perform a Ukrainian dance, the Gopak, squatting on his haunches. 'When Stalin says dance, a wise man dances,' said Khrushchev. Such revelries did not calm Stalin's hatreds. In January 1953, a new conspiracy, the 'Doctors' Plot', was unveiled. Nine Kremlin doctors were said to be plotting to kill the leadership. Seven of them were described as 'rootless cosmopolitans', Sovspeak for Jews. Anti-semitism had broken surface again in Russia following the war; the great Yiddish actor Solomon Mikhoels had been murdered in Minsk, and all Yiddish publications and the Yiddish theater were shut. Confessions were obtained of 'conspiracy' with an American Zionist organisation; two of the doctors died under interrogation. People stopped going to the doctor, thinking they would be poisoned; louts threw dead mice at the daughter of one of the arrested men, accusing her father of taking pus from corpses to infect healthy Russians. Rumors spread that all Jews would be deported to Siberia.

Stalin was in good form for a long revel with the four cronies on February 28, 1953. The eating and drinking went on until five or six in the morning. He was cheerful after the meal. 'He joked a lot,' Khrushchev remembered. 'He prodded me in the stomach, calling me "Mikita" … We left in a good mood too, for nothing had happened during the dinner, and those dinners had not always ended on such a happy note.' Khrushchev awaited the usual summons the next evening. None came. Stalin had signaled

Factory workers stand in silence *to show their respect during the funeral of Stalin in 1953. The country was deeply shocked by his death; in Moscow, sealed off by troops, people were crushed to death in the immense crowd as they queued to pay their last respects.*

Stalin's body lies in state *(above right) in Moscow in March 1953. Within a few years, the dictator would become a non-person, like Trotsky. His coffin was taken from the Lenin Mausoleum, secretly, at night, and buried in a deep pit covered with concrete.*
[PHOTO: V. YEGOROV]

'Make tea' to the servants' quarters, but this had not been followed by the signal 'Bring tea in'. His bodyguards were too frightened to enter his private quarters; a servant went in, and found him unconscious on the floor. The four Party men were summoned to the dacha where he lay in a coma on a couch.

He had suffered a cerebral hemorrhage and took four days to die, slowly suffocating, his features becoming dark and twisted, his lips black. At the last moment, his daughter said, he opened his eyes and cast a 'terrible glance, insane or perhaps angry and full of fear of death.' He raised his arm as if, she thought, to bring down a curse, and then died.

The death was announced on March 6, 1953. The body lay in state on a flower-draped bier in the Hall of Columns; Muscovites were crushed to death in the swelling queues outside. The lights went out in the slave pits of the Gulag, as a mark of mourning and respect; the zeks, celebrating the death, launched a wave of revolts in their camps.

The Kremlin pathologist Dr Yakob Rapaport telephoned from the lobby before climbing the stairs to his apartment; he had been awaiting execution in the Lubyanka for his part in the Doctors' Plot, and he was anxious to prevent his family from fainting at his sudden appearance.

NIKITA

Khrushchev was the essential Soviet man, the perfect prole, born in a cabin near Kursk in 1894. 'Whenever I see shepherds tending their sheep,' he wrote, 'my own childhood comes back to me.' He looked after livestock and was taught in a one-room schoolhouse until he was fifteen. His father, grindingly poor, moved the family to a new coal town in the Donbass area of the Ukraine, and there risked his hand as a coal miner. It was a hard place whose tenements swarmed with ex-peasants seeking a grimy fortune. Khrushchev got a job as a fitter in a German-owned factory.

His progress in the Party had a classic ring to it; the borrowed copy of the *Communist Manifesto* at sixteen; the instant conversion to the cause, emergence as a strike leader in the plant; the sack in 1912 when the strike was broken. The Donbass pits educated him, he said. They were 'a working man's Cambridge, the university of the dispossessed of Russia.' Blacklisted by factory employers, Khrushchev found work in a chemicals plant and as a fitter in a pit. He was established as a radical miners' leader at the end of his teens; then he was elected to the local soviet after the February revolution; after the Bolshevik coup, he joined the Party and became chairman of the metal workers' union. Volunteering for the civil war, Khrushchev fought in the south as political commissar to a Red division. His wife died in the typhus year, 1921; the Donbass was ruined, the pits flooded, the winding gear destroyed. 'There was famine in the mines,' he said, 'and even isolated cases of cannibalism.'

Khrushchev became Party organiser for a group of sixteen pits; to rebuild them with semi-literate and famished labor was a harsh task, he admitted, 'sometimes requiring sacrificing moral principles as well as material comfort.' By 1925 the ex-cowherd was finding his awestruck way round Moscow as a Ukrainian delegate to the 14th Party Congress. The Party in Kharkov felt that the local leadership had too many intellectuals, but was light on 'proletarian elements'. Khrushchev fitted the bill for promotion to area organiser, though he fretted at the paperwork. 'I'm a man of the earth, a man of action, a miner,' he said. 'I hate having to go through a pile of forms and files to see the flesh-and-blood-world.'

Ambitious, impulsive but persistent, he moved on to Kiev and then to the Industrial Academy in Moscow. His timing was sweet; with the Five Year Plan came rafts of appointments for Party men with qualifications, especially if, like Khrushchev, they were devoted Stalinists. Before her suicide, Stalin's wife was a fellow-student at the Academy. She and Nikita Sergeevich got on well, so he met Stalin at family dinners. He wrote, 'This was why I stayed alive when most of my contemporaries lost their lives because they were regarded as enemies of the people.' Another useful patron was Lazar Kaganovich, former Ukrainian leader, who became Moscow Party boss. By 1934, Khrushchev was a Central Committee member and took over from Kaganovich as Moscow boss. He was tough, hard-working and he adored Stalin: 'I was a hundred per cent faithful to Stalin as our leader and our

guide,' he said. 'I believed that everything Stalin said in the name of the Party was inspired by genius.'

Moscow was a construction site for most of the Thirties; bulky skyscrapers, broad boulevards, slabs of offices and apartments were thrown up in fevered and slapdash haste. So was the Moscow Metro, built at a pace that killed and injured well over a thousand workers, but to a standard that made it the grandest system on earth, a subterranean marble palace of Communism. Over it presided Nikita Sergeevich, round-faced, with eager little eyes above a floral Ukrainian collar, striking at purged colleagues with cobra fangs: 'These despicable traitors infested the party apparatus …' As city boss, he toured the cells with NKVD officers, meeting men he had worked with and knew well as they waited for execution. The show trials were held in Moscow, on his turf. Khrushchev said nothing for almost twenty years. 'I was literally spellbound by Stalin,' he excused himself. 'Everything that I saw and heard when I was with him bewitched me.' He was, he said, 'absolutely bowled over' by the mass murderer's 'charm'. He came close to feeling a cold barrel in the neck himself; Stalin once said that Nikolai Yezhov, the NKVD boss, had him marked down as an ethnic Pole, at a time when the execution squads were running through Polish Communists as class enemies. He survived to become Party leader in the Ukraine in 1938, swearing the good Stalinist's oath: 'I pledge to spare no effort in seizing and annihilating all agents of fascism, Trotskyites, Bukharinites, and all other despicable bourgeois nationalists in the Ukraine.' In 1939, with the Soviet invasion of Poland, he was busy purging and collectivising the western Ukraine.

The war was good to Khrushchev. He was political commissar at Stalingrad; a lieutenant-general, he re-entered liberated Kiev on November 5, 1943 as it was still burning; he stayed on as the Ukrainian supremo, owning allegiance to none but Stalin. There were more deportations to the Gulag of Catholics, Poles, and guerrillas of the Ukrainian Insurgent Army who continued fighting Red army patrols into the 1950s.

After Stalin's death, there was no one dominating figure among those who had been closest to him. Beria was the greatest danger to Khrushchev's survival. A 'moon-faced idiot' to Beria, he was caught off balance when Beria proposed Malenkov as prime minister, whilst Malenkov returned the compliment by nominating Beria as head of the MVD and MGB. The secret policeman's minions guarded the borders, the Kremlin and the nuclear weapons dumps; he could call on ten MVD divisions. Personally a pervert – he interrogated many prisoners himself, gaining pleasure from their pain, as well as indulging a taste for under-age girls, redheads and black bedsheets – Beria was politically liberal by Kremlin standards, sympathetic to nationalists in the republics and to the reformers in East Germany. He disliked collectives, and favored giving the peasants larger private plots. He was eager for détente with the West and he admired the US.

Beria was canny; since he was Stalin's chief executioner and Gulag proprietor, many millions had reason to do him harm, and

Nikita Khrushchev *sports a Ukrainian shirt and a white hat at the height of his power in 1959.*

caution was a second skin to the snake. When East Berlin revolted in June 1953, he was sent to East Germany on June 17 to put it down. He found out that a routine Presidium meeting was to be held in the Kremlin on June 18. Mistrustful, he seized an aircraft in Berlin and flew back to Moscow for the day, but such foresight did not save him. Khrushchev astutely won backing from Malenkov, and Beria was to be arrested at a Kremlin meeting on July 10. Khrushchev turned up for the meeting with a gun in his pocket; Marshal Zhukov was charged with grabbing Beria. He waited in a sideroom with ten men, whilst Khrushchev accused the shocked Beria of a string of crimes, including spying for the British. At a signal from Malenkov, Zhukov's posse burst into the room and led Beria off to be interrogated and held in an air raid shelter. Two tank divisions were stationed at the main intersections to prevent rescue. Beria's men were picked up in their country dachas, city apartments and hospital beds. Those who tried to protect their chief were shot.

The secret trial was as bizarre as those of his victims. He was tried under the same law as them – a decree of 1934 which denied the accused representation in court and which stipulated summary execution – and on the same ragbag of charges: working for foreign intelligence, terrorist murders and plots, and other catchalls. He was guilty of innumerable crimes; but many of them, the murder of Jewish artists, the deportations from the Caucasus and Crimea after the German retreat, the more recent killings in Leningrad, were not mentioned, for the pointing fingers that accused him were stained with the same blood. Only one of his victims was named.

A chief prosecution witness, A. V. Snegov, arrived in the courtroom direct from an Arctic labor camp in Kolyma. News of Beria's arrest had reached the Gulag; Snegov, who knew many of the secret policeman's crimes, detailed them in letters that were smuggled to Khrushchev and Mikoyan in Moscow. When Beria saw him in court he shouted: 'What, are you still alive?' 'Your organisation didn't do its job properly,' Snegov spat back. Snegov was questioned closely on Beria's past; the Gulag, from which he had so recently been sprung, was not mentioned. After a fulsome confession the death sentence was passed and Beria subsided into cowardice; the torturer begged for mercy. He is thought to have been shot whilst gagged, for fear he would compromise Khrushchev and his fellow-conspirators in front of the army firing squad.

Beria's death was the work of the gangster state, but reform now started and victims were gradually 'rehabilitated', as the word had it. They could not be pardoned, for most had committed no crime, but they were released from the camps or, if already beyond help, they were restored to public memory. Molotov's wife Polina came back from the camps, where she had been sent for spying for the US and Israel; she had been seen talking to Golda Meir, Israel's first ambassador to Moscow. Khrushchev's daughter-in-law, who had been arrested as a 'Swedish spy' after his son was killed in action, also returned from a camp.

The Kremlin was opened to the public; under Stalin, it had been a crime even to photograph it. Anyone could buy a ticket to view its treasures. Khrushchev, with an eye for public relations,

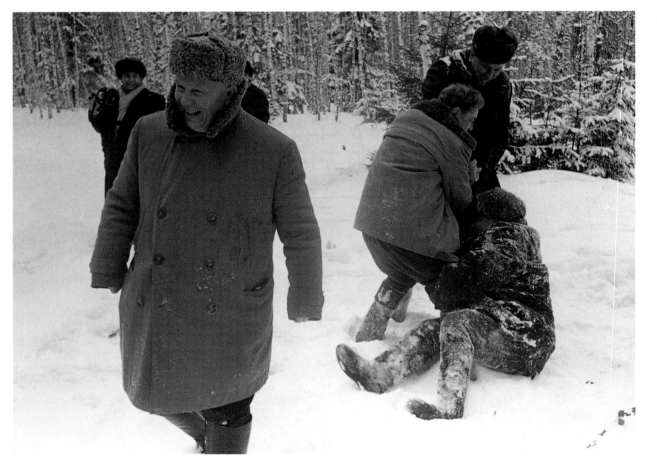

A playful snow fight (*left*) *in 1963, involving Leonid Brezhnev, the man who would replace Khrushchev, seen here walking away. Although he could be roused to sarcastic fury, Khrushchev had a cheerful and sunny disposition and a flair for populism unknown in earlier Party leaders.*
[Photo: V. Yegorov]

Marshal Tito, *the Yugoslav leader (opposite), with Khrushchev after a successful day's hunting in 1963. Marshal Malinovsky, who had captured Budapest at the end of the war and was now the Minister of Defense, is on Tito's right, while Andrei Gromyko, the Foreign Minister and former Ambassador to the US, is on Khrushchev's left. On the extreme right is Marshal Chuikov, the Hero of Stalingrad.*
[Photo: V. Yegorov]

held a New Year's Eve ball, with bunting and fairy lights, for young people. He maneuvered well politically, outflanking Malenkov who resigned as prime minister in February 1955.

There was no more recourse to the execution cellar for disgraced politicians. Malenkov survived as director of a Siberian power station. Molotov was sent as ambassador to Mongolia when Khrushchev eased him from power. Terror slowly wound down in the Gulag. At a closed meeting of the 20th Party Congress on 25 February 1956, Khrushchev read a speech entitled 'On the Cult of Personality and its Consequences'. Though called his 'secret speech', its content was soon known in the Soviet bloc and in the West. Khrushchev savaged every step of Stalin's career. He hinted that Stalin had planned Kirov's murder. He detailed the arrests and killings of the purges. He blamed Stalin's terror for the early disasters of Barbarossa which 'followed Stalin's annihilation of many military commanders … because of his suspiciousness and through slanderous accusations.' He revealed that it was only Stalin's death that had prevented a further surge of purges. Khrushchev's claim to be 'amazed' at Stalin's crimes was nonsense; he knew intimately what was happening in the purge years. But Khrushchev was an emotional man, with a streak of idealism. The speech, and the release of millions of zeks that followed it, was an act of basic humanity. It was accompanied by an outpouring of

poetry and literature in Russia of prodigious scale and quality.

Liberalising a Communist regime was a risky business, however; the speech helped inspire an autumn rising in Hungary. On October 23, thousands marched to the statue of the poet Petofi in Budapest, to read his emotional poem 'Arise Hungarians!' Many wore the red, white and green cockade of the national colors. In the evening, they were ordered to disperse. 'Someone had an idea and lit a newspaper,' reported a Hungarian émigré working for the BBC. 'In a minute or two about 100,000 newspapers were lit and Parliament Square flared in a sea of yellow, menacing flames.' The crowd moved on to another statue, this time of Stalin. It was torn down and broken up into souvenir-sized pieces. Only the boots remained. The rebels rapidly took over the country. The mechanics of repression were on show for the first time as the Soviet-trained secret police were hunted down. Gyor, a provincial town, had a police headquarters identical to scores in Russia. A torture chamber was found, a brick cavity connected to an adjacent boiler by a steam tube that could flay a man like paint stripper. Cells – foul, tiny – were thrown open to 'let out the stench of many years'. A large room was equipped like a telephone exchange, with equipment to record forty phone calls simultaneously. Rows of tapes were stacked on shelves, each with a card on it rating the conversation: 'interesting', 'suspicious', 'to be followed up'. The secret police were found to be subject to their own Five Year Plan; required to enlist six new informers every three months.

Khrushchev, whatever his views on his predecessor, was not in the business of liquidating Communism. Soviet armor was ordered into Hungary; to the accompaniment of small arms fire and flaming Molotov cocktails, it ground onto the streets of Budapest in the pre-dawn of Sunday November 4, 1956. By mid-afternoon, a Hungarian reporter was telexing Vienna: 'Help … SOS … People are running up to the tanks, throwing in hand grenades … It is only a pity we cannot last. What is the United Nations doing? The tanks are coming in, masses of them …' The prime minister, Imre Nagy, was tricked into leaving his sanctuary in the Yugoslav embassy, seized and eventually hanged.

To pacify the home front, Khrushchev promised that the country would catch up with the Americans in the production of meat, milk and butter per head within three or four years. It was an empty boast – US beef production was three times higher than Russian – but Khrushchev believed it with fervor. There were vast acres of virgin land, in northern Kazakhstan, western Siberia, the northern Caucasus and the Urals. Plow it – Khrushchev, who did not think small, had plans for thirty million acres – and the Americans would be tumbled from their perch. Fodder would be needed for the huge increase in beef cattle and for this Khrushchev had another miracle cure, maize. No matter that maize was currently grown only in those parts of the Ukraine where it ripened properly. It was made compulsory to grow it; had not Catherine the Great been obliged to force the peasants to grow potatoes? His enthusiasm became boundless on his 1959 American tour, when he visited lush maize fields in Iowa. He was known as *kukuruznik*, the maize freak, even growing it in the grounds of his Moscow dacha. Thousands of young Communists were persuaded to pioneer the virgin lands, swarming into Kazakhstan and Siberia. They had no experience of farming, no tools and little backup. Many of the areas where they pitched their tents were marginal, with thin, arid soil. The locals loathed them. The Kazakhs grazing cattle in the northern vastness of their republic now feared they would be racially swamped by Russians, and the grasslands would be plowed.

A woman volunteer *(far left) in the Virgin Lands, the previously untilled lands of Kazakhstan and western Siberia. The drive to exploit new farmland was part of Khrushchev's empty boast in 1957 that the Soviet Union would overtake the US in the production of meat, milk and butter within four years.*

Volunteers celebrate *the completion of a new village in the Virgin Lands (left) in 1956. The expansion turned from apparent triumph into disaster when the natural fertility of the soil was exhausted. Once plowed, it was subject to dust storms which ruined millions of acres in Kazakhstan.*

Promoting maize, *Khrushchev at Chernigov (right), in his native Ukraine, in 1961. His passion for the plant brought him the nickname of* kukuruznik, *the maize freak, and was totally misguided, forcing up the price of meat and dairy products. Food rioters in Novocherkassk, shouting 'Cut up Khrushchev for sausages!', were shot down by troops in 1962. It helped to topple him.*
[PHOTO: V. YEGOROV]

In six years, 103 million acres of land were plowed. Khrushchev went on morale-boosting agro-tours and he tampered endlessly, in classic Soviet style, with the bureaucracy. It became an alphabet soup as he dissolved the State Committee of Agricultural Procurement, SCAP, in favor of an All Union Committee for Agriculture, AUCA, which supervised a new hierarchy of Territorial Production Associations, TPAs. Nine in ten kolkhoz chairmen were Communists by 1958; the average collective had a Party cell of twenty members. They gathered by the ten thousand at conferences in the Palace of Sport in Moscow. Khrushchev was a believer, a conviction politician to whom such a concentration of Communists was in itself a guarantee of success. Professional agronomists warned that shortage of rainfall and herbicides made it essential to leave fields fallow for much of the crop cycle, and to sow late. The Party hack Trofim Lysenko sang of early sowing, and intense cultivation without fallow periods. Khrushchev, captivated, told the professionals that they needed a flea up their shirts to wake them up. A good Communist could thrash an American; look at those yields in Iowa, and beat them!

Individual kolkhozes, regions and republics swore to double and triple production. Khrushchev pointed to the Ryazan region, which in 1959 carried out its promise to triple the amount of meat sold to the state to 150,000 tons. He made the Party First Secretary there, Alexei Larionov, a Hero of Socialist Labor. Larionov shot himself the following September. He had reached his target by sending breeding stock and milch cows to the slaughterhouse, by buying cattle from peasants and selling them back and buying them again, to inflate book figures. The Ryazan collectives were ruined. Rustling became common as kolkhozes and regions competed to fulfill their targets and meat production fell. The early-sowing, no-fallow policy brought massive weed infestation that choked off grain. There were no herbicides to deal with it. A drought caused the topsoil in the Kazakh virgin lands to dry out and 15 million acres were ruined in summer dust storms that swept inches of topsoil into the foothills of the Sayan mountains. Eighty-five million acres of maize were planted at Khrushchev's direct orders. Only sixteen million could be harvested ripe; Communism could not overcome climate. Hay

Talking to the cosmonaut Valentina Tereshkova *as she orbits the earth. She was given the call sign of* Chaika *(seagull) and this became her nickname. She was also given a black Barguzine sable fur coat. Only six other women have one, including Queen Elizabeth II, Jacqueline Onassis and Elizabeth Taylor. Khrushchev is flanked by Leonid Brezhnev and Anastas Mikoyan. The Soviet domination of early space flight was a huge achievement. Mikoyan, one of the most senior Politburo members, was the brother of the great aircraft designer Artem Mikoyan. MiG fighters, named for Mikoyan and Mikhail Gurevich, remain among the world's best.*

yields disappeared under the plow, cutting this source of animal feed so that meat and dairy prices were increased by a third in 1962. Workers in Novocherkassk, in the northern Caucasus, marched on the local Party headquarters. Troops opened fire into the air. Children began to fall to the ground from trees like fruit; they had climbed them to get a better view, and had been shot. The crowd rushed the soldiers and the next volleys were aimed straight into them.

The Soviet system was paying for its coercion and bigotry on the land. It did better in space. When the Americans talked of putting a man on the moon, the Russians said that he would be met on arrival by a short, fat man who would tell him how to grow maize there. Khrushchev and the Russians were rocket men, while the Americans remained devoted to the manned bomber. 'We were like peasants in a market,' Khrushchev said of the space plants. 'We walked around the rocket, touching it, tapping it to see if it was sturdy enough – we did everything but lick it to see how it tasted.' Intelligence reports of a rocket based on a German V-2 being launched on a Kazakhstan proving range reached Washington as early as November 1947. A Council of Chief Designers was established to manage the Russian rocket effort that year. Its members do not have the fame they merit: Sergei Korolev, designer of the first ICBM, liquid-propellant engine designer V. P. Glushko, control systems specialist A. N. Pilyugin. By 1955 the Americans were getting consistent reports of big advances in Russian missile programs. On October 4, 1957 the world's first satellite was launched and the word Sputnik was coined; the US was more than a year behind. It gave a distinctive radio call-sign. Russians went up to Americans on Moscow streets, grinning triumphantly: 'Beep beep.' A month later, a satellite with the dog Laika aboard was launched; there was no re-entry system and Laika died after a week in orbit when her oxygen supply ran out. Test launches of ICBMs accelerated, bringing the continental US within nuclear strike range.

In 1959, Lunik succeeded in landing on the moon. Lunik III soon took the first pictures of the dark side of the moon. The same year, the Strategic Rocket Forces were established. The new unit was the cream of the cream, outranking all other services; but its first commander, Marshal M. I. Nedelin, was killed the following year when a new booster exploded on launch at the Tura Tam missile range. The booster was to improve performance in hitting US targets. In May 1960 a Soviet spacecraft weighing 4.5 tons orbited the earth. An American fell into Russian hands the same month. For all the paradoxical intimacy of the Cold War – the mutual obsession, the colossal ritual effort, the ballet between American pilots and Russian missiles over Vietnam, and Russian pilots and American missiles in Afghanistan, the eyeballing at Checkpoint Charlie in Berlin, the exchange of cavitational signatures by deep-diving nuclear submarines – very rarely had one side physically come in contact with a member of the other. Hence the significance of the capture of Gary Powers. The pilot of a U-2 reconnaissance aircraft, he took off from a base in Pakistan to fly to Norway. He penetrated Soviet air space east of Samarkand, flying at a height of 19,750 meters. No Russian interceptor could get within 15,000 feet of him. He was nearing Sverdlovsk, the Romanov deathplace, when he heard a dull explosion and the aircraft went out of control. He was equipped with a poison pin with shellfish toxin, but did not use it. His parachute filled and he landed in a field, then was happily paraded by the Russians at a Sverdlovsk photo opportunity. The CIA discovered that the Russians had developed a successful surface to air missile, the SAM that would figure so largely above Israel and Vietnam.

Three months later a spacecraft with two dogs aboard returned safely from orbit. On April 12, 1961 Cosmonaut Number One, Yuri Gagarin, soared into the sky, strapped into a spacecraft atop a missile rocket. The Reds, the ex-peasants, had stolen a lead on the industrial Titans.

Journalists are shown space dogs *Chernushka and Zvyozdochka (top left) after their return from a space flight on March 28, 1961. The success of the mission opened the way for the first manned flight by Gagarin a few days later.*

Cosmonaut's wedding *(top right). Khrushchev proudly attends the wedding of the cosmonaut Valentina Tereshkova to her fellow cosmonaut Andrei Nikolaev, whilst a uniformed Yuri Gagarin looks on and Brezhnev peers over a head behind him. These were happy and confident days, with Soviet prestige high and the Communist system seemingly capable of mounting a challenge to capitalism.* [Photo: A. Ustinov]

Yuri Gagarin *(left) became the first man in space on April 12, 1961 after completing an orbit of the earth in the Vostok spacecraft. Born near Smolensk, he was killed in a training accident in an aircraft in 1968. He remains a Hero to Russians of all political persuasions.*

John F. Kennedy *looking slightly glazed by Khrushchev's rhetoric when the two most powerful men on earth met at the Soviet embassy in Vienna in June 1961, shortly after the abortive US-backed Bay of Pigs invasion of Cuba. Khrushchev, unimpressed by Kennedy in Vienna, began the installation of Soviet missiles in the Caribbean island the following year.*

American-backed exiles landed at the Bay of Pigs on the southern coast of Cuba on April 17, 1961, Khrushchev's 67th birthday. They were poorly armed, lacking anti-tank weapons and air cover, and were soon driven into swampland and killed or captured. This confirmed Khrushchev's view that the Americans were 'too liberal to fight'. The Americans had missiles in Turkey, a 'pistol pointed at the head' of the Soviet Union. Why should the Russians not do the same to the Americans in Cuba? Relations with the Cuban leader Fidel Castro warmed. 'We gave them as many arms as the Cuban army could absorb,' Khrushchev noted. At first, these were conventional, but in July 1962, after Castro's brother Raul had made an unexplained visit to Moscow, US aircraft tracked a significant number of Russian merchantmen steaming for the Cuban port of Mariel. On October 14, a U-2 reconnaissance aircraft flew over the San Cristobal region of Cuba and photographed what appeared to be medium-range missile sites. Two Russian lumber-trade freighters were spotted at sea, riding too high to be carrying timber. Their hatches were wide enough to load seventy-foot missiles.

By October 17, President Kennedy had firm evidence that missiles with a range of 2000 miles, enough to penetrate as far as Montana, were going into Cuba. And they were not protected by silos, which meant these were first-strike weapons. Khrushchev had fallen for the temptation to give the Americans 'a little of their own medicine'. The thought behind his action, a dangerous cocktail of self-pity, pride and moral superiority, was profoundly Russian. Everything the Russians had, they felt that they had died for. They had paid in blood, on battlefields, in execution cellars and camps, in famine and epidemic, for every advance.

Consolation prize. *Fidel Castro with Khrushchev (right) on a tour of Georgia in 1964. When Khrushchev stationed missiles in Cuba, Washington warned that it was 'ready to convert the USSR into a radioactive heap of rubbish within thirty minutes.' The missiles were shipped back to Russia, to be followed by Castro on his consolation tour.* [PHOTO: V. YEGOROV]

They had suffered in the rocket race. Thousands of zeks had toiled on the test ranges and died in the uranium mines. American rocket designers were famous figures on big salaries whereas Sergei Korolev had been arrested in 1937 and served time in the Arctic camps of Kolyma before working in a special prison with the aircraft designer Tupolev; he had been rehabilitated on Stalin's death but his name was kept secret. The Americans had got their place in the world on the cheap. The mixture of jealousy and admiration for the US was – remains – a Russian constant. America fascinated Khrushchev on his visits; just as he, earthy, energetic, a hard drinker and full of life, fascinated Americans.

On October 22, Kennedy revealed the missile build-up on television. At the same time, Khrushchev heard from the Soviet Ambassador in Havana that Castro was predicting an American airstrike within hours. 'Castro suggested that to prevent our nuclear missiles being destroyed,' Khrushchev wrote, 'we should launch a pre-emptive strike against the United States.' Kennedy announced a naval blockade of Cuba; force would be used if Soviet freighter captains refused to heave-to. 'I would not be candid', Dean Rusk told ambassadors in Washington, 'if I did not say that we are in as grave a crisis as mankind has ever been in.' Ninety B-52 bombers with nuclear payloads were airborne, and nuclear warheads were readied on 157 US Atlas and Titan missiles. All US forces were at Defcon-2, a Red Alert one step below actual war. The Americans were prepared to go to war; Khrushchev had miscalculated. Dean Rusk thought it a considerable victory in itself that he was 'still alive' on October 23; a naval attaché at the Soviet Embassy in Washington said that, having fought in three wars already, 'I am looking forward to fighting in the next.' Khrushchev was not; the bluff had failed. 'Cuba was eleven thousand kilometers from the Soviet Union,' Khrushchev admitted. 'Our sea and air communications were so precarious that an attack against the United States was unthinkable.' He decided to withdraw the missiles. Castro heard the news from a Soviet broadcast. 'He was hotheaded,' said Khrushchev. 'He was very angry with us.' Six months later, Khrushchev took Castro on a tour of Russia as a consolation.

Khrushchev was becoming increasingly erratic. He was both

radical and reactionary. He agreed to erect a monument to Stalin's victims; he permitted a former zek, D. Lazurkina, to make a speech to the 22nd Party Congress claiming that the ghost of Lenin had appeared to her, to say that 'It is unpleasant for me to lie next to Stalin' in the Red Square mausoleum. Delegates agreed to remove Stalin's body; to leave it there longer 'would be an act of blasphemy'. The mummified corpse was removed by soldiers at night and placed in a deep pit dug near the mausoleum. The hole was filled, not with earth, but with truckloads of concrete, as if only this would ensure that its grisly occupant stayed put. The poet Yevgeny Yevtushenko recorded it in his poem *The Heirs of Stalin*:

> *Silent the marble.*
> *Silent the glass scintillates.*
> *Silent stand the sentries*
>   *in the breeze like bronzes poured.*
> *And the coffin smolders slightly.*
> *Through its chinks breath percolates.*
> *As they carry him through the mausoleum doors,*
> *Slowly floats the coffin,*
>   *grazing bayonets with its edges.*

Several thousand placenames, rivers, lakes, collective farms, towns, factories, streets, were renamed. Stalingrad, ex-Tsaritsyn, became Volgograd. A thirty-year-old delegate from Stavropol, Mikhail Gorbachev, was attending the Congress. It was his first. Also present was Leonid Brezhnev, a wartime crony of Khrushchev who was moving slickly up the power structure: 'The daily activity of Nikita Sergeevich Khrushchev is a magnificent example of tact and sympathy …'

Traditionalists were appalled; Stalin's crimes were best ignored, they felt, for too many prominent men were implicated in them. They were unamused, too, at the flow of evidence; the novels, memoirs, stories and articles on the Gulag that Khrushchev allowed to be published. He had helped hound Boris Pasternak, whose great novel *Dr Zhivago* was smuggled out of Russia to an Italian publisher in 1957. When he handed the manuscript over at his dacha in the writers' colony of Peredelkino outside Moscow, Pasternak said: 'You've invited me to my own execution.' Like most inconveniences, the book was officially ignored inside the country, although grubby typewritten copies circulated as *samizdat*, a 'self-published' book. In 1958, Pasternak was awarded the Nobel Prize; the system was obliged to take note of that. Khrushchev did not read the book until much later; he was fed passages critical of Red October by officials. *Pravda* dismissed Pasternak's classic as 'a political lampoon', whose hero was a 'moral freak' and whose author was 'a pig who has fouled his own sty'. Pasternak was thrown out of the Writers' Union, so he could not work. His lover Olga Ivinskaya was no longer used as a translator.

A joke did the rounds: 'Moscow is suffering from three plagues: rak, Spartak and Pasternak.' Rak is cancer; Spartak a Moscow football side that was playing badly. Pasternak's fellow writers denounced him as 'a literary Judas who has betrayed his people for thirty pieces of silver.' Pasternak, wounded, forced to refuse the Nobel Prize, was soon dead.

It was a disgraceful throwback to Stalinism; Khrushchev sensed it, and took a different line with a second great Russian writer. The magazine *Novy Mir* ran Alexander Solzhenitsyn's Gulag novella, *One Day in the Life of Ivan Denisovich*. The magazine sold out. It was allowed to be published as a book; the book sold out. It was, a critic said, something greater than a literary event, than the discovery of a great new writer; 'it was a major event in public life.' Evgenia Ginzburg's *Into the Whirlwind*, a heartbreaking narrative of the purges, also had a profound impact. Khrushchev was pleased at the success. 'I wish I'd handled the Pasternak affair the way I dealt with *Ivan Denisovich*,' he wrote. 'I read the book myself. It is very heavy but well written. It made the reader react with revulsion to the conditions in which Ivan Denisovich and his friends lived while they served their terms.'

At the same time, he went out of his way to repress the Church and modern art. Thousands of churches were closed including the Monastery of the Caves in Kiev, the holiest place of the Orthodox faith. He ordered Moscow's finely domed Church of the Transfiguration to be demolished to make way for a Metro line. The artist Ernst Neizvestny recalled that Khrushchev, when visiting an exhibition of modern art in Moscow, 'swore horribly and said "a donkey could do better with his tail." He said that I devoured the people's money and produced shit. I told him he knew nothing about art …'

Agriculture stagnated; winds stole the Kazakh topsoil; wheat imports increased. Industry had seemed set to challenge the United States in the Gagarin year of 1961. The 22nd Party Congress that year declared that the stage of building socialism was complete; the final stage of pure Communism, of wealth and plenty, would be reached within twenty years. Planning, fine for rockets and rifles, ran into the swamps with consumer products. Furniture was scarce, but overstuffed, enormous sofas abounded. They would not fit into tiny Russian apartments, but they were the easiest items for the furniture factories to make, because their plan was based on ruble value. Small light fittings were unobtainable; instead, there was a glut of chandeliers so heavy they would pull down the average apartment block ceiling. The plan for light fittings was designated by tons.

A personality cult started; a film, *Our Nikita Sergeevich*, was put on general release, his official portraits became larger, his 70th birthday in April 1964 was marked by sycophantic outpourings. This was orchestrated by Leonid Brezhnev, now Head of State, who was soon plotting to overthrow him. Khrushchev was toppled in October 1964, the Presidium speaking of his 'harebrained schemes, hasty conclusions, rash decisions and actions based on wishful thinking'.

He was not shot, nor sent in disgrace to Mongolia. That much he had changed in the system; for all his faults – the failures in foreign policy, in farming – ordinary Russians were fond of a man human enough to have roundly insulted the loathsome East

German leader, Walter Ulbricht, and to have called Mao Tse-tung 'an old boot'. He kept his city flat and country dacha, together with bodyguards and servants, and was given a meagre 400 rubles a month pension and an ancient car. Both flat and dacha were bugged; three cosmonauts were in orbit when Khrushchev was dismissed, and he panicked Brezhnev by setting off in his car when they returned to Moscow. The plotter feared that his disgraced victim was heading for Red Square to take part in the festivities, though in fact the car swung off for his dacha. The bugging was amateur – the circuits were wrongly wired, so that the tapes the KGB men played to pass the time blared out through the microphones in the walls – and did not prevent him from writing his memoirs.

'I am old and tired,' Khrushchev said. 'I've done the main thing. Relations among us, the style of leadership, has changed drastically. Could anyone have dreamt of telling Stalin that he didn't suit us anymore, and suggesting that he retire? Not even a wet spot would have remained where he had been standing ...' His own epitaph was short and fitting: 'The fear's gone. That's my contribution.'

Rudolf Nureyev *(above) was born on a trans-Siberian train in 1939. The stifling artistic uniformity that persisted under Khrushchev repelled him and, to furious Party embarrassment, he defected in 1961. His spectacular debut with Margot Fonteyn at Covent Garden in 1962 rubbed salt in the Soviet wound.*

Mstislav Rostropovich *(right), the cellist and composer, was awarded the Lenin Prize in 1964. However, he left Russia in 1974 and was stripped of his Soviet citizenship in 1978. He returned during the abortive coup of 1991, to stand atop a tank and bolster the morale of the democrats.*

Boris Pasternak *(left) celebrates with his wife on winning the Nobel Prize in October 1958. Dr Zhivago, his epic story of the Revolution published that year, set off a political explosion. It was banned; he was described as a 'reptile', expelled from the Writers' Union, and forced to refuse his Nobel Prize.*

Yevgeny Yevtushenko *(above), cult figure of the younger generation during Khrushchev's half-thaw. His poem 'Zima Junction' helped spark a spiritual renaissance, and he publicly supported Solzhenitsyn on his arrest. Shostakovich set five of his poems, including his attack on Russian anti-Semitism, 'Babyi Yar', to music as his Thirteenth Symphony.*

Mikhail Sholokov *(top) wrote a single masterpiece before alcohol and sub-servience to the Party put paid to his powers. And Quiet Flows the Don gave a splendid picture of the Cossacks in the years of war and revolution. He protested to Stalin about the killing of the kulaks, but by Khrushchev's time he was complaining that the State was too soft on the dissidents.*

Sergei Prokofiev *(above) went into exile for 18 years. He returned to Moscow in 1936, writing film scores for Eisenstein, his opera War and Peace, and Peter and the Wolf. Though he wrote a cantata 'Hail to Stalin', his wife was sent to a labor camp and his work was condemned. He died 3 hours before Stalin: only then could his last opera be performed.*

11
THE BIG SLEEP

THE COUNTRY WANTED NO FURTHER ALARMS AND EXCURSIONS and it yearned rather for stability and perks; cheap food, cheap rents, jobs for life and 3-ruble vodka. They were provided by Leonid Ilyich Brezhnev, the Ukrainian steelworker's son from Dneprodzerzhinsk. The system had helped him to prosper and, corpulent at 58, his coarse features blotched with good living, indolent, he was happy to leave it be. The purges had given him dead men's boots to climb in, as he rose from junior engineer to Party secretary of a big industrial region of the Ukraine in thirty months; at 33, he was a powerful figure, a good organiser in his prime. Khrushchev took a shine to him and sent him to Kazakhstan to oversee the Virgin Lands project, elevating him to the Politburo on his return. He neatly distanced himself from his patron shortly before Khrushchev's fall, and replaced him after it.

He was vain; vanity, the importance of appearance, was the key to his era. He had a modest, noncombatant war as a political adviser, but loved uniforms and medals, which he awarded himself. He won Lenin Prizes for Peace and for Literature; he became a Marshal of the Soviet Union. Films were made of his 'heroic' wartime past, although cynics suggested that he should be buried in the Tomb of the Unknown Soldier, on the grounds that it was unknown whether he had really been a soldier. It was the form, not the substance, that was important to him; on the surface, at least, the country prospered under him.

Things had never looked so good since the revolution. The economy was the world's second largest, after the US. Meat and milk production climbed by a third. Consumption of fish and eggs doubled; that of alcohol quadrupled. Prices were stable. Wages doubled, but the price of meat remained pegged at 1962 levels. There was an explosion in internal travel as Aeroflot became the world's largest airline, its rugged prop aircraft flying from rough strips in outlying settlements to feed the new Ilyushin and Tupolev jets serving the cities. Airplane tickets were dirt cheap; as late as 1990 it cost less than $15 to fly from Kiev to Vladivostok, further than New York to Honolulu. Apartments rented at $5 a month; heating, in cities with six-month winters, was included. Socialism had been a struggle and now here was the pay-off.

As distant oil and mineral reserves were exploited, hard currency tumbled into Soviet coffers with the huge increases in world energy and precious metal prices. The country became the world's largest oil producer, and Muruntau in the Uzbek wilds was its largest gold mine, producing eighty tonnes a year. Norilsk, the northernmost city in the world, its high-rises built on piles above the permafrost, saw its population of miners and

A shopping spree in Moscow *in the mid-Seventies. People came from all over the USSR to shop in Moscow and other big cities for the food and clothing unobtainable in smaller places. Trains were filled with shoppers, and since air tickets were kept dirt cheap by subsidies, aircraft also were packed with housewives and their overstuffed cases.*
[PHOTO: I. GAVRILOV]

Women workers *(left)*
at a smelting plant in the
Brezhnev era. Women
continued to provide
much of the muscle in
heavy industry as well as
in snow clearance,
roadmending and
fieldwork.
[PHOTO: V. SHCHEKOLDIN]

Oil workers *(opposite)* **in**
the Siberian fields. *They*
were recruited from across
Russia with the lure of
high wages, but they
worked twelve-hour days
in teams and shifts were
six months on, six months
off. May Day was the
only official holiday in
the oilfields; the men
worked all other days.
[PHOTO: I. GAVRILOV]

Winter on a new oil field
at Ussinsk in Siberia
(left). Massive new oil
deposits were discovered
in Siberia; the country
became the world's
largest oil and gas
producer. Although
workers in the northern
oil fields were well paid
by Soviet standards,
living conditions
remained tough.
[PHOTO: I. GAVRILOV]

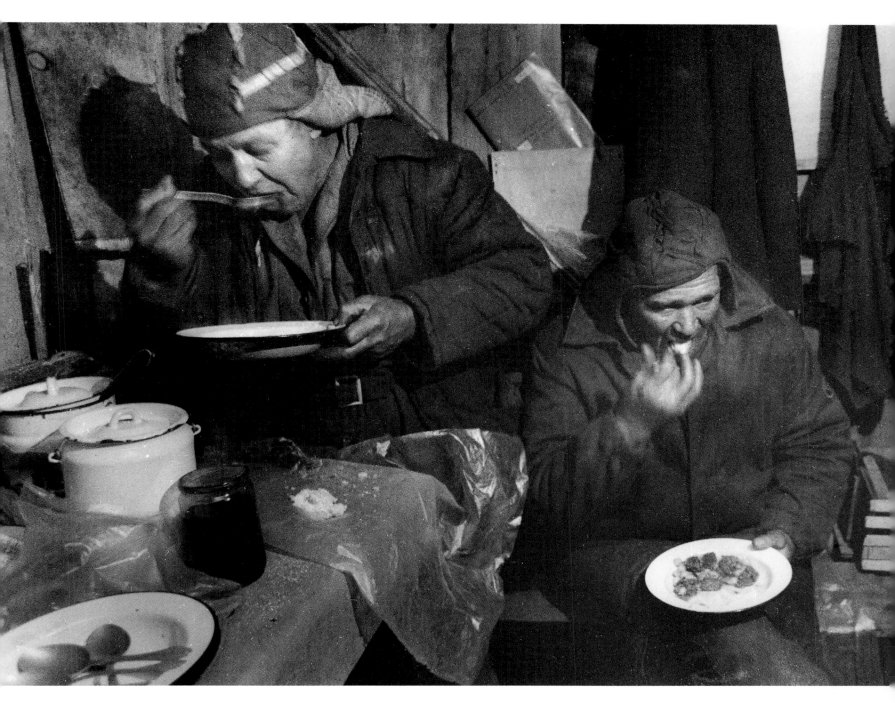

steelworkers soar to 140,000. Surgut, the center of a huge oil zone in the middle reaches of the Ob, boomed from a village settlement among frozen marshes and soon outgrew Anchorage, Alaska; toolpushers on the Samotlor field it serviced could make $18,000 a year, phenomenal money. Bratsk, heart of the Siberian power industry, quadrupled its population, whilst that of Yakutsk, deep in the permafrost zone, grew to 100,000, with a university and a branch of the Academy of Sciences.

By the mid-Seventies, it was reckoned that the Soviet worker had a living standard a third that of an American – and half that of a German; he was at the same level as a blue-collar American at the start of the Twenties. A Westerner might think that dirt-poor – only 1 in 46 had a car; the average per capita living space was 72 square feet, 17 times less than in the US – but Russians felt good enough. In the first five years of the decade, the number of private cars doubled to 3.6 million. Waiting lists were huge, costs

horrendous; tinny Zhigulis, badly made Fiat copies, sold at $10,000, four years' average salary. But the mere existence of family cars was gratifying to people who for decades had feared the automobile as a Party and KGB transporter. Two thirds of families had a television, three fifths a sewing and washing machine; half owned a refrigerator.

Life was sweet for the members of the nomenklatura. The Party always looked after its own. 'A worker-agitator who is at all gifted and promising *must not be left* to work eleven hours a day in the factory,' Lenin said. Brezhnev confirmed them as aristocrats, fussed over by batmen and chauffeurs, eating special rations in large apartments. They were becoming hereditary as their children went on from special schools to envied foreign postings, Brezhnev's son to Sweden, KGB chief Yuri Andropov's to a doctorate in the US. 'Trust in cadres' was Brezhnev's motto; the *cadres*, the Party professionals, helped themselves.

The Aeroflot fleet. *A plane (above) takes on passengers at an airstrip in the Caucasus. The State-owned airline was a colossus, the world's largest with a fleet of some 15,000 aircraft. More than anything else, the vast country was stitched together by Aeroflot. Provisions arrive by Aeroflot helicopter (opposite) in the Arctic zone of eastern Siberia. The figure in the foreground is a reindeer herder. A huge region* *of eastern Siberia, the size of the United States, had no all-weather roads and no railroads. When the rivers froze, aircraft were the only practical means of transport. Aeroflot pilots flew into some 8000 airports and airstrips, serving the most isolated communities. The gigantic effort, where the furthest-flung sable hunter could get himself to Moscow by helicopter and jet airliner, was a great* *achievement. It drained resources, however, since fares were so low that traders could jet thousands of miles from the Black Sea coasts to Moscow with a single suitcase of oranges, and still turn a profit.*

[PHOTO, ABOVE: Y. RASKOPOV]
[PHOTO, RIGHT: S. BURASOVSKY]

Home life. *A working mother (left) with her daughter in 1983. Single-parent families were common, with a high divorce rate. But once unheard-of luxuries – a telephone, a radio set – became commonplace under Brezhnev, and the dream of the car seen in the poster on the wall came closer to reality. (Opposite) Brezhnev as the family man with his grand-daughter at one of his dachas. These homes in the countryside and forests had become one of the great perks of the* nomenklatura, *their size increasing as the pecking order was climbed. Stalin had a modest wooden one outside Moscow. Brezhnev had five, including one on the Black Sea in Georgia, like the Tsar's Livadia Palace in the Crimea.*
[PHOTO, LEFT: A. TAMBULIDIS]
[PHOTO, RIGHT: V. MUSAELYAN]

Special stores provided brown-paper wrapped parcels of caviar, sturgeon, imported brandies and perfumes, Japanese cameras, English woollens. A network of shops in Moscow and other cities, without names or window displays, provided discreet services from laundering to picture framing and hairdressing. The powerful received the *kremlevsky payok*, the Kremlin ration of succulent foodstuffs and wines. The *Upravleniye Delami*, the 'Administration of Affairs' of the Central Committee, maintained apartment houses, guesthouses, rest homes, clinics, car pools and servants.

The intricate pecking order was reflected in the height of apartment ceilings; in the type of chauffeured car, Zil for the cream, Chaika for others; in the size of hotel rooms. The largest room in a Black Sea hotel used by vacationing officers, with big refrigerator, color TV and working telephone, was assigned to the commander of the Kiev military district. Edward Lozansky, the son-in-law of a general, qualified for lesser quarters with a black-and-white TV and a phone that did not work. Lozansky found himself moved to the best room; his father-in-law had been promoted. As one of the *Vlasti*, the powers that be, the nomenklatura member might qualify for a special flight from the VIP's own Moscow airport, Vnukovo II. The less exalted could bump people off overbooked Aeroflot flights and out of sleeping berths on overnight expresses. Their cars sped down the green-marked central lane of main streets reserved for VIPs, known as 'the Chaika lane'. They could watch American or European movies, banned to other Russians, in special cinemas. They could read Green, White and Red *Tass*, which in ascending order of detail provided daily news reports suppressed from ordinary newspapers.

Lenin's corruption had taken a spiritual form. Stalin had no time, and no need, for money; he allowed his salary to pile up unopened in envelopes on his desk. Khrushchev was too earthy to

be deflected by wealth. Brezhnev, and his grasping family, liked baubles. Ambitious Party officials gave him presents of diamonds and antiques; Western visitors gave him sporting guns, and automobiles for a collection that included a Citroen-Maserati, a Lincoln, various Mercedes and a Rolls Royce Silver Cloud. Foreign cars were a symbol of the Brezhnev elite. The KGB journalist Victor Louis had a Rolls Royce, though his was secondhand; President Podgorny made do with a Mercedes 600; the planning supremo Nikolai Baibakov sported a Chevrolet Impala.

They had dachas, too. That of Ukrainian party boss Pyotr Shelest ran to four stories and a half-mile of shoreline at Yalta; Anastas Mikoyan, survivor and trade minister, had one close by with fresh and salt water marbled pools. Brezhnev had one near Usovo, another at Pitsunda on the Black Sea; he shot boars from one in the hunting region of Zavidovo, where Henry Kissinger was a guest; he had a pinewood retreat near Minsk and a Finnish-built guest house close to Leningrad. In one story, he showed them off to his mother, astonished by the luxury after her humdrum life in provincial Dneprodzerzhinsk. 'Well, it's good, Leonid,' she says nervously. 'But what'll happen if the Reds come back?'

The good life was withdrawn at a hint of dissent. The Brezhnev years were warm, mollycoddled for those who conformed; the system, the poet Yevgeny Yevtushenko wrote, 'buys us off with things like big children'. Everyone had to give way to the compromise within him, to comrade Kompromis Kompromisovich:

He buys us off with apartments,
Furniture, showy fashions,
And we're no longer belligerent.
We raise a noise – only when we're drinking.

A motorboat trip on the Black Sea: *Brezhnev on his summer holiday in 1974. The country had been living off its nerves, reeling from crisis to crisis, but Brezhnev brought it stability. Everybody kept their job and their perks, most of all the country's plump and well-pleased leader. (Right) He dances with his daughter Galina* at a reception in 1976. He was indulgent of her; she in turn indulged in her taste for men and for the bottle. The three main photographs on this spread were taken by his personal photographer and were not seen during his lifetime.*

[PHOTO, ABOVE: V. MUSAELYAN]

[PHOTO, RIGHT: V. YEGOROV]

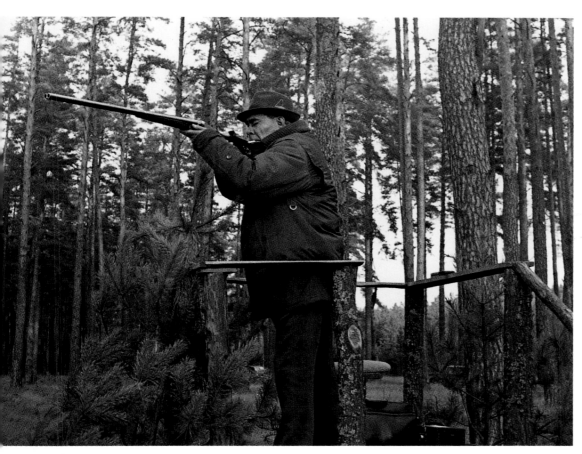

Brezhnev on one of his frequent hunting trips. *In Yuri Andropov, head of the KGB, he had an efficient and loyal man watching his back, which meant he was relaxed enough to leave the Party to its own devices and to take time out to go hunting. (Below) Brezhnev free from the cares of office on a skimobile. He had a passion for the internal combustion engine.* [Photos: V. Musaelyan]

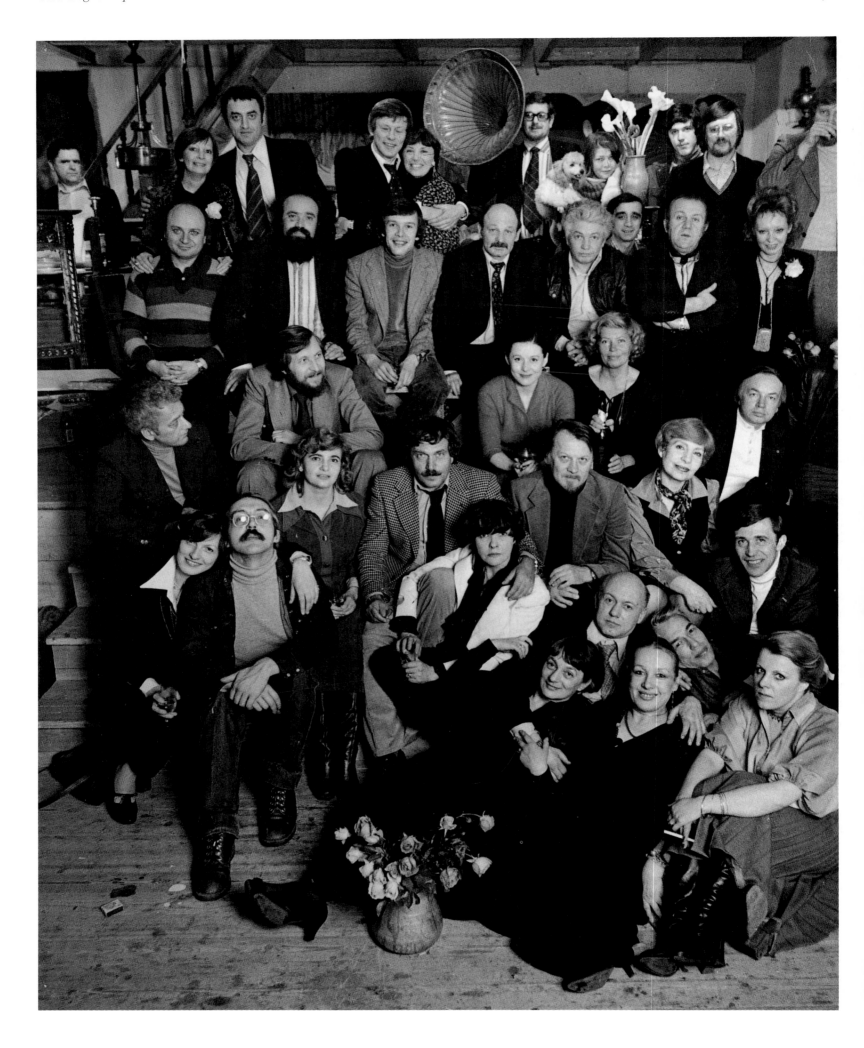

A group of dissidents *(left) from the arts world involved with the banned* Metropol *magazine, photographed in Moscow in 1979. The woman, center front in a white jacket, is the famous poet Bella Akhmadulina and she is seen (right) giving a party in her studio for the visiting Italian film director Michelangelo Antonioni (in spectacles). She is furthest right. Vladimir Vysotsky, Russia's Bob Dylan, is at the end of the table, with a jagged fringe. He died of drink in 1980.* [PHOTOS: V. PLOTNIKOV]

The consequences for those who rebelled were severe. Andrei Sinyavsky and Yuli Daniel were sentenced to five and seven years in labor camps for 'anti-Soviet propaganda'; they were no more than satirists. Brezhnev, and his KGB chief, Yuri Andropov, puritanical, severe, a philosopher among secret policemen, drew lines; those who strayed over them were struck down. Psychiatric punishment was perfected. It had been used since the late Thirties when the NKVD built a 400-bed penal wing in the grounds of a mental hospital in Kazan. To oppose Communism was so bizarre and irrational that, as Khrushchev had put it, it was 'frequently caused by mental disorder … Clearly the mental state of such people is not normal'. They were thus confined to mental hospitals. Thirteen or more Special Psychiatric Hospitals opened under Brezhnev and the West became aware of them through Valery Tsarsis's book *Ward 7*. They were controlled by the MVD, the interior ministry, rather than by the health ministry. Professor Andrei Snezhnevsky, director of the Institute of Psychiatry at the Academy of Medical Sciences, provided a pseudo-academic argument for labeling dissent as schizophrenia. The definition of criminal dissent was broadened by Article 69 of the revised constitution introduced under Brezhnev. This obliged Soviet citizens positively 'to safeguard the interest of the Soviet state and to enhance its power and prestige'. Failure to act in support of the regime could be an offense in itself. 'In our country it is not forbidden to "think differently" from the majority,' said Brezhnev, before adding a brutal rider: 'It is quite another matter if a few individuals who have actively come out against the Soviet system embark on anti-Soviet activity with the help of imperialist subversive centers.' The wards were filled with Christians, writers, Baltic nationalists and pacifists.

What was true for a person applied also to a country. In April 1968, the Czech leader Alexander Dubcek declared that the Party was not the 'universal caretaker' of society. To make the heresy worse, he added that the right of free speech, a free press and travel abroad must be guaranteed. This was the 'Prague Spring'; a Czech Party congress to confirm it was called for September. If the reforms were to be reversed, the Russians would have to move before then. 'Socialism with a human face,' as Dubcek put it, was not on Brezhnev's agenda. In August, Soviet 'tourists' in stout boots began arriving in large numbers in Prague; tank movements were reported from the East German border. Shortly after 10 pm on August 20, the control tower of Prague airport was taken over by Soviet commandos who landed in an Aeroflot civilian airliner. A tank column, shepherded by a black Volga from the Soviet embassy, reached Dubcek's office at dawn. Eight soldiers with sub-machineguns broke in and cut the phone lines. 'I, who have devoted my whole life to collaborating with the Soviet Union, now they do this to me!' said Dubcek, who had been raised in Russia by his Communist father. He was taken in handcuffs to a KGB prison in the Ukraine – and then to the Kremlin, where he was kept in a small room, naked to the waist, limp and sedated. Brezhnev told him: 'For us the results of the war are inviolable and we will defend them even at the risk of a new war.' He flung a last contemptuous line – 'we have already got the better of other little nations, so why not yours too?' – and walked out, the rest of the Politburo following him 'like a line of geese'. Dubcek cracked; he agreed censorship ('ideological supervision') could be restored and accepted the 'temporary stationing' of the invasion forces.

In Russia too, the best and the brightest were muzzled or forced abroad. Iosif Brodsky, the best young Russian poet, was driven to emigrate in 1972. Viktor Nekrasov, author of *In the Trenches of Stalingrad*, followed; so did 100,000 Soviet Jews.

Mikhail Baryshnikov *trains with the Kirov ballet in Leningrad in 1973. His American dreaming became real. He defected the following year whilst in Canada, to dance with the American Ballet Theater and to become the ultimate symbol of Americana, a Hollywood star.*

Solzhenitsyn had one article and one short story published in Russia under Brezhnev. He was expelled from the Writers' Union in 1969 and in 1974 he was bundled on an airplane to Switzerland, ultimately to make his way to Vermont. The poet Alexander Tvardovsky was fired as editor of *Novy Mir*; his brave magazine did not show sufficient Party-mindedness, *partiinost*, in its writing. The brilliant cellist Mstislav Rostropovich, disheartened by the quarantine imposed on him for defending Solzhenitsyn, left Russia in 1974 with his wife, the soprano Galina Vishnevskaya; he became conductor of the National Symphony Orchestra in Washington. The lead dancer of the Kirov, Mikhail Baryshnikov, defected in Canada; he had wanted to dance Schoenberg in Leningrad, but the deadhand culture ministry ruled it 'unsuitable for ballet'. Those left in Moscow felt themselves as lonely as on the moon. The Moscow Art Theater, where Chekhov and Stanislavsky had worked, staged *Steelworkers*, a tale of heroic Bolshevik foundrymen; *The Hottest Month*, playing in Moscow moviehouses, showed how the Five-Year Plan for steel was achieved. The poet Andrei Voznesensky caught the air of the age; it was 'a great fast of the spirit'. The Strugatsky brothers disguised criticism as science fiction, others reworked 19th-century novels for the stage, where the parallel between a Tsarist Okhrana agent and the contemporary KGB would be clear to the audience, but not specific enough for the censor to intervene. KGB men tracked down the sources of *samizdat*, the 'self-publishing' by dissidents who laboriously copied novels and essays onto thin yellowing paper with antique typewriters. The parallel process of *magnitizdat* produced cassette recordings of protest songs and satire. *The Chronicle of Current Events*, put together by a group of friends in a Moscow apartment, was closed; its Ukrainian equivalent, the *Herald*, went the same way. In the forests of Latvia, Baptists printed half a million copies of the Bible before they were discovered.

The economy sagged beneath a veneer of flattering statistics. Huge investment went into fertilisers and farm machinery, but millions of soldiers and townspeople had to be mobilised for the harvest each year, while the machines broke and fertiliser designed for sugar beet was sprayed on fields of rye. Peasants were forced into 'agrotowns' from *neperspektivnye* villages, 'futureless' hamlets that Moscow bureaucrats emptied with a stroke of the pen. The peasants loathed them and took their revenge in classic Soviet fashion. They idled, and they stole from the State. *Izvestiya* estimated in 1975 that over a third of private motorists were driving on stolen State gasoline. The black economy was almost the only source for quality fruit and meat, fashionable clothes, effective medicines, car mechanics, television engineers. In the mad world of Soviet pricing, it was hugely profitable to fly by jet from Georgia to Moscow with a single suitcase of oranges for sale; the black marketeers who did so, in silk shirts and Cuban boots, would stand each other salted salmon, caviar and vodka with champagne chasers in the bar of the National Hotel.

Bribery, *vzyatka*, the take, was rampant. Party officials sold jobs and permits. The Party boss in Georgia, Eduard Shevardnadze, clamped down on corruption, arresting 25,000 in the early Seventies; death threats obliged him to travel in a blastproofed car. A huge fraud was uncovered by satellite pictures in Uzbekistan; where cottonfields should have been, the camera found only desert. For years, officials had lined their pockets from false claims of increasing harvests. Cotton had become a poison in Central Asia. Water from the rivers feeding the Aral Sea was diverted into the fields. The sea receded, leaving the fishing village of Aralsk thirty miles inland. While fertilisers and pesticides sprayed on the cottonfields soaked into the water table, storms blew salt and chemical dust from the areas where the sea had dried out, and dumped them on farmland hundreds of miles to the southwest.

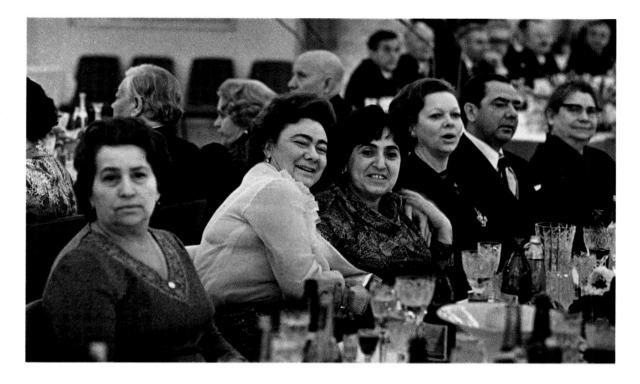

Kremlin wives: *Galina Brezhnev with friends at her father's 70th birthday party. Her husband Yuri Churbanov was Shchelokov's deputy. After Brezhnev's death, he was convicted of corruption in a four-billion-ruble Uzbekistan cotton scandal.* [Photo: V. Musaelyan]

Most goods were *shtampny*, stamped-out, mass produced rubbish; refrigerators without freezer compartments, washing machines with no automatic cycle or spin dry. New apartment blocks came complete with standard defects: floors built of green lumber that had already warped, the plaster peeling off the walls, the bath leaking, the toilet broken and none of the power points working. Women spent two hours a day in queues; walkers out for a stroll went equipped with large amounts of cash and an *avoska* by-chance bag, in case they ran across something rare for sale, boots that fitted, a rug, Polish toothpaste.

The profits of oil and precious metals were squandered on the 'metal eaters', as Khrushchev called the defense industry. At the end of the Sixties, the Russian ICBM force was growing by 300 silo launchers a year. In the fourteen years after Cuba, the Russians built 1323 naval vessels; in the same period, Washington built 302. Under Soviet naval escort, Cuban troops landed in Angola as Soviet surrogates in 1975. The following year, they were in Ethiopia. By the end of the Seventies, there were ten Marxist states in Africa. Nicaragua saw Marxism reach the American mainland. Middle East terrorists were trained at Simferopol in the Crimea. Russia was also a great Asian power; it twice equipped armies fighting the Americans, in Korea and in Vietnam. Vietnam was a triumph for Brezhnev, costing him less than a thirtieth of the treasure paid out by Washington, but he failed to draw the lesson of superpower vulnerability from it. After dark on Christmas Eve 1979, Soviet paratroopers landed at Kabul airport and by December 27, 5000 heavily armed Russian troops were there. They attacked the interior ministry, and the old royal palace where the Afghan president Hafizullah Amin was based. He was cornered with his mistress in a bar on the top floor and shot. By the time Brezhnev's successors called it a day, Afghanistan had cost the Kremlin a failed Olympics and billions of rubles.

The vast military and political effort – Cuba alone was costing $4.5 billion a year by the start of the Eighties – was extracted from a country in which consumer goods were chronically *defitsitny*, in deficit. No recognition came from a geriatric Politburo. Brezhnev was in physical and mental limbo for his last six years after suffering a stroke. 'Lies snowballed, both petty daily lies and big State lies,' wrote the diplomat Alexander Yakovlev. 'To succeed in anything one had to be sly, to lie, to violate rules and laws. What was the right way to live? To answer the question, one at least had to know the true state of affairs. And no one knew what it was like – both those who had been lied to, and those who had lied.' When he died in November 1982, his replacement also came from the living dead. Yuri Andropov was 68, a tall, stooping man, for fifteen years the master of the KGB but so little known in the West that it was not clear whether he was a widower or still a married man. Gray and waxen, he was dying of kidney disease. He was soon confined to a special suite in the Kremlin clinic at Kuntsevo west of Moscow. What vigor was left him he invested in an ineffectual campaign against drinking and slackness. In January 1983, Party activists in red armbands searched cafes, baths, department stores and cinemas for people who should have been at work; a raid on a Moscow bathhouse netted two generals. The crackdown infuriated women who had no alternative but to shop in working hours because of the lengthening queues. Trying to win back favor, he slashed the soaring price of vodka back to 4 rubles 70 kopeks; in gratitude, the fiery liquid became known as 'Andropovka'. He died in February 1984, the year of the heaviest losses in Afghanistan, with 2343 officers and men returning home as 'military cargo 200' – in coffins. Andropov's successor, Konstantin Chernenko, breathless and wheezing with advanced emphysema, was too weak to raise his hand to his predecessor's coffin as it was carried into Red Square. He was dead by March 1985.

Politicians in a civil defense exercise *in Vologda (left) simulating a Nato gas attack in the early Eighties. The Soviet obsession with American attack seemed unreasoning, but the century had shown that evils came from the West: Germans and Austrians in 1914; British, French, Americans and Japanese in 1919; Poles in 1920; Germans, Rumanians, Italians in 1941.*
[Photo: S. Donin]

Goose-stepping infantry *(left) parade outside Moscow in 1984. 'We will bury capitalism,' Nikita Khrushchev once threatened. Communism had the men and the machines to achieve it. The Soviets outnumbered the Americans in ground troop numbers by four to one.*

A fighter pilot *at the test pilots' training school at Orenburg, where Yuri Gagarin was a pupil. Russian pilots had the run of eight interceptor types to the American Top Guns' three. In surface-to-air missiles, the Soviets outdid the* *Americans by twelve types to six; in ICBM types by seven to three. This immense load was placed on an economy in which light bulbs and toothpaste were in chronic shortage.* [PHOTO: I. GAVRILOV]

Waiting for bread to arrive *in the early Eighties. The villagers in this picture are noticeably not talking to each other. Village life remained distorted by memories of the brutal process of collectivisation and the purges. The sense of community was destroyed by the fear of informers. Agriculture remained maimed by the collectives; the largest country in the world, a grain exporter in Tsarist days, was unable to feed itself and had to depend on American, Canadian and Argentinian imports to ensure enough bread to go round.*
[PHOTO: B. MIKHALYOVKIN]

12
THE LAST BOLSHEVIK

MIKHAIL SERGEYEVICH GORBACHEV WAS THE VERY ROLE MODEL of *Homo Sovieticus*; assured, incisive, at times debonair, with his redhead wife, the superstar who unleashed Gorbymania among Western crowds. But he was born a peasant in the rolling southern steppelands of Stavropol, reared in a two-room mud cabin in a back-country village whose straggling main street was dust, mud or ice according to season. No tarmac road came within fifty miles of Privolnoe and its wheat and sunflower fields. Gorbachev's southern accent was as noticeable as the purple birthmark on his forehead.

The village was collectivised in 1931, the year he was born. His childhood was classically Russian, with its surf-beat of Stalinist and then Nazi horrors. The first savaged his paternal grandfather, Sergei, given nine years in the Siberian camps after a village informer claimed he had hoarded forty pounds of grain. The latter did for Gorbachev's oldest brother, killed in the great tank battle at Kursk. His paternal grandmother told him as a child of the night they came to take his grandfather. As an adult, he remembered it with such force that he choked with tears at the scene in the anti-Stalin movie *Repentance* where the innocent hero is arrested. He also saw the splits that marked so many Soviet families. His maternal grandfather was the first chairman of the local collective farm; far from being flung to Siberia by Stalinism, he rose on its back.

He was an ambitious boy – 'magnetic', an early girlfriend said. He had to start work during the harvest at 14, as helper to a combine driver, washing down after a blazing day in a barrel of muddy water. But he stayed on at high school, walking ten miles a day to lessons in which he excelled. He won a place to Moscow State University, the pinnacled Stalinist skyscraper that looms from the heights above the city like a Fifties sci-fi backdrop. He read law; an unusual choice in a country where 'Socialist justice' – the Gulag, the execution cellar – had for so long taken precedence over juridical nicety. But then, as his friend, the Czech Zdenek Mlynar who shared his university dormitory, commented, 'Gorbachev was a Stalinist at the time, like everyone else. To be a true Communist reformer, you have to have been a true Stalinist first.'

The Party was the best route up the cliff face and he began collecting its acronyms. He joined *Komsomol*, the Young Communists, soon becoming *komsorg*, youth organiser, for the law faculty. A lively girl from Siberia, the daughter of a railroad engineer, was reading philosophy at the university. Gorbachev married his Raisa. Room in Moscow was desperately scarce, the simplest hotel beyond their means; by tradition, Gorbachev's room-mates bunked down elsewhere so that the newlyweds could

Mikhail Gorbachev *atop Lenin's mausoleum on Red Square. Ambitious and charismatic, he remained a Communist and said that he had no intention of presiding over the death of the Party. But he proved to be the last Soviet leader, victim of the forces unleashed by his own tolerance.*
[PHOTO: J. TORREGANO]

Furling the Red flags: *a
Party loyalist collects the
banners after a sparsely-
attended rally in 1985.
As the economy groaned,
harvest yields tumbled,
and absenteeism soared,
support for the Party
shrank. It lost contact
with the young, and those
who remained loyal, as
much out of habit as
conviction, were mainly
elderly.*
[PHOTO: S. PODGORKOV]

have one night together. In June 1955, the couple graduated and
moved to Stavropol where Gorbachev's Party links paid off and he
got a job as a Komsomol organiser. Self-improvement was part of
his politics; when he was Party leader, he was to have Dale
Carnegie's *How to Win Friends and Influence People* translated
specially. He now went to night school to win a degree in
agriculture.

Gorbachev spent twenty-three years inching up the Party
rockface in Stavropol. The effort was well spent; the Moscow
bureaucracy was renowned for its spite and backstabbing, and a
provincial could have a clearer run at power. But even in the sticks
a Party man had to keep his nose clean; when Zdenek Mlynar sent
him a postcard from fraternal Prague, the local police chief
delivered it personally. Foreign greetings aroused suspicion. As a
young official, Gorbachev was part of the system as it reached the
heights; foreign empires, British, French, were dying; the
Americans were being beaten in space while the economy was
expanding steadily. As he matured and rose, he was aware of the
Brezhnev inertia and its 'sputnik rhetoric', the high-flying boasts
that burned out as they neared earth.

By 1971, he was Party boss in Stavropol. As such, he met the
Moscow grandees who came to vacation in the Caucasus, Yuri
Andropov among them. The puritanical KGB chairman took to
Gorbachev; he liked his lively intelligence, the lack of corruption
that meant his mother still lived on the collective farm and his
brother was a mere army captain. Most Brezhnev bureaucrats
would have wangled a Stavropol apartment for mother, and a
colonelcy for brother. Gorbachev himself lived in a modest one-
story block opposite the Stavropol KGB building. He came to
Moscow's attention with an agro-industrial scheme, involving the
use of mobile fleets of harvesters, trucks and tractors. It had a
grandiose ring to it which appealed to the Brezhnevite mentality;
by the time it was proved a flop, he had moved safely on. At
Andropov's urging, Brezhnev made a stopover at the spa town of
Mineralnie Vody on Gorbachev's patch in 1978. Brezhnev,
Andropov, Chernenko and Gorbachev – four Soviet leaders –
talked on the low platform of the Tsarist railway station. Two
months later, Gorbachev was summoned to Moscow and made
responsible for agriculture, at 47 the youngest member of a
geriatric team. In 1980, he became a member of the Politburo. He
was 50; his appointment brought the average age of its members
down to 70.

His record at agriculture was miserable. Grain harvests
slumped and imports soared; primitive storage saw a fifth of the
grain crop and a third of the potato crop rot. More than half a
million tractors were built each year; they broke down so easily
that the number in working order on the farms stayed steady. But
so much else was wrong – drunkenness, corruption, the poisoning
of rivers, the evaporation of lakes, the grotesque subsidies that
made it worthwhile for a man to buy a 3000-mile round ticket on
a jet in order to sell a suitcase of oranges in Moscow – that no
blame attached to Gorbachev. He shone more brightly when
Andropov became leader. His patron groomed him, involved him

in foreign affairs, sent him to Canada, that other great northern country, so that he could see how socialism was failing.

Andropov, dying of kidney failure, disappeared in September 1983; he was not seen again until his corpse lay in state the following February. Konstantin Chernenko, his successor, was so ill that he too reminded Russians of the living dead. He was 72; his prime minister was 79, the defense minister 75, foreign minister Andrei Gromyko 74. Chernenko reverted to his Brezhnev origins, celebrating the opening of the Baikal-Amur railroad with a golden spike in 1984, when in truth it was not completed for a further five years. He went into hospital in January 1985 and Gorbachev flew back from Britain, where Raisa had astonished people used to dumpy Soviet wives with her gold lamé sandals and cream satin two-piece. By March, Chernenko was dead and Gorbachev was Soviet leader. 'Comrades,' said Gromyko, 'this man has a nice smile but he's got iron teeth.' Russians knew little about him, but felt relief that he was 54 and fit.

He was inexperienced, and he inherited a palsied system that leached out vigor and talent. The old work ethic, 'building Socialism', was long since buried. Workers had had too many demands, too many lies, too much terror. Cynicism and skiving replaced it. 'Our rockets can find Halley's comet and reach Venus,' said Gorbachev. 'But our fridges don't work.' A brand-new apartment block on the Moscow river, a prestige building for the elite, was almost uninhabitable; the roof leaked, the lifts were broken, the doors had warped, the ceiling panels were coming off. Alcohol consumption had rocketed fourfold in the past two decades. The average life expectancy for Soviet men had fallen from 67 under Khrushchev to 62; it was the first drop ever recorded in an industrial society in peacetime.

Alcohol was no more than a symptom, but Gorbachev went for it. Opening hours for liquor stores were reduced, and the lines outside them swelled to a mile and more. Restaurants could only serve drink with food; alcohol was banned from official receptions and banquets; 900,000 acres of vineyards were plowed under. For angry drinkers, the *Generalny Sekretar* became the *Mineralny Sekretar* (mineral water in Russia is often salty and near undrinkable). Official alcohol sales dropped, and with them valuable revenue; home brewing took off, with queues for sugar matching those outside the remaining liquor stores. The amount of moonshine being distilled was put at 150 million deciliters a year; enough to lead to 11,000 fatal poisonings over the Gorbachev era. The puritanism bit into the popularity Gorbachev won for his Western-style walkabouts and his flesh pressing. The only favor alcohol did him was to destroy the career of his rival and friend of the arms industry Grigori Romanov, who got roaring drunk whilst out boating with a blonde singer thirty years his junior and was picked up by a Finnish patrol boat when he crossed into Finnish waters.

Gorbachev had an entertainer's flair. His first year in power was a triumph in the West; the new media star escorted Raisa to dinner at Versailles, negotiated arms reductions in Geneva. At

Happily drunk Russians *stagger through spring mud. Alcohol consumption quadrupled under Brezhnev; Gorbachev attempted to cut it back, for which he was nicknamed 'Mineral Water'.* [PHOTO: O. ZAITSEV]

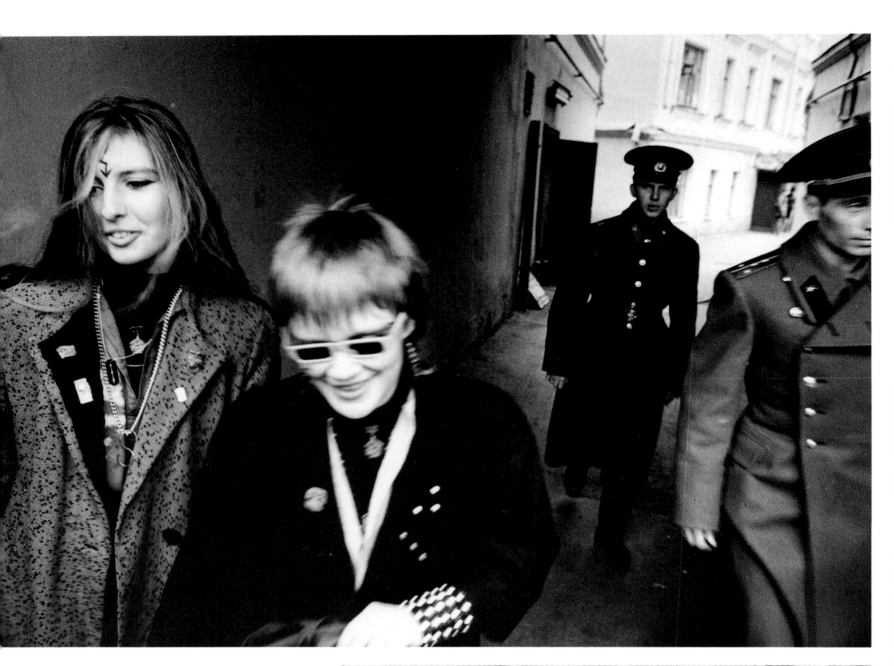

Girls on a Moscow street *(above) trying to look as Western as possible. The young reveled in being able to shock their elders, without risk of being sent to the Gulag, for the first time since 1917.*

[PHOTO: I.MOUKHIN]

English graffiti *and what looks like a drug deal in Vilnius in Lithuania (right). Drugs became a major problem as the young copied the West.*

[PHOTO: I.MOUKHIN]

A stylish rock musician *on a street in Leningrad in 1986. Russian rock stars commanded huge audiences at home; unlike Russian triumphs in classical music and dance, none succeeded on the world stage.*
[PHOTO: I MOUKHIN]

275

home, thousands of members of the nomenklatura were sacked, but there was no visible change. 'The problems that have accumulated in society are more deeply rooted than we first thought,' he admitted. The nomenklatura was happy to allow him enough rope to hang himself.

In the early hours of Saturday April 26, 1986 an explosion destroyed the number four reactor at the Chernobyl nuclear power station in the Ukraine. When firemen arrived from Pripyat, the nearest town, the graphite core of the reactor was ablaze and flames shot 200 feet into the air. It was not until late on Sunday morning that the evacuation of Pripyat's 40,000 people was ordered; before, children had played football and the open air swimming pool had been full of people enjoying the spring sunshine. Helicopter pilots dumped thousands of tons of sand,

boron and lead on the burning reactor. On the morning of Monday April 28, workers at a Swedish nuclear power plant 700 kilometers away detected radiation levels four times above normal. Meteorologists confirmed that the wind bearing the radioactive particles was blowing from the Soviet Union, yet the Swedish embassy in Moscow ran into a wall of denial. It was not until 9 pm on April 28 that a single-line statement referring to an accident at Chernobyl was read out during the main TV news from Moscow.

The human cost was thirty dead in the first few months; the cash cost of the rescue operation and clean-up has been put at more than $2 billion. The damage to Soviet pride was immense. The system had failed spectacularly at every level. A month before the incident, a Ukrainian newspaper had quoted experts

Workers at Chernobyl:
*they wait for buses (left)
to take them away from
the crippled reactor at the
nuclear power plant eight
days after it was wrecked
by an explosion in 1986.
Clean-up teams were sent
to Chernobyl without
training and with only
the flimsy face-masks
worn by this group for
protection. Radiation
levels were so high that
bus drivers refused to go
near the plant. The clean-
up teams had little idea
of the risks they were
running; when they
returned to their home
regions and fell ill,
communications were so
poor that local hospitals
did not realise that they
were dealing with
radiation sickness. An
inadequately-protected
clean-up worker (right)
at the disaster site. There
were several instances of
heroism by volunteers, but
the overall incompetence
was enough to damage
Gorbachev's reputation at
home where it mattered,
if not in a still adoring
outside world.*
[PHOTOS: I. GAVRILOV]

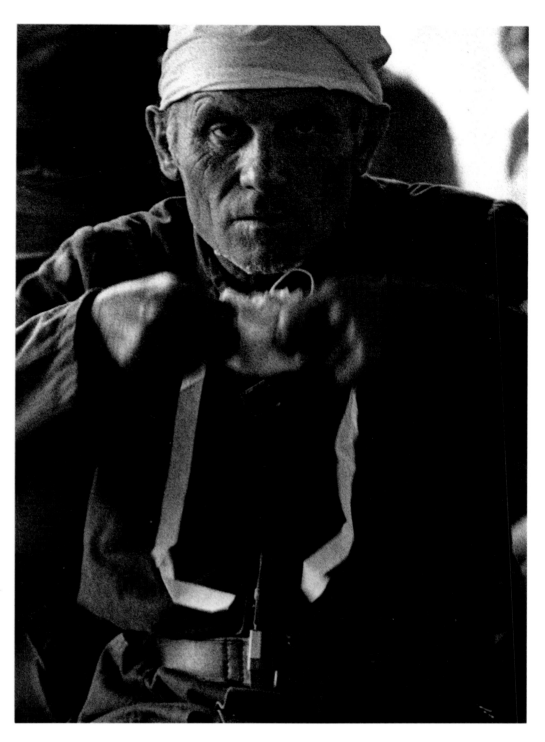

who said that the nuclear complex had been shoddily built of sub-standard materials. Nothing had been done. It was not until May 5 that pregnant women and children in the area were warned to stay indoors; the announcement induced a panic in which thousands of children were sent to Moscow by worried parents.

Steeped in idleness and comfortable corruption, the nation was indifferent to Gorbachev's attempts to reverse its drift. In Rostov-on-Don, local worthies showed their contempt for reform when they flocked to follow the coffin of an official who had died whilst serving a prison sentence for corruption, and extolled the departed hero with graveside eulogies. Gorbachev spoke angrily of a plant in Cherkassy where a manager tried to introduce new equipment and working methods. He was fired from the job; when he wrote to Moscow to complain, the letter was intercepted

at the Cherkassy post office. 'As far as talking is concerned, everything is fine,' Gorbachev complained. 'But there is no real change.' He tried to bypass the Party hierarchy by appealing direct to the rank and file through *glasnost*. The word means openness, transparency; its lack had been cited by dissidents like Solzhenitsyn as evidence of the sickness in Soviet society. It was a dangerous weapon. Senior officials and managers feared glasnost as the precursor of a purge aimed at the privileges, the special stores, the cronyism that made their lives comfortable; those beneath them dismissed it cynically as another empty slogan.

It was appreciated most in the arts and media. From the summer of 1986 on, a liberated and lively press reported on a flood of once-banned movies, novels, poems and essays. *Dr Zhivago* was at last published in Pasternak's birthplace; Vladimir

Nabokov's *The Defense,* first published in 1930, appeared. Anna Akhmatova's *Requiem* at last fulfilled the promise she had made to another mother waiting for news of her son in a Leningrad prison queue thirty years before: 'the truth will be told, and I shall tell it.' Selling out each new 100,000 printing, Anatoly Rybakov's *Children of the Arbat* became *the* book of the Eighties. It had been finished in 1967, but its pitiless exposure of Stalinism was too strong meat for those days. Its author, now in his mid-seventies, said that he wanted to live a few years more to be sure that the dictator was done for. 'I want to drive a stake through his heart so that he can never rise again,' he said. 'I want to help kill once and for all the system he created.' The system lingered – one human rights activist, Anatoly Marchenko, died on hunger strike in prison; another, Yuri Orlov, was stripped of his citizenship and dumped on a New York-bound jet; the sculptor Vadim Sidur, whose works included the haunting *Monument to Those who Died by Violence,* died himself with no public exhibition held in his lifetime.

But ghosts and non-persons from the Terror returned. Trotsky and Bukharin strolled the stage in Mikhail Shatrov's *Dictatorship of Conscience*; Stalin and Beria became the leads in a musical farce that drew on Stalinist melodies. The devil pair haunted *Repentance,* the hugely successful movie by their fellow-Georgian Tengiz Abuladze, into which was cut eerie footage from the Thirties. Marshal Zhukov's memoirs were published with the references to the Terror restored; Alexander Bek's long-banned novel *A New Appointment* was unfrozen; Vasili Belov's *The Last Day* dealt with the bestialities of collectivisation. An exhibition of paintings by Pyotr Belov served as a requiem for the graveless victims of the purge; in his painting *The Hourglass,* Stalin watched skulls mark the progress of time in place of sandgrains. The evils of the system were talked over in hundreds of new debating clubs, informal affairs where people met in city apartments simply to discuss; in the countryside, correspondence clubs started and lively debates were carried on by mail.

Party ultras did not take this lightly. The novelist Yuri Bondarev said that glasnost was creating 'civil war in Soviet literature'; it allowed 'liars' and 'civilised barbarians' to emerge from the shadows where they should be kept to threaten national pride and values. 'When all the nightingales are slain, an owl begins to sing,' he wrote. Not all the new associations were liberal; they included *Pamyat*, Memory, a throwback, anti-Semitic, anti-foreigner, anti-Gorbachev, a sort of Bolshevik Black Hundred whose members were skilled in the midnight telephone call, the thuggish demonstration outside the offices of glasnost symbols like Moscow News, the yell of 'Jew' and 'Freemason'. Neither did the KGB change its spots, waiting until Gorbachev was on a Black Sea vacation to arrest the US journalist Nicholas Daniloff and to do its bit to jeopardise the increasing rapprochement between Kremlin and White House. Gorbachev was not intimidated. In December 1986, he released the leading dissident Andrei Sakharov. A Nobel peace laureate, a nuclear physicist who was a father of the Soviet H-bomb, Sakharov had

Fishing boats *lie in sandy wastes thirty miles from the waters of the Aral Sea in one of the worst Soviet ecological disasters. The diversion of rivers to irrigate cotton projects, and the indiscriminate use of fertilisers, have shrunk the great inland sea and killed off its fish and wildlife. Winds whip the sand into dust clouds that poison fields hundreds of miles away.*
[PHOTO: V. SIOMIN]

been sent into internal exile under Brezhnev for criticising the invasion of Afghanistan in 1980. He was held with his wife Yelena Bonner in Gorky, where the KGB made his life miserable and force-fed him during his hunger strikes. Gorbachev telephoned him to ask him to return to Moscow; it was a remarkable personal act of atonement by the Soviet leader.

It was easier to release a dissident than to turn round the sagging economy. 'Perestroika is not proceeding easily,' Gorbachev admitted as another well-known dissident, Anatoly Shcharansky, was allowed to leave for Israel. 'The main obstacle is the mentality.' Glasnost and *perestroika*, the effort to reorganise industry, were double-edged weapons; for each could hurt the other. Under glasnost, newspapers were able to report the corruption and waste that riddled industry; this seemed to confirm that perestroika was not working. *Komsomolskaya Pravda* was able to remind its readers that Russia had ranked seventh in the world in per capita consumption in the last days of the Romanovs – and was now seventy-seventh. 'We have to admit,' it added, 'that from the viewpoint of civilised, developed society the overwhelming majority of the population of our country lives below the poverty line.' Other secrets, sensed but suppressed, came out: the existence of *bomzhi*, homeless vagrants; the drying up of the Aral Sea, its expanse now reduced by a third, its barren wastes producing poisonous dust storms 250 miles long and thirty wide; the flood level of theft – it was estimated that a third of motorists were driving on petrol stolen from the State.

Under Brezhnev, the country could forget its woes in a haze of cheap vodka. Now alcoholics were obliged to move on to shoe and metal polish, thinners and coolant. Eau de cologne became a favorite cocktail; the director of a perfume plant at Kuibyshev on the Volga complained that customers insisted on buying it by the boxload, whilst shops restricted sales to one or two bottles per customer. An army veteran lobbied for Red army heroes to be allocated a regular perfume ration. At Perm in the Urals, a shop

manager refused to accept glue deliveries because he was besieged by alcoholics who had turned to glue sniffing. In Belorussia, sales of window cleaning fluid doubled.

The Party was also recidivist. Gorbachev's anti-corruption drive gathered some sacrificial victims. General Yuri Churbanov, Brezhnev's son-in-law and a deputy chief of the Interior Ministry, was charged with accepting $1.1 million in bribes whilst in Uzbekistan. At the trial Churbanov admitted accepting a briefcase stuffed with $200,000. He was sentenced to twelve years in a camp near Nizhny Tagil. Brezhnev's secretary, Gennadi Brovin, also fell with a nine-year sentence for corruption. Gorbachev laid about senior Party figures who abused their office for personal gain, 'and some of whom become accomplices, if not organisers of criminal activities.' The most obvious mafiosi in the Politburo went; but Gorbachev could not reform the Party root and branch. The rot, and the resentment, went too deep. 'I wanted to return the money, but to whom?' Churbanov said of the suitcase. The remark had some ring of truth; bribes were paid to Party men for jobs, for Party positions ($150,000 to become a regional Party secretary in Central Asia, so the magazine *Smena* claimed), for the Order of Lenin ($165,000 to $750,000 according to the same source), for permission to open a restaurant, for a place in a cemetery. Where was an honest man to be found in the Party?

Sverdlovsk, the industrial city in the Urals where Gary Powers fell to earth, had produced such a person, perhaps. Boris Yeltsin was famous for rare energy and honesty whilst the Party boss of the city, until Gorbachev had brought him to Moscow at the end of 1985. Word of his sixteen-hour workday, his outspokenness and contempt for privilege made him popular in the capital; his attacks on perks and corruption turned this into adulation. He was the same age as Gorbachev, a big blond Siberian, energetic, open, who also liked a drink – 'Boris Yeltsin thinks America is a bar three thousand miles long' a journalist wrote of a trip to the US. He was a showman. With camera crews in tow, he visited Moscow's premier food store after he knew it had had a veal

delivery. Told that there was no veal, he called the police who discovered it selling in a private market at four times the official price. A newspaper ran an exposé of Moscow's 'special schools'; equipped with saunas, swimming pools, language laboratories and English-speaking staff, they were supposedly open to specially gifted children. The newspaper revealed that almost all the pupils were the pampered children of senior officials, who bartered American chewing gum for Western porn magazines in class breaks. A parent, the wife of a ranking bureaucrat, wrote a poison pen letter to the newspaper: 'we shall tear the puny sails of your perestroika to pieces'. Yeltsin insisted that the letter be published.

Muscovites loved it. They snapped up, too, his autobiographical sketch *Against the Grain*, which described his own house, a typical bigwig's spread with private movie theater, a 'kitchen large enough to feed an army', so many bathrooms that 'I lost count.' The politics of envy worked perfectly with an audience living without privacy in crowded rooms and shared kitchens and toilets. The big Siberian did not stop his populist

Returning from the wars: *Red army men carry the bodies of comrades fallen in Afghanistan. The failure of the Afghan invasion, and its transformation into a Soviet Vietnam, lowered morale. When Gorbachev ordered the troops out, it had an unraveling effect on the Russian position in eastern Europe – and in the Soviet republics.*
[PHOTO: M. ROGOZIN]

Cruise and Pershing missiles out of Europe. It was brilliant international public relations; Gore Vidal thought that Gorbachev's address was 'the most intelligent public speech ever heard'.

Hardliners had more to fear. Gorbachev had already called Afghanistan 'a bleeding wound'. When he visited Czechoslovakia later in 1987, his spokesman was asked what was the difference between his thinking and that of Alexander Dubcek, martyred architect of the Prague Spring in 1968. 'Nineteen years' came the answer, to the discomfort of the ultra Czech leader, Gustav Husak. Erich Honecker fretted in East Berlin; Nicolae Ceaucescu was publicly hostile in Rumania. In the satellites, only Poles and Hungarians approved of Gorbachev's New Thinking.

It was clear that the military brass was in for a tarnishing. Gorbachev had given the address at Chernenko's funeral without the traditional senior officer at his side. Admiral Sergei Gorshov, who had presided over the fabulously costly expansion of the Soviet navy for twenty-nine years, was let go with the briefest of paragraphs in the army newspaper *Red Star*. In May 1987, the teenage German Mathias Rust flew a $70,000 Cessna from Finland to a safe landing in Red Square, thus cocking a snook at several billion rubles' worth of radar systems, air-defense aircraft and surface-to-air missiles. Gorbachev took immediate advantage of Rust to sack the head of air defense and the defense minister, whose job went to an obscure general from the Far East, Dmitri Yazov. The military had more to suffer: in a unilateral Christmas gesture, Gorbachev announced a cut of half a million men and 10,000 tanks from his order of battle.

Since Stalin, the military had lived off the fat of a lean land. In the civilian economy, *Izvestiya* noted in 1987, 'by turns or in combinations towels, toothpaste, toilet paper, lotions, sugar and light bulbs have disappeared from the shelves. Now you cannot buy detergent and cheap soap.' The Russians had eight air defense interceptor types to the Americans' three; twelve SAM types to four; eight classes of attack submarine to one American. The surfeit of armor was such that the ratio of tanks to infantry was the highest ever recorded, in war or peace; four vast but ramshackle fleets had made a maritime power of a country with few maritime interests. The effort had distorted the economy; the military had the cream, of research, investment, facilities, labor; civilian industry got – and produced – junk.

'We are going into the unknown, and people are trying to stop us,' said Abel Aganbegyan, Gorbachev's chief economic advisor. 'It is as if life is forcing you to live in the water and you don't know how to swim.' Oil production was falling rapidly; so was the birth rate in the industrialised western part of the country. Measured by the health of its people, the Soviet Union had ceased to be a developed nation. It was on a par with Jamaica, Mexico and Costa Rica; life expectancy was six years lower and the infant mortality rate three times higher than in Western Europe. Russian women, the *babushkas*, outlived their men by an extraordinary average of eleven years. Nostalgia grew for the Brezhnev days. 'Life grew richer, spiritually and materially,' said

attacks at marble-lined Politburo houses with their fine crystal and porcelain and imported Swedish kitchens. He named names. 'Why has Gorbachev been unable to change this?' he said. 'I believe the fault lies in his basic cast of character. He likes to live well, in comfort and luxury. In this he is helped by his wife.' Raisa Gorbachev was another object of envy; for her good looks, her Western clothes, her shopping trips, her supposed vanity.

For the moment, Gorbachev could discipline Yeltsin. His own magic, if it no longer worked on Russians, still cast its spell on foreigners. Gorbachev gathered them from eighty countries early in 1987 to attend a three-day seminar, 'For a World without Nuclear Weapons, For Mankind's Survival'. It was held in the Grand Kremlin Palace and it attracted an extraordinary phalanx of celebrities: Gregory Peck, Yoko Ono, Graham Greene, Kris Kristofferson, Claudia Cardinale, J. K. Galbraith. Sakharov attended, fresh from his Gorky exile. Petra Kelly and Gert Bastian, the German Greens and nuclear campaigners, were there – Gorbachev made a special point of holding Bastian's hand, for the German ex-general was crucial to the Soviet desire to keep US

Women kneel *(above) in front of the famous Procession of the Cross from the Kursk monastery, renowned throughout Russia. Christianity revived strongly under Gorbachev's new tolerance.*
[PHOTO: V.SIOMIN]

Muslims pray *on Freedom Square in Groznyy (opposite) at the moment the self-declared Republic of Chechnyia broke from the Soviet Union in 1991. Many Chechen had been deported by Stalin to Kazakhstan; others were dominant in the gangs of the Soviet mafia.*
[PHOTO: V.SIOMIN]

Yegor Ligachev, a powerful conservative voice in the Politburo. 'If you ask me about those years, that was an unforgettable time, when we lived a genuinely full life.'

Glasnost helped old nationalism and ethnic hatreds to resurface. Latvians demonstrated for independence in Riga's central square. Tartars deported by Stalin for collaborating with the Germans marched in Red Square to demand to be returned to the Crimea. The Baltic tension spread to Lithuania and Estonia; in the Caucasus bloody fighting broke out between Christian Armenians and Moslem Azerbaijanis. The Fergana region of Uzbekistan exploded. The KGB chief, Viktor Chebrikov, was openly worried at the prospect of the country disintegrating. Party unity was fracturing; Boris Yeltsin denounced Ligachev in such violent terms that Gorbachev dismissed Yeltsin in late 1987. The conservative press attacked Yeltsin in traditional Stalinist manner; he was a political adventurer, a demagogue. The attacks helped confirm him as the people's hero. Censorship tightened; an *avant garde* sculpture exhibition was closed down, and *Pravda* muttered about the dangers of democracy leading to catastrophe.

Gorbachev was *Time*'s Man of the Year for 1987; 'Gorbymania' was well under way in the West. He announced that all Russian troops would be pulled out of Afghanistan by February 1989. The anti-corruption campaign continued; it was announced that 400,000 Party and government officials would lose the cherished perk of a black Volga sedan and chauffeur. The surplus cars were to be sold to the public or turned into taxis. In another dig at privilege, Soviet citizens with hard currency were no longer to be allowed to shop in the Beriozka stores for foreigners. Brezhnev's name disappeared from street signs and his statues vanished at night. Soviet TV usually reserved its most popular programs for Easter as a way of keeping people out of church. Now live coverage was allowed of the midnight Easter service at the Yelokhovsky Cathedral in Moscow; the mounted police who normally stopped crowds from reaching the Cathedral were withdrawn. The fourteenth-century monastery of Optina Pustyn was returned to the Church; since 1917 it had been used as a concentration camp, a prison, a barracks and a technical college.

The resurgence of religious feeling led to pogroms as well as joy. In Sumgait, a sweaty oil city on the Caspian, a wild crowd of Azerbaijanis was fed rumors of the murder of fellow Muslims by Christian Armenians. The mob set on Armenians, beating thirty to death. A mob also burst into Nagorno-Karabakh to loot and burn and prevent the Christian enclave from joining Armenia. Anti-Russian rioting broke out in Kazakhstan. Glasnost had its dangers; this was the message aimed at Gorbachev by an article in *Sovyetskaya Rossiya*. A 'letter' from 'a Leningrad university lecturer' took up a whole page to attack the thaw in censorship, permissiveness, rock and roll and drug culture, the denigration of Stalin. With Gorbachev abroad, Ligachev called a meeting of Soviet editors to discuss Party policy in his role as acting general secretary. He criticised glasnost and praised the article; the news agency Tass suggested that editors should run it. Forty-three did

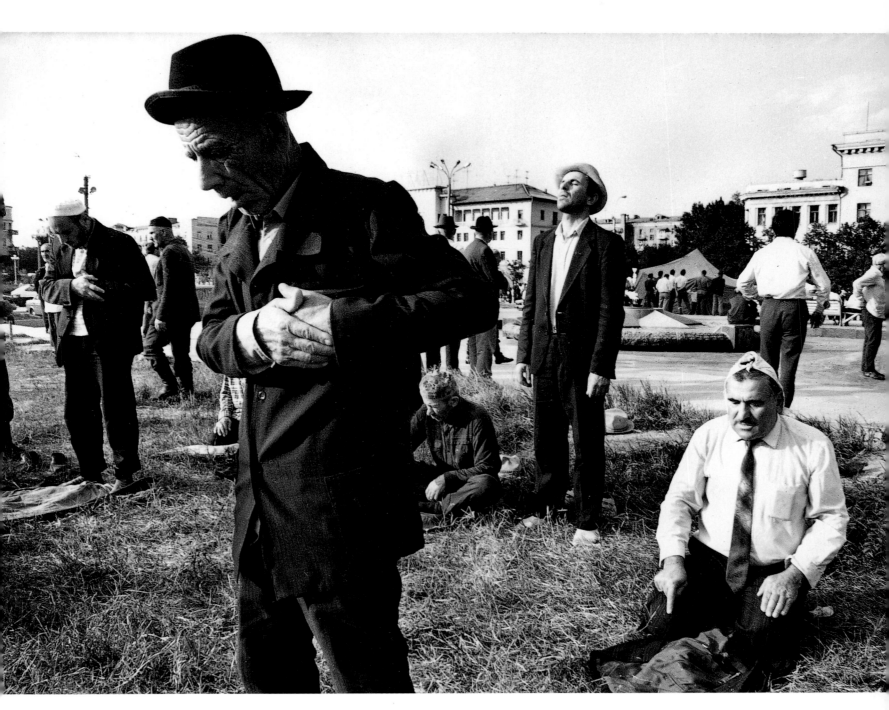

so; in East Berlin, heartened that the Russians were showing some Bolshevik backbone, the German Communists reprinted it in the Party sheet *Neues Deutschland*. In Moscow, *Pravda* supported Ligachev. The hardliners were confident that they had damaged Gorbachev. He had a reply to the *Pravda* article drafted by Alexander Yakovlev, his closest advisor and a former ambassador to Canada. *Pravda* refused to run it. Gorbachev gave the Politburo warning: follow him, or replace him. For the moment, the threat worked, as *Pravda* caved in and ran the Yakovlev riposte.

The tide of reform ran on. All conversation, all thoughts were possible; KGB plain clothesmen stood by as soapbox orators discussed the return of the Romanovs or the abolition of the Party. Maximum tax rates, fixed at 90 per cent to discourage entrepreneurs, were repealed as private restaurants and shops were opened. Masha Kalinina, a seventeen-year-old Muscovite,

became 'Miss Perestroika' in the country's first beauty contest; the actress Natalya Negoda posed as a *Playboy* cover girl. A Week of Conscience was held in Moscow to commemorate Stalin's victims; in the Kuropaty forests near Minsk, troops began to exhume thousands of bodies dumped there by Beria's killing squads. Sotheby's held Moscow's first post-revolution auction of fine art. Ronald Reagan, who had talked of the 'evil empire' five years before, made a dreamlike visit of friendship: 'there is no way I really can explain how I come to be here.' The crowds loved him, as they continued to love Yeltsin and his savaging of Ligachev and the conservatives. Gorbachev revealed plans for a 'fundamentally new State' headed by a new executive chairman or president, a role he clearly saw for himself.

Old demons could not be laid to rest by liberalism. Nationalists in Karelia and Moldavia now added to the mass movements in the Baltics and the Caucasus. Inflation was rolling;

A woman crosses herself *(left) in a re-opened church undergoing restoration near Moscow in 1991. Onion domes await completion behind her and (right) one is replaced on the roof of the same church. Christians were persecuted more at some times, such as the Thirties and under Khrushchev, than at others, but always suffered from the Bolshevik distaste for a rival creed. Churches had been grain stores, prisons and cinemas; hundreds were restored to their old uses under Gorbachev.* [PHOTOS: M. ROGOZIN]

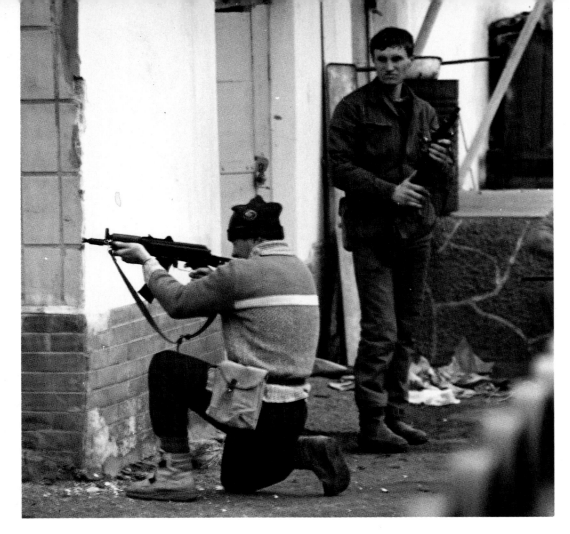

Fighting in Moldova, *as Moldavia renamed itself, adding to the nasty little wars in the Caucasus and Central Asia. The large Russian minority in the republic wanted to maintain contact with Moscow, whilst Moldavians wished to rejoin Rumania.*
[Photo: D. Borko]

Russian troops resting *during a lull in riots at Dushanbe, the capital of Tadzhikistan in Central Asia. They were trying to police the inter-communal violence there.*
[Photo: B. Bulgakov]

production fell with a wave of factory sit-ins. The 1988 harvest was a disaster. Hard currency earnings were squandered on grain imports, when 50 million tons of Soviet wheat rotted at railheads or fell through holes in trucks and freight cars. Half of the fruit and vegetables sent to Moscow rotted before it reached the shops; elsewhere, Gorbachev said, 40 per cent was wasted. But the private enterprise program was running headlong into public envy. Outside Moscow, a private pig farm was torched by neighbors jealous of its success. In the cities, the high salaries paid to workers in cooperative restaurants and markets heightened resentments. The manager of the first cooperative restaurant in Moscow, on Kropotkinskaya Street, was regularly denounced to the police for profiteering. Jewelry and alcohol sales, and videos and publishing, were put off-limits to entrepreneurs. On a tour of Siberia, Gorbachev was shocked by the deep anger over food shortages, shoddy public transport and housing, pollution, disintegrating medical care. He felt threatened enough to relax the restrictions on alcohol sales.

An earthquake in Armenia killed 25,000. The tremors were of medium strength, only 6.9 on the Richter scale, but tatty modern buildings collapsed and aid and medical efforts were slow and slovenly. The clear-up cost was greater than Chernobyl, while the fall in the world price of oil and gold savaged hard currency earnings. Glasnost in the press was revealing genetic deformities in Kazakhstan caused by nuclear testing, and a huge infant mortality rate in Uzbekistan resulting from defoliants used on the cotton crop. Russians accounted for less than half the Soviet population for the first time; Russian minorities in the Caucasus

and Central Asia were nervous. Gorbachev had become president and executive head of state and he had shifted Ligachev and Chebrikov sideways, but his personal position was deteriorating quickly. Inflation and nationalism were on the up; production continued to fall. A bitter little ditty showed that the public realised the consequences of his arms concessions to the West:

There is no meat
There is no sausage
There is no vodka
Perhaps soon there will be no rockets either.

Instead of being 'Upper Volta with rockets', the country was becoming simply Upper Volta.

The last Russian to die in Afghanistan was an NCO called Igor Lyakhovich. He was killed on February 7, 1989; his comrades put his body on the deck of an armored fighting vehicle, covered it with a tarpaulin and drove it back to Russia as the final troops withdrew.

The satellites spun out of orbit and the Kremlin spokesman Gennady Gerasimov referred to the 'Sinatra doctrine' for eastern Europe; the countries were free to go 'My Way'. The system unraveled in six months. Poland and Hungary threw out the Party first. In September 1989, Gorbachev warned Erich Honecker in East Berlin that those who failed to change with the times would be punished by them. Honecker was thrown from power in mid-October. Bulgaria's Todor Zhivkov and Gustav Husak in Czechoslovakia also went peacefully; the dissident playwright Vaclav Havel, who had spent five years in Communist jails, became president of Czechoslovakia. Killing was necessary to get

A demonstrator faces troops *in Yerevan at the start of the Armenian campaign for independence from the Soviet Union, as the fault lines that riddled the huge country became evident once more.*
[PHOTO: I.GAVRILOV]

Specially trained KGB troops *of the Dzerzhinsky division stand by at a demonstration in support of democracy in 1990. The new freedom brought rioting and sporadic repression in its wake as ethnic and political passions, frozen for three-quarters of a century, burst out again.*

[PHOTO: T.SHAKHVERDIEV]

Old hatreds. *As the veil of Soviet brotherhood was ripped away, religious and racial enmities swiftly re-established themselves. (Above) An old man is helped by a soldier to escape communal rioting in Tadzhikistan in 1989. Lenin, on his plinth in the background, had preached a different hatred, based on class. (Left) Tent City in Red Square in Moscow. Mostly fleeing ethnic violence in the Caucasus, its refugees also included Russian families who had been victimised in Central Asia. (Opposite) A man bandaged after ethnic clashes in Baku in 1990.*
[Photo, top: A. Lomakin]
[Photo, left: S. Podgorkov]
[Photo, opposite: F. Titov]

A Georgian saint? *This sixteen-year-old girl (left) was the youngest victim of a massacre during the fighting in Georgia. Lying almost in state in the intensely Christian country, she was declared a candidate for canonisation after her funeral.*
[PHOTO: V. IVLEVA]

Andrei Sakharov *(right) lies on his bier whilst his wife Yelena Bonner looks on after his death in 1989. Sakharov was the youngest-ever member of the Soviet Academy of Sciences in 1953. Disenchanted with the regime, he began a vigorous campaign for peaceful co-existence and civil rights, and was awarded the Nobel peace prize in 1975. None of this endeared him to the Kremlin. He was sent into internal exile in the closed city of Gorky from 1980 to December 1986. He continued to fight for civil rights and was elected a People's Deputy shortly before his death.*

rid of Rumania's Stalinist dictator; by Christmas 1989, Nicolae Ceaucescu and his wife had been executed and replaced by Ion Iliescu, once a Moscow university student with Gorbachev. The Cold War was over. The *Time* editorial for the 1990 New Year described Gorbachev as 'the Copernicus, Darwin and Freud of Communism all wrapped in one'. It made him the Man of the Decade. In his own country, the bestselling weekly *Argumenti i Fakti* said that he did not reach the Soviet top ten in popularity.

Boris Yeltsin said that those who remained Communists were fantasists, and that he regarded himself as 'a social democrat'. 'I

am a Communist, a convinced Communist,' Gorbachev retorted. 'For some that may be a fantasy. But for me it is my own goal.' It was a fateful remark. Soviet Communism did not allow of half measures; compromise had no part in its character, it had no human face. Gorbachev fell prey to a sapping ambivalence. He welcomed the new freedoms in the satellites, but not in the Baltics. 'To exercise self-determination through secession is to blow apart the Soviet Union,' he warned, 'to pit people against each other and to sow discord, bloodshed and death.' The Soviet State from its earliest time had been glued together by violence

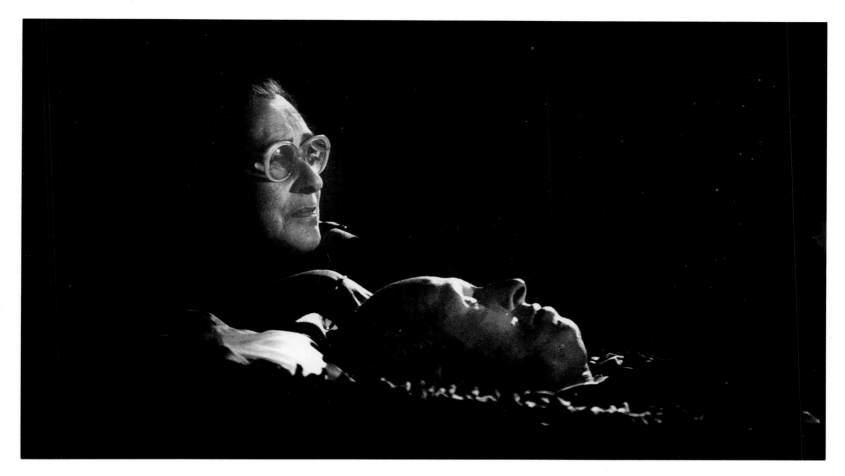

and centralism; remove them, and many thought it must fall prey to its immense centrifugal forces. It was the same with Gorbachev's desire to preserve some of 'the culture of Marx and Lenin', to keep entrepreneurs and wild capitalism in check; to restrain the new whilst vigorously shaking the old. His ceaseless tampering with the system irritated all interests at all levels.

Whilst Gorbachev visited Lithuania – whose nationalist leaders continued to insist that the Russians 'give back what was stolen', their independence – an Azeri mob in Baku slaughtered Christians. The Armenians responded by killing Moslems. Azeris carrying pictures of Ayatollah Khomeini rioted and attacked Soviet troops. Seventeen thousand reinforcements were sent in and 200 died in street fighting before the military reimposed control. Protesters demonstrated with banners reading 'Gorbachev The Butcher of Azerbaijan'. Rumors that Gorbachev would quit sent world stock markets reeling. Russians fleeing from Moslem Tadzhikistan after ethnic riots were joined by others caught in anti-Russian pogroms in Tuvinska on the Mongolian border. The satellites had gone; the Soviet Republics were following as nationalism surged in the Ukraine and in the Russian Republic itself.

Right and left, ultra and liberal polarised. Gorbachev, vulnerable, had a foot in both camps. Hardliners were infuriated when the Party's formal monopoly of power was deleted from the constitution. Liberals mistrusted his continuing links with the conservatives. 'Mikhail Sergeyevich, which side are you on?' ran the banners of Yeltsin supporters demonstrating against Ligachev outside the Kremlin wall. Gold and diamonds were dumped on declining world markets to buy food as rumors of impending starvation multiplied. Television showed ethnic bloodshed, rail and mining strikes, queues, army trucks sent to try to rescue another poor harvest. Prices increased, supplies dwindled; collapse could be felt in the pinch-faced queues where bitter citizens traded rumors of Raisa Gorbachev's luxury lifestyle. Things looked fine viewed from the West. Gorbachev had slain the Communist dragon. But in doing so, said Alexander Bukhanov, influential and unhappy editor of *Sovyetskaya Literatura*, he had 'destroyed everything we believed in, everything that kept us together. Gorbachev hasn't built anything new, he hasn't thrown us a lifebelt! Everyone, me included, is on a sinking ship, on a plane that is crashing, and that's what terrifies us.'

A street joke had a chicken farmer going to Gorbachev for advice when ten of his chickens died. 'Give them aspirin' came the reply. More died. 'Give them castor oil.' Further deaths. 'Give them penicillin.' All were now dead. 'How sad,' said Gorbachev. 'I had so many more remedies to try.' It raised a laugh from both left and right; Gorbachev was friendless in the decaying center. At the May Day rally in Red Square, protesters shouted 'Resign' and 'Shame' as he stood unnerved above Lenin's mausoleum. He seemed blurred, indecisive, telling Margaret Thatcher that he could not sleep at night; 'I would like to sleep in the afternoon.' Boris Yeltsin was elected President of the Russian Republic; the *lèse majesté* left Gorbachev visibly shaken. 'Our ship has lost its anchor,' he told visiting US Congressional leaders. 'So we are all feeling a little sick.' Rivals were circling, Yeltsin, Ligachev; the center could not hold. A coup was close.

13
RU$$IA

As statues of Lenin were melted for scrap in Georgia, the Ukraine and the Baltics, article six of the constitution, which confirmed the Party's 'leading role', was dropped. 'Hands off Lenin!' read banners at a rally in Gorky Park, and Gorbachev issued a decree against monument desecration, but no notice was taken. One in five of youngsters called up for military service failed to report at induction centers. Troops were pulling out of Czechoslovakia and Hungary, 125,000 of them: too many to house, so they were put in tents when they arrived. Rockets were dismantled, and thousands of tanks melted down in Karaganda, to honor Gorbachev's arms cuts.

Citizenship was restored to the chess grandmaster Victor Korchnoi and to Mstislav Rostropovich, who played concerts in Moscow. Alexander Dubcek made his first visit to Moscow since his drugged humiliation in 1968, and Gorbachev welcomed him personally. Older specters came back to haunt Party loyalists. Guilt for the massacre of 15,000 Polish officers in the forests of Katyn was admitted for the first time; details emerged of how KGB executioners, uniformed in brown leather hats and aprons and elbow-length gloves, had killed them at a steady 250 a night. A pro-Romanov movie was made; the basement massacre of 1918 was discussed in liberal newspapers, and called a crime. In rallies across the Ukraine, portraits were displayed of the anti-Soviet guerrilla leader Stephen Bandera; he had been a non-person for decades, murdered in exile in Munich by a KGB agent. Andrei Golitsyn, artist progeny of the famous princely family, formed the Union of the Descendants of the Russian Nobility. He intended to reconstruct the Russian nobility, no less. As to Party ghosts, a waxworks opened in Moscow where Lavrenty Beria was modeled playing chess with his fellow torturer Malyuta Skuratov, 16th-century henchman of Ivan the Terrible. Old ethnic hatreds were warmed back to life in the liberal thaw, especially in Asia and round the Black Sea. The Baltic States were claiming independence and their Communists pulled out of the Soviet Party.

Immorality, so hardliners had it, was swamping the country. A show of erotic art was held in a Moscow theater. The centerpiece was a 'Cake Girl', a model smeared with confectionery for the audience to lick. Gorbachev signed a decree at the end of 1990 against 'pornographic and pseudo-medical publications and erotic videos.' *Playboy* imports flourished. McDonald's opened a branch in Moscow; the queue beneath the Golden Arches stretched for four blocks as up to 50,000 Russians a day were introduced to hamburgers and apple pie. Rock culture swept the young; Victor Tsoy, lead singer with Kino, dead in a car crash, became a Soviet James Dean. The first service since 1917 was held at the Cathedral of the Dormition in the Moscow Kremlin

A Lenin lookalike *in a Moscow strip club in 1993. He makes a good living from advertising campaigns. The scene is enough to have set the great Bolshevik's mummified remains spinning in the mausoleum on Red Square. The girls in the club trained at Russia's first school of striptease. In an atmosphere reminiscent of the political cabarets of pre-Nazi Berlin, other lookalikes drinking casually in the club included Stalin and Adolf Hitler.*
[Photo: F. Gubayev]

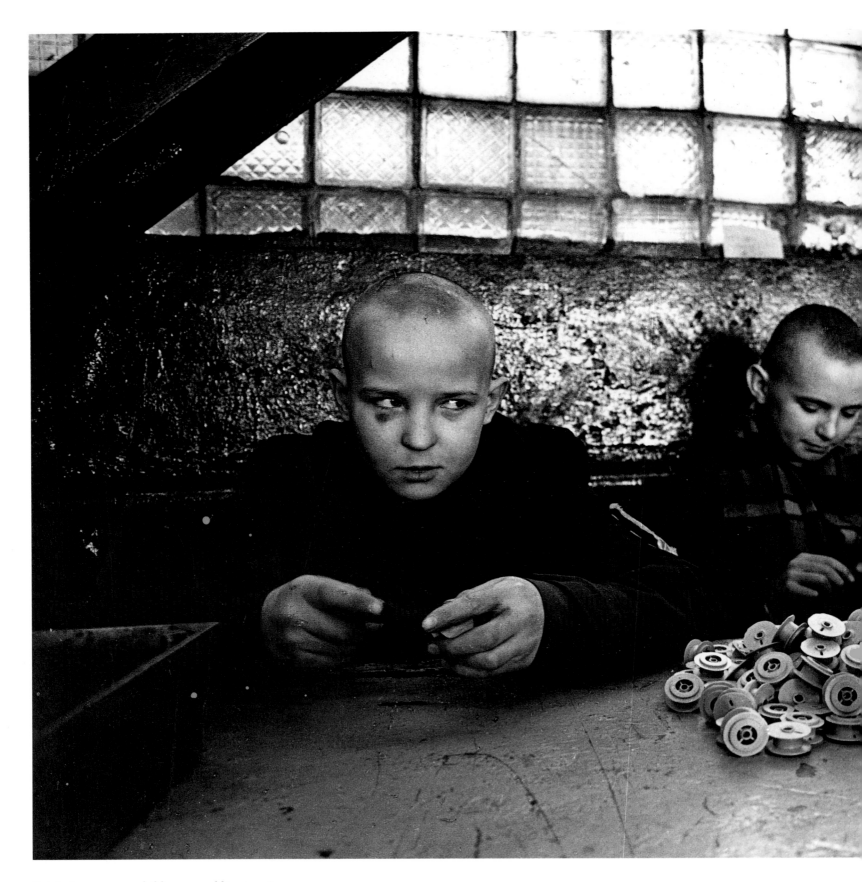

Catch them young: *children assembling toys in a juvenile detention center in Kazan for boys under seventeen. Punishment is severe, a regime of labor and study. The 12-year-old at left is serving a two-year sentence for stealing a car radio. The old Soviet Union was corrupt in its upper reaches, but the pervasive system of police and informers kept street crime low. High-level corruption remains, and petty crime, thefts and assaults, have exploded.* [PHOTO: F. GUBAYEV]

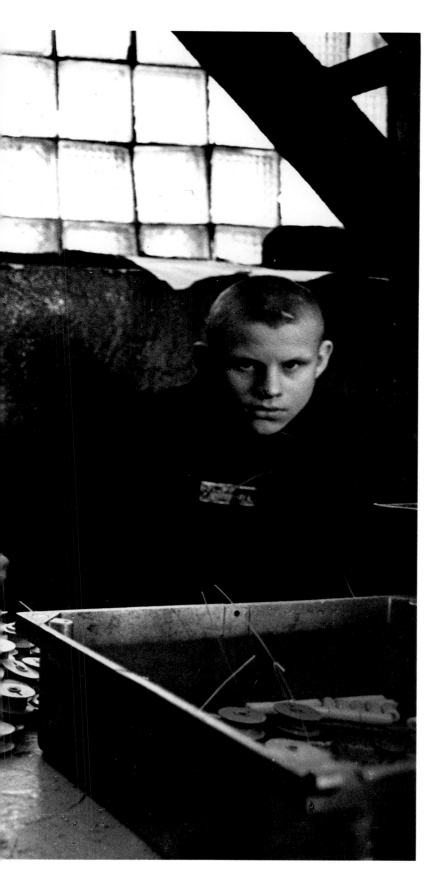

itself, while the Great Ascension Church was restored after years as a high-voltage laboratory.

Statistics, published for the first time, made unhappy reading. Road deaths were running at 58,000 a year; an American level of slaughter achieved with less than a tenth the number of vehicles. Health was deteriorating with the Soviet Union coming 58th in the world in post-natal survival. Ninety-five million tons of pollutants were being released into the atmosphere and 300 million cubic meters of untreated waste were pumped into the Volga each year. The number of registered alcoholics reached 4.5 million.

The new openness in the press showed that the penal system was in crisis; four major prison riots were reported, including one in Dnepropetrovsk where it took riot squads six days to restore order in a smoldering complex wrecked by 2000 prisoners. Serious crimes increased by 42 per cent in 1990 and the rise in street crime was 65 per cent. The arrest of traffickers was reported as the size of the drug problem became clear. Details of mass murders were once repressed, but now papers splashed the pretty face of Tamara Ivanyutina on the front pages. She was a school dishwasher who poisoned eighteen children and teachers when she was stopped from taking leftover food home to feed her piglets.

Most worrying for Gorbachev was a figure produced by the All-Union public opinion center in January 1991. In response to the question 'What does the Soviet Union give its people?', 68 per cent said: 'Shortages, queues and poverty.' He was in trouble. By mid-1991, Yeltsin, his rival and tormentor, had become Russia's first elected president. Yeltsin could be careless and destructive; as an eleven-year-old, he had experimented by hitting a hand grenade with a hammer, losing his thumb and forefinger to gangrene when, to his surprise, it exploded and wounded him. He attacked Gorbachev and the hardliners with equal venom; not through policy, but because he was like that, a renegade. He drew radicals and the young away from Gorbachev whose style was professional, bureaucratic. Yeltsin was all heart and mouth, the construction worker's beefy son. To Gorbachev's right his own appointees had started to conspire against him. Ministers, generals, his own chief of staff, Valery Boldin, with him since 1978, were meeting in KGB safe houses to plan his overthrow. There were warning signs. When Gorbachev went to Oslo to receive the Nobel peace prize, troops in Lithuania set up provocative roadblocks against his instructions. This led to his being embarrassed by hostile questioning at his Oslo press conference. Hardline newspapers declared the Motherland to be 'dying, falling apart and plunging into darkness and nothingness.' The plotters had special phone lines installed in their apartments and dachas.

The Americans were warning Gorbachev of an impending putsch by late June 1991. He disregarded them and left Moscow by air for a Crimean vacation at the beginning of August. The conspirators, meeting for a final briefing over whisky and vodka at a KGB sanatorium outside Moscow on August 17, were all

Old Faithful: *hardline Communists (above) demonstrate against Boris Yeltsin behind the hammer and sickle in Moscow in 1992. Although many former Party bosses have nominally changed allegiance, the rank and file has no hesitation in declaring its undying belief in Communism. Food shortages and inflation have kindled nostalgia for the Brezhnev days. Rising crime has bred an older yearning, for the 'disciplined' days of Stalin.*
[PHOTO: P. GORSHKOV]

The young claimant to the Russian throne, *Prince George Hohenzollern (left), is greeted with incense by Orthodox priests in St Petersburg in 1992 after the death of his grandfather, Prince Vladimir Kirilovich Romanov. Prince George's mother, Princess Maria of Russia, stands behind the boy. Prince Vladimir, who used the title of Grand Duke, claimed his grandson to be Tsarevich and heir to the throne. Other Romanovs contest the claim. For three centuries, loyalty was owed to God, Romanov and Russia. All were subsumed in 1917 into the Godless and republican Soviet Union. God and Russia have been restored. Those who wish to restore the Romanovs are regarded as a lunatic fringe; but so, the monarchists point out, were the Bolsheviks in 1917.* [PHOTO: V. SIOMIN]

The power of the Cross. *An Orthodox priest (above) blesses the crowd in Kursk in 1992, during an annual procession with an ikon. The scene is part of the vivid resurgence of Russia's oldest faith. The Church reached its lowest point with the mass purges of priests in the Thirties. It was attacked again under Khrushchev, who closed more than ten thousand churches.* [PHOTO: G. BODROV]

Gorbachev's appointments; some he had handplucked from obscurity to great office. They ordered handcuffs from a factory in Pskov, a quarter of a million pairs. As well as radicals, the putsch would round up the new class of *spekulanty* and *biznesmeny*. Kryuchkov, head of the KGB, prepared a secret underground room in the Lubyanka for use as a headquarters in case of resistance. He doubled KGB pay and ordered its officers back from vacation. Gorbachev relaxed in ignorance at his compound in the resort town of Foros which had cost $20 million to build. The main house ran to marble; the guest house accommodated thirty and an escalator ran all the way down to the beach.

It was the telephones at Foros that gave the first intimation of trouble; they all stopped working at 4.50 pm on August 18. At the same time, servants announced an unexpected visit by a

delegation including Boldin and the general commanding ground forces. Raisa Gorbachev thought of the Romanov murders long ago. Boldin told Gorbachev that an emergency committee was to rule the country; it would be announced that he had resigned 'for reasons of health'.

The conspirators started drinking on the plane back to Moscow. Vice-president Gennady Yanayev was drunk by the time he signed the State of Emergency elevating himself to acting president in the early hours of August 19; he sat up drinking with prime minister Pavlov. Marshal Yazov sent off a coded telegram ordering all units to be on alert and for troops to return from leave. TV and radio announced that Gorbachev was ill and that a State Committee for the State of Emergency had taken over; the announcers were nervous and uncertain. A Kremlin doctor was summoned to Pavlov's dacha at 7 am. 'Pavlov was drunk,' he later

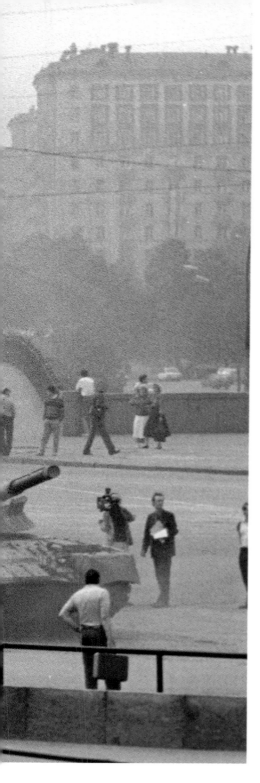

Bolshevik blunderers: *tanks roll through Moscow at the start of the attempted coup in August 1991. Lenin and his colleagues had bungled one coup attempt in July 1917; much of Red October had been a shambles. The Party hardliners who aped them in 1991 did no better. They gagged Mikhail Gorbachev, but failed to arrest Boris Yeltsin or storm the White House, the Parliament building on the Moscow River that became the focal point of resistance.*
[Photo: S. Anipchenko]

testified. 'But this was no ordinary, simple intoxication. He was at the point of hysteria.'

Yeltsin was told of the coup whilst breakfasting in his country dacha. He donned a bulletproof vest and set off for the 'White House', the high-rise block on the Moscow River that housed the new Russian parliament. Tanks and armored cars rumbled into the city and took up positions outside the city hall, TV stations and newspaper offices and the White House. Yeltsin drafted an appeal denouncing the coup with Ruslan Khasbulatov, chairman of the parliament. Alexander Rutskoi, hero of the Afghan war and Yeltsin's vice-president, broadcast from a make-do studio in the White House. Just after noon, Yeltsin climbed atop a T-72 tank of the Taman Guards division outside the White House and spoke in a gruff bellow: 'Citizens of Russia … The legally elected president of the country has been removed from power … We are dealing with a right-wing, reactionary, anti-constitutional coup d'état …' The tank crews spun their gun barrels away from the White House; they now provided it with defense, not threat. 'You can build a throne of bayonets,' Yeltsin taunted the plotters, 'but you cannot sit on it for long.'

The coup degenerated into shambles. The plotters failed to make arrests; Gorbachev was their only prize. Radio stations opposing them continued to broadcast; CNN and the BBC provided continuous coverage and, after fisticuffs in the print room, *Izvestiya* appeared carrying Yeltsin's appeal to resist the coup. The military in Leningrad refused to move their men into the country's second city. Moscow seemed normal, apart from the crowds and barricades outside the White House. Yeltsin's office was guarded by Mstislav Rostropovich, the cellist, clutching an AK-47 rifle. He had no need of it; an assault would have been a bloody business and the conspirators had no stomach for it. An air force commander warned them that if they sent in the KGB's elite Alpha group, he would bomb the Kremlin. Yanayev was too

Boris Yeltsin roars defiance *at the coupmakers from outside the White House in Moscow on August 19, 1991 while a bodyguard holds up a piece of armorplating in a briefcase to protect him from snipers. His courage was a decisive factor in crushing the plot, and in endearing the bulky Siberian to rank-and-file Russians. His scorn for the plotters rapidly communicated itself to the tank crews surrounding the parliament building.*
[Photo: S. Anipchenko]

The line outside Lenin's mausoleum in 1970. *Once, people came from all over the vast land and from abroad to pay their respects to the mummified body in Red Square. They would then move on to the nearby Lenin Museum. It was a Socialist pilgrimage, a ritual at a time when the faith was still kept.* [PHOTO: V.SOBOLYEV]

drunk to recognise voices over the telephone. Casualties were limited to three Yeltsin supporters killed in a clash with a tank on the Garden Ring Road. In Foros, Gorbachev listened to the coup unraveling on his Sony transistor. By 1 pm on August 21 it was over; long convoys of tanks were pulling out of the city in wild scenes of joy.

Gorbachev returned to Moscow, not in the Soviet presidential Ilyushin 62, but in a smaller Tupolev of Boris Yeltsin's Russian Republic. He still spoke of the Soviet Union and of a 'renewal' of the Party, but in reality both were doomed. At a triumphalist session of the Russian parliament on August 23, Yeltsin obliged Gorbachev to read out a transcript of the meeting of the Council of Ministers five days before. Gorbachev's residual authority evaporated as he read how all but two had betrayed him. 'On a lighter note', said Yeltsin in high good humor, 'shall we now sign a decree suspending the Russian Communist Party?' Gorbachev, humiliated, could only mutter: 'What are you doing? ...' Outside

the Lubyanka, a crane toppled the statue of Felix Dzerzhinsky. The Lenin Museum closed for 'reconstruction'. The gardens of the Tretyakov art gallery filled with other toppled statues. The plotters bungled even their suicides; Marshal Sergei Akhromeyev, Gorbachev's putschist personal military adviser, needed two attempts to hang himself; interior minister Pugo finished himself off, but left his wife badly wounded. On August 24, Gorbachev quit as Party general secretary and dissolved the central committee. Then the Party was banned, and its property seized. The Baltic states, together with Moldova and Georgia on the Black Sea, became independent; the leaders of the ten other Soviet republics agreed to create a decentralised confederation. Gorbachev wished to direct a common defense and foreign policy, but Yeltsin would have none of it. The presidency would be strictly ceremonial; 'something like the Queen of England'. Gorbachev's nameplate was removed from his Kremlin office on Boxing Day.

By 1991, only a solitary babushka *kept vigil, her sparse posy of flowers behind her. Her banner reads: 'We are with you.' Events would later prove that many agreed with her, but now they were keeping a low profile.*
[Photo: V. Siomin]

The Russian flag flew once more in a city named St Petersburg; in Moscow, the Lenin Hills reverted to Sparrow Hills. In the flea market traders sold off heads of Lenin cut from velvet banners, military watches with portraits of Gagarin on the strap, sniper sights, field glasses, army greatcoats and ties gaudily lettered 'KGB Agent' and 'I love Boris'. Gorbachev remained a superstar abroad; at home, he was ridiculed. Yeltsin played with him, taking away his perks – his limousine, the grand building on Leningrad Prospekt he used as offices – at whim.

Yeltsin's brave new Russia inherited the old problems. All-Union government had collapsed but the center retained an immense payroll – millions of servicemen, bureaucrats, workers in arms plants. Its ability to raise money was circumscribed so it resorted to printing money on a massive scale. Inflation rocketed out of control. The dollar bought 32 rubles the month after the attempted coup; by the start of 1992 it had reached 90 and it hit 1000 in mid-1993. Two societies were spawned. Ruble Russia

squatted in the ruins of the Soviet Union, immense, impoverished and angry. Above it was another world, Ru$$ia, small and sleek, peopled by those with access to dollars – tarts, touts, taxi-drivers, traders. Security guards kept the two sides apart. Bulky young men in tight-fitting uniforms defended the Ru$$ian settlements: $350 a night hotels, casinos, nightclubs with $150 Scotch, Mercedes concessionaires, stores packed with perfumes, cashmeres, video cameras. The guard and the single word 'Currency' on the door served to keep out dollarless Russians; in old Shanghai, signs reading 'No dogs or Chinamen' served the same purpose.

Social imbalance became grotesque. It was not only the old and the poor who were beggared and driven into the queues. In Western-owned hotels aerospace engineers became barmen and pediatricians bellhops for the hard currency tips. Alexei Abrikosov, a theoretical physicist and Academician, earned 1000 rubles a month. That was good money for ruble Russia yet he

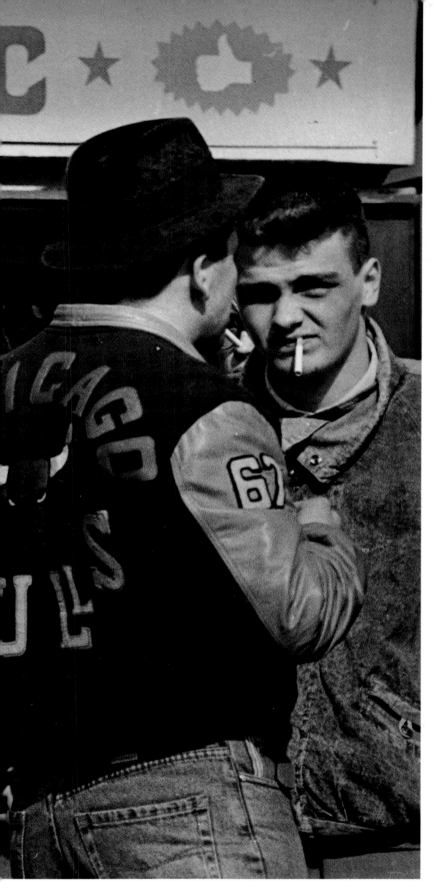

emigrated to Chicago. 'If you spend all day trying to find food,' he said, 'it doesn't stimulate theoretical research.' A *valutnaya*, a currency girl, on $200 a trick could earn four years' average earnings in an hour; a $20 cab ride from the airport to downtown Moscow translated into four months' wages in ruble Russia. Speculators bought seats on new commodity exchanges across the country; the Rolls Royces and high-number Mercedes weaving their dark-windowed way through the tinny, smoke-belching traffic hinted at the killings to be made in oil and strategic metals. The old Central Post Office in Moscow became the Russian Commodities and Raw Materials Exchange; a forgotten bust of Lenin surveyed the trading floor from a lofty plinth. Seats cost 60,000 rubles when it was set up in October 1990; a year later they were changing hands for 4.4 million. The auctioneer called his audience *gospoda*, gentlemen, an expression not used since 1917; they bid hectically for steel reinforcing rods, oil, cottons, trousers, trucks, anxiously asking foreigners : 'Is this like it is in Chicago?'

An old breed, the mafia, multiplied and acquired a new uniform; cropped hair, trainers and shell suits whose pockets harbored wads of green money and, increasingly, as *biznesmeny* and *konsultanty* were murdered, guns. Mafia groups separated on ethnic lines: Russian, Georgian, Chechen, Armenian. Some were old Party men; at 1.30 am as damp snow settled on Leninsky Prospekt, a black Zil, an old-regime car, drew up outside a ruble casino. 'They've come for the charity money,' said the owner as he handed over a thick wad of rubles wrapped in a napkin to the steel-toothed driver. They creamed off 20 to 60 per cent of turnover from restaurants and discos. They ran in cars and computers stolen by Poles and Volga Germans in western Europe.

The Russian birth rate fell 30 per cent on its 1989 level. Suicide and drug addiction multiplied. So did vegetarianism, Buddhism, faith healing. The televised 'healing' sessions of the 'psychotherapist' Anatoly Kashpirovsky attracted huge audiences; a million people wrote in to Yuri Tarasov, 'the Russian wizard', who claimed to heal diabetes, skin complaints and nervous disorders with a laying on of hands. Pirate TV stations aired Russian rappers, and a transsexual Marilyn Monroe

Toughing it out: *street scene (above) shows the old Russian hardness in the faces mixed with the new American image in the baseball jacket and 'Serve Yourself' shop sign. Streets now are filled with intimidating men, with crew-cuts and a swagger that shows their willingness to use their fists or a weapon.* [Photo: D. Borko]

Poverty and inflation *stalk the new freedoms. This woman (right), who has saved her girlhood hair, sells it in a special shop in St Petersburg. It will be exported for use in Western hairpieces and wigs. Her hair is worth slightly more than the $16 to which inflation has reduced her monthly pension.* [Photo: S. Demianchuk]

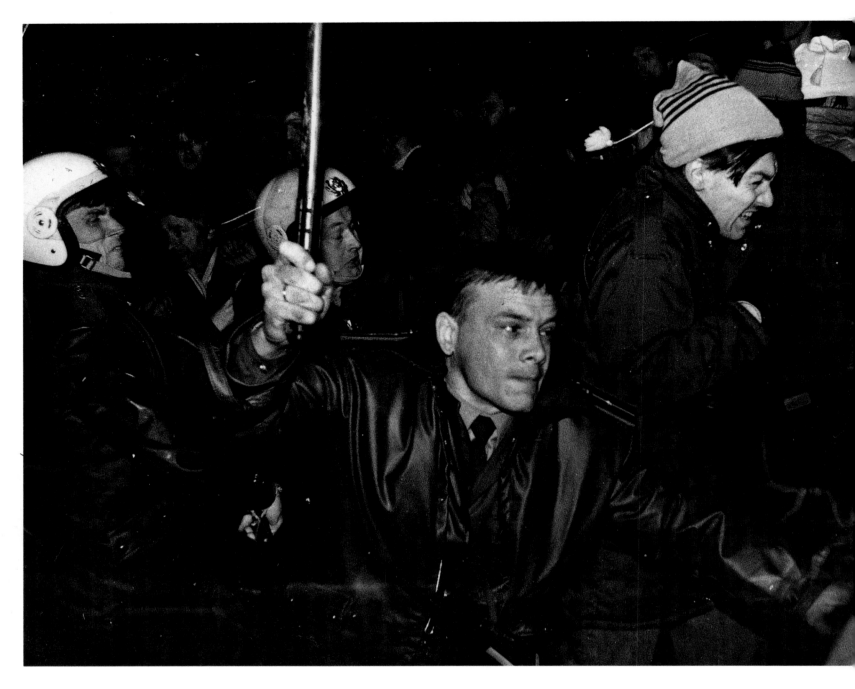

impersonator. Lookalike Lenins were hired for evenings of mockery.

Wars continued in the Caucasus. Armenia was bloodied and bankrupt; Eduard Shevardnadze, who had basked in reflected glory in the West as Gorbachev's foreign minister, fled from victorious Abkhazians in his native Georgia. In Estonia, the sizeable Russian minority complained of discrimination and ill-treatment; the Estonians angrily denied it, but the Russians dragged their heels over troop removals. Russian troops remained in eastern Germany; there were no barracks to rehouse them at home. Russian officers, from regiments that had stormed the Reichstag forty-odd years before, were seen returning supermarket trolleys for the one deutschmark it earned them. Russia and the Ukraine haggled over who owned missiles and the Black Sea fleet; nuclear stockpiles were deteriorating dangerously from Belorussia (Belarus) to Kazakhstan. 'Yugoslavia with nukes,' shuddered James Baker, the American Secretary of State.

Only a quarter of the deputies in parliament reliably supported Yeltsin. A 'red-brown' group of hardline Communists and extreme nationalists coalesced into the National Salvation Front to oppose him and frustrate reform, as relations deteriorated with his fellow heroes from the putsch, Alexander Rutskoi and Ruslan Khasbulatov. Economic policy – shock therapy, slashed subsidies and market prices – ran into the sands. The military-industrial bosses refused to turn their weapons into plowshares; with memorable contempt, a shipyard director said he would not switch from 'beautiful' naval vessels to tankers because the latter were 'sea-going biscuit tins'. Meat rotted at packing plants that ran out of tin for cans; machines rusted on the farms for lack of spares, and milk was fed to pigs because poor roads and a truck shortage prevented its distribution to humans. Gorbachev, bitter, preening, called the Yeltsin government 'an insane asylum', but there were real lunatics on the loose. Vladimir Zhirinovsky had won six million votes as an

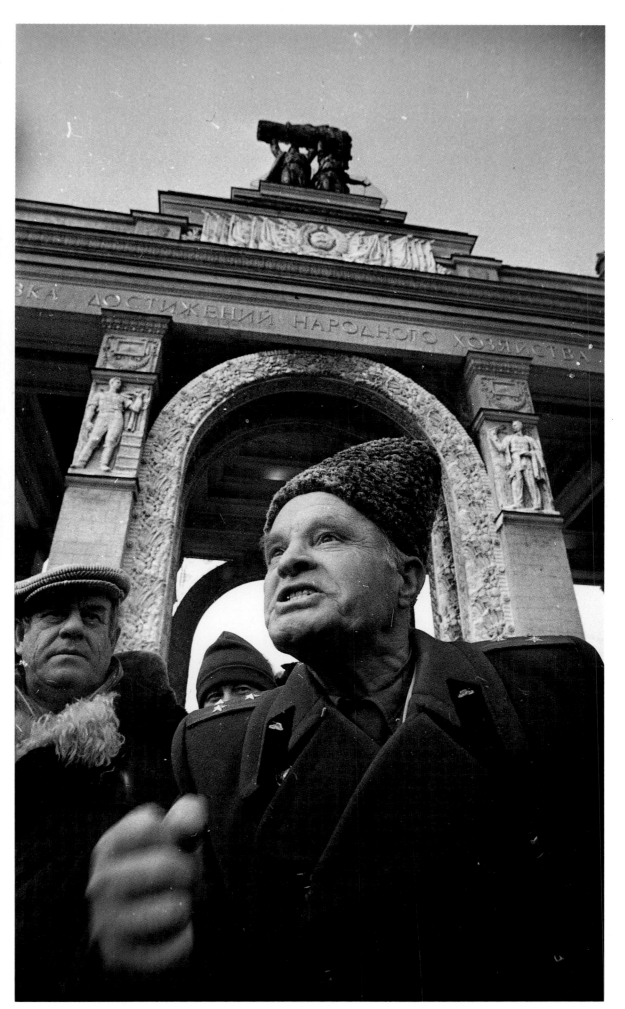

Police break up a demonstration *by Communists and extreme nationalists.* [PHOTO: D. BORKO]

A hardline colonel, *a militant Communist, slams the Yeltsin government to the crowd at the Exhibition of Economic Achievements in Moscow, as tension mounts in September 1993. The exhibition ground became a center for anti-Yeltsin rallies, the language increasingly violent as parliamentary deputies hostile to Yeltsin barricaded themselves into the White House.* [PHOTO: D. BORKO]

In the besieged White House:
Ruslan Khasbulatov (center) and Alexander Rutskoi (right) hold their final press conference in the parliament building on October 3, 1993. [PHOTO: D. BORKO]

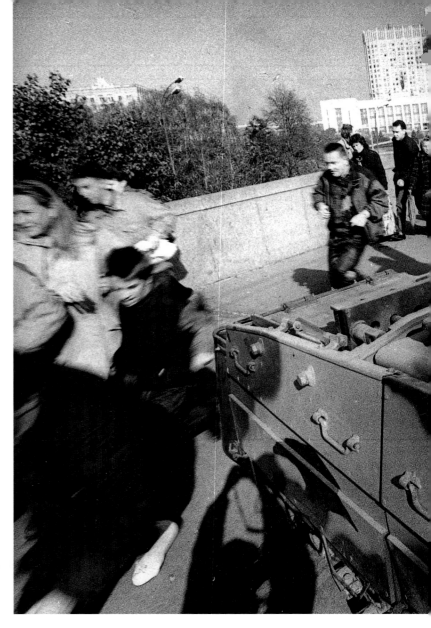

A tank loyal to President Yeltsin *on a bridge over the Moscow River. People run past as shelling breaks out. The fire-damaged façade of the White House is in the back-ground. It was held by Yeltsin's opponents and tanks fired at close range into it.*
[PHOTO: S. PETROUKHIN]

extreme nationalist standing against Yeltsin in the 1991 Russian presidential election. His 'solution' for the Baltic states was simple; he would put nuclear waste along the borders and run powerful fans at night so that the Balts would die of radiation sickness. He would solve the Muslim problem by resurrecting the Afghan war. Russian officers would drive Uzbek and Tadzhik troops forward against the Afghans until they were all dead. Any demagogue could acquire a following; they were an item not in *defitsit*.

No clear constitution existed; no developed legal system, no business law, no tested chain of authority. The power play between Yeltsin and the parliament, unresolved, headed towards crisis. The White House had seen Yeltsin's greatest triumph; now, blocking and frustrating him, it provoked fresh crisis.

On September 20, 1993, parliament announced plans to strip Yeltsin of much of his authority, and to pump more rubles into inflationary subsidies. Yeltsin reacted to this double slap in the face the next day, dissolving parliament and calling for fresh elections in December. Parliament impeached him and elected Rutskoi president. The deputies occupied the White House. An uneasy standoff lasted for a week. Yeltsin then issued an ultimatum: the deputies should leave the building by October 4, or the interior ministry troops who were now surrounding it would forcibly remove them. Moscow went about its business, oblivious to the drama taking place in its heart. The opposition was united in its loathing for Yeltsin and reform, and it could mobilise support on the streets.

Events slid out of Yeltsin's control on October 3. Hostile demonstrators burst through the cordon surrounding the White House and linked up with the deputies inside the building. The

Attack on the Ostankino television center *(top). Hardliners tried to take over key TV installations to broadcast their defiance of Yeltsin. Journalists and TV crewmen (above) were killed in* *the crossfire between them and forces loyal to Yeltsin outside the Ostankino building on October 3, 1993.*
[PHOTO, TOP: D. BORKO]
[PHOTO, ABOVE: A. ZAMAKHIN]

interior troops fled. An armed mob then moved to Ostankino, the main television center, where they smashed down the doors with trucks and tossed grenades inside. The troops guarding the studios fired back. Sixty-two were killed in the long firefight that followed, including Western television journalists. Gaidar, fearing that the mob would now turn on the seat of power, appealed to Muscovites to defend the Kremlin. Ten thousand turned up, but there was near panic when news of the storming of Ostankino spread. Yeltsin's arrival by helicopter had little effect on morale; there was astonishment that he had been relaxing in his dacha whilst his enemies were drumming up armed thugs. A state of emergency was belatedly proclaimed, but it was only at 5.20 am on October 4, when the first tanks growled their way to the Kremlin, that it was clear that Yeltsin would survive.

He had the army with him; or, more accurately, the Kantemir and Taman Guards divisions, and some paratroops. The pro-Yeltsin armor took up positions on the roads surrounding the White House and then opened fire on the upper stories where the malcontent deputies were holding out with armed guards. The building was soon on fire, whilst the tank rounds sent glass slicing back down the corridors. Another fifty were killed before white flags were seen and the rebel parliamentarians surrendered. Alexander Rutskoi and Ruslan Khasbulatov were led out under arrest from the smokestained building.

Yeltsin and the reformers seemed to have won a mighty victory. An opinion poll showed that 72 per cent supported the president; only 7 per cent sided with the disgraced deputies. But support was soon drifting away. The reformers split into four parties; they campaigned more vigorously against each other than against the conservatives. They spent much time in Moscow offices, playing

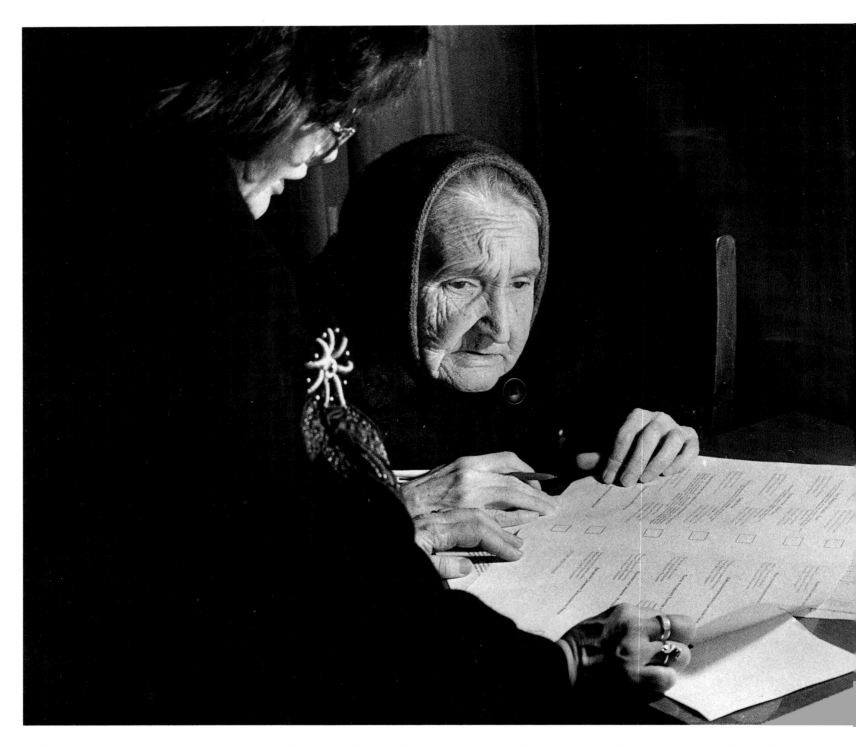

with computers; most were not seen out on the stump. They paid little attention to Vladimir Zhirinovsky and his so-called Liberal Democrats, writing him off as a neo-fascist madman.

His foreign policy was simplistic. The Japanese? 'I would bomb them ... I would sail our large navy round their small island and if they so much as cheeped, I would nuke them.' The United States? 'You Americans must leave the Balkans and the Middle East,' he warned. 'If you do not, one fine day you'll find yourself on a court bench facing another Nuremberg.' The Jews? 'Sometimes Russia has been overwhelmed by anti-Semitism. This phenomenon was provoked by the Jews themselves. Russia is a kind nation.' What made such weird views chilling was the chord they struck with millions of Russians.

A natural self-publicist, he backed his talent for the

outrageous with hard cash. He spent 300 million rubles, or a quarter million dollars at the then exchange rate, on television time. Zhirinovsky made sure that an electorate suffering a surfeit of politics took note of him; he appeared with a bottle of vodka and a condom, declaring that alcohol and sex was 'All that Gorbachev has left us.' He appealed to all those who had lost out in the reduction of state subsidies and who had gained nothing from the fitful functioning of market forces. The military, coal miners, people in remote regions and people in rustbowl industries were his natural constituency. It was a large one. He won 15 million votes, a two-and-a-half-fold increase on 1991; 93 per cent of the cadets at the Russian Military Academy, and three quarters of the elite Strategic Rocket Forces voted Zhirinovsky, in a country that still possessed 8972 ballistic missile warheads. His

Which party to vote for? *An old woman puzzles over the question in the parliamentary elections of 1993. Almost as old as the century, she was too young to have voted in Russia's last free elections in 1917. This is the first free vote she has enjoyed in her ninety years.* [PHOTO: D. BORKO]

Boris Yeltsin's *authority as president crumbled slowly through ill-health, sudden sackings of prime ministers, and unsteady public appearances (right). His problems were awesome – an economy in near-terminal decline, separatists at home, collapsing influence abroad – and his eccentric reponses worsened them.*
[PHOTO: G. PINKHASSOV]

meaningless, Khrushchev had given the Crimea to the Ukraine on a whim. In January 1994, Crimeans voted overwhelmingly for a party committed to quitting the Ukraine and rejoining Russia. Control of the Black Sea fleet and over nuclear weapons were other running sores in relations between Russia and the Ukraine.

The Ukrainian economy was in such crisis that its people were envious of Russia; eight-engined Antonov jet freighters, the world's largest aircraft, flew airlifts of cash from Western banknote printers in an attempt to keep up with inflation. Armenia, devastated by the 1988 earthquake, was blockaded by Azerbaijan over its support for ethnic Armenians in the Nagorno-Karabakh enclave. In turn, a fifth of Azerbaijan was controlled by Armenian troops. Twenty thousand Russian troops were fighting Islamic guerrillas along the Afghan border in Tadzhikistan. As Russia reasserted itself in the crumbling republics, Yeltsin said pointedly: 'Everyone must realise that this border is effectively Russia's, not Tadzhikistan's.' In Belorussia, where inflation was 50 per cent a month and accelerating, a Popular Front was formed to promote a 'Baltic-Black Sea community' with the Ukraine and the Baltic states to combat resurgent Russian influence.

In Moscow, parliament voted in early 1994 to amnesty the coup makers of 1991 and the diehards who had been blasted out of the White House in 1993. The one-party state had become pluralist with a vegeance, with a total of 43 political parties and blocs contesting the State Duma elections in December 1995. The Communists emerged as the largest single party, though they

Liberal Democrats were the largest party in the new parliament elected in December 1993. These were the first free parliamentary elections since November 1917; the lunatic fringe that year had been the Bolsheviks, but the electorate had ensured that they were far from the most popular party.

The poll revealed a fault line stretching along the 54th parallel. Those above it, in Moscow, St Petersburg, the mineral-rich areas of northern and western Siberia, supported Yeltsin. Below it, in the impoverished heavy industrial areas and the corn belt, people voted against reforms that brought them no advancement. This was in Russia; the cracks in other republics were often worse.The Ukraine was split between its nationalistic western half and the heavily industrialised and Russified eastern provinces. In the centralised days when local autonomy was

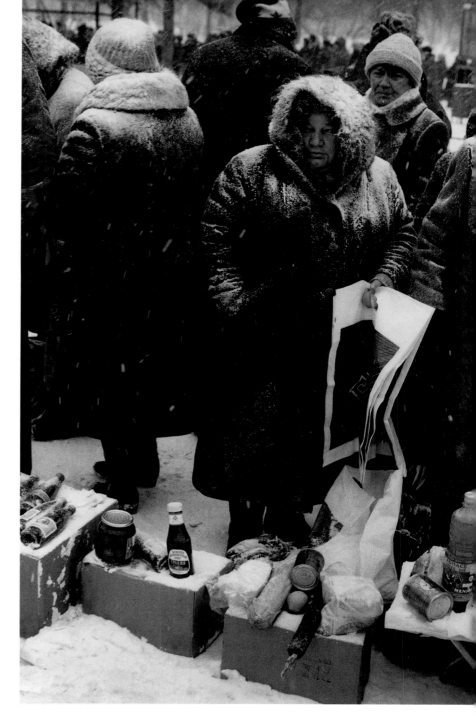

were well short of an overall majority, and the reformist Anatoly Chubais remained Prime Minister. However, Communists and ultra-nationalists had much in common – nostalgia, outrage at what they saw as moral decline, loathing for the new rich glimpsed riding between bodyguards in high-number Mercedes or shopping for designer clothes in Moscow's booming boutiques, and a conviction that all could be put right by some old-fashioned coercion. Their hatreds and beliefs picked out popular chords.

The old state system had effectively become a vast estate in bankruptcy, and there were rich pickings to be had by the few able to exploit it. They consisted in the main of three classes : the grandees of Soviet days with connections and political clout, the robber barons running protection and other rackets, and the ambitious and well-educated young, whose optimistic business flair was untempered by experience of the downsides of capitalism. A string of financial scandals heightened resentment against these so-called New Russians. The chief of the committee controlling state property resigned amid allegations of bribe-taking. The Uneximbank, headed by the government's former first deputy chairman, picked up lucrative stakes from the government sale of the state telecom company Syvyazinvest and the big mining company Norilsk Nickel; large advances for books were paid to key figures by a publishing house controlled by the bank. Business ill-will was marked, not by the lawyer and the writ, but by the professional assassin, by car bombs or gunfire in the coffee shop of a luxury hotel in St Petersburg. Politicians and journalists who exposed the mafia became its victims, too.

The doses of economic liberalism prescribed by the government and the International Monetary Fund were resented by many who, far from being cured by the medicine, felt a great deal worse. Inflation slashed salaries in sectors where they were still paid. Sometimes, they were not. Huge nationwide protests were held in 1997 to demand back wages. Miners from Arctic coalfields descended on Moscow to complain that they were paid in coal, not cash. Servicemen's pay was often months in arrears; Western aid had to be sought to pay for the dismantling of redundant nuclear weaponry. The potential for disaster was underlined when the electric power to ageing and inadequately mothballed nuclear submarines of the northern fleet was cut off by the power company for non-payment of charges. Crisis was only averted when an admiral threatened to use force if electricity was not restored.

Nonetheless a decision was taken to send demoralised troops to fight separatists in the breakaway republic of Chechnya. Some 15,000 well-armed Chechens were led by General Dzokhar Dudayev. The Russians took Grozny, the Chechen capital, in January 1995 after a costly assault involving several thousand civilian casualties. Rebel resistance continued in the southern mountains; in June, Chechen gunmen broke into the city of Budennovsk more than 100 miles over the border and took a thousand hostages in the city hospital. The Chechens demanded that the Russians hold talks with Dudayev. About a hundred were killed before a cease-fire was agreed, and the rebels returned to Chechnya with a column of 'volunteer' hostages who were released once the border was crossed. A pattern of broken cease-fires and hostage taking followed; Dudayev was killed, a passenger ferry seized, Red Cross workers murdered. All Russian troops were withdrawn by January 1997. The war had cost some 80,000 lives and created half a million refugees. A formal peace treaty was signed by Yeltsin and the new Chechen leader Aslan Mashkadov in

May the same year, but sporadic violence continued. Yeltsin's representative in the region was kidnapped in 1998.

Despite the tensions, Yeltsin provided continuity, winning once more in the presidential election of 1996, after a scare in the first round when he only narrowly defeated the Communist leader Gennady Zyuganov. He suffered recurring heart problems; bouts in hospital and lengthy convalescence alternated with public appearances whose eccentricity sometimes appeared to be alcohol-fuelled. As reform waxed and waned, governments and men of influence likewise came and went; Chubais, his ally Vladimir Potanin and his rival Boris Berezovsky, the popular general Alexander Lebed, a supporter of a grateful Yeltsin in the second round of the presidential election but sacrificed as a Chechnya scapegoat, Viktor Chernomyrdin, prime minister and energy supremo, succeeded by the young and hitherto unknown Sergei Kiriyenko. Yeltsin rose from his sickbed to appoint the last, amid public astonishment. The IMF complained that big companies and rich men were not paying taxes. The stock market boomed. A multi-layered luxury shopping complex, a subterranean Rodeo Drive, was built beneath the Kremlin walls. Russian tourists were seen in numbers in Monte Carlo for the first time since the summer of 1914; another sort of tourist plied her trade in Dubai; the piled-up blonde replaced the steel-toothed commissar as Russia's visible presence in the Middle East. Yeltsin and Bill Clinton met in Helsinki to agree to begin negotiations for a further reduction in nuclear weapons; Yeltsin and Ryutaro Hashimoto, the Japanese Prime Minister, agreed to conclude a peace treaty by the year 2000 that would bring the Second World War – still technically in progress due to a dispute over the Kurile Islands – to a formal end. The ruble stabilised; there were days early in 1998 when its dollar exchange rate strengthened.

And then gravity intervened. The market and the ruble crashed, almost on the day that *Vogue* magazine, symbol of the

Chechen separatists *demonstrate (above) in the capital, Grozny, which fell to Russian troops after a bloody assault. Although Yeltsin survived an attempted impeachment blaming him for the war and the break-up of the Soviet Union, the Chechnya bunglings undermined the status of democracy in Russia.*

'Up and Down' – *the name of the disco where these girls are auditioning – speaks for the country itself. They have arrived from the provinces to take part in an unofficial Miss Moscow competition, and to be looked over by the businessmen controlling the event (right).* [PHOTO: LISE SARFATI]

rich, famous and well-clad, launched a Russian edition. Long lines of stunned depositors queued forlornly outside banks that remained shut. Kiriyenko was replaced by a bleaker figure, Yevgeny Primakov, the former director of the Foreign Intelligence Service, no lover of free markets or the West. Yeltsin's authority slowly crumbled away. In April 1999, he sacked his prosecutor general, Yuri Skuratov, after a TV station friendly to the president aired a videotape allegedly showing Skuratov in bed with a pair of women. Skuratov retaliated by issuing an arrest warrant for Boris Berezovsky, whose lucrative companies were closely linked to Yeltsin's entourage, and particularly to the president's daughter, Tatyana. Told that he

was being charged with money laundering, Berezovsky retorted that the prosecutor's office was run by 'men who do not have a pair of trousers to their credit.' Communists pressed for Yeltsin's impeachment. The cat-footed Primakov kept his silence; in accepting the premiership at all, he said, before losing it, that he had already reached 'the limits of lunacy'.

Like the orbiting Mir space station, however – battered, creaking, solar panels awry, its continued existence a source of wonder to the cossetted sensibilities of visiting American astronauts – Russia is still there and still manned. The giant land is freighted with broken dreams; the century has been long and achingly cruel, but it has been survived.

Optimistic Russians *at a*
wedding toast the future in
home-distilled vodka.
[Photo: F. Gubayev]

ACKNOWLEDGEMENTS

There are many people to whom thanks are due for their help in the creation of 'The Russian Century'. We owe our greatest debt to the photographers, archivists, curators and collectors in the former Soviet Union who were so generous with their time and their work. We thank not only those whose photos appear in the book but all those who so kindly and patiently entrusted us with their prints.

Special thanks must go to the photographers Farit Gubayev, Vladimir Siomin and Igor Moukhin, not only for showing us their pictures but also for establishing a network of introductions which set us on our way. We are also indebted to Lara Stoyanovskaya and Mischa Smetnik, our two intrepid Russian interpreters. We thank them for their excellent translating skills, for their initiative and also for their humor which saw us through the difficult moments.

We are also particularly grateful to the families of Dmitri Baltermants and Georgi Zelma for the loan of material; to Varvara Rodchenko and Nicholai Lavrentyev for the loan of Alexander Rodchenko's photos; to Yevgeny Khaldei for producing images every bit as powerful as his famous picture of the raising of the flag on the Reichstag in 1945; to Alexander Ustinov for personally printing up his equally memorable World War II photos; to Vasily Yegorov for his intimate photographs of Khrushchev; to Vladimir Musaelyan, Brezhnev's personal photographer, for revealing a Brezhnev the West has never seen; and to the collector Slava Katamidze for filling our every last-minute gap with a suitable image.

In addition, we wish to acknowledge our gratitude to the following individuals and institutions: Andrei Baskakov and Leonid Bergoltsev of the *Union of Art Photographers, Moscow*; Irina Orlova of the *Museum of the October Revolution, Moscow*; Veronica Akopdjanova of the *Literature Museum, Moscow*; Tatyana Ivanova, Dr Alexander Shkurko, Irina Saltykova and Tamara Igumonova of the *State Historical Museum, Moscow*; Galina Nossova of the *Lenin Museum, Moscow*; Natalya Metelitsa and Ejba Norkute of the *State Museum of Theater and Music, St Petersburg*; Elena Barkhatova and Vladimir Zaitsev of the *National Library of Russia, St Petersburg*; Alexandra Golovina, Ludmila Protsai and Elena Dzuba of the *State Archive of Film and Photographic Documents, St Petersburg*; Evgeny Raskopov of the *Mirror Club, St Petersburg*; Lyudmila Zapryagayeva of the *Russian State Archive of Film and Photographic Documents, Krasnogorsk*; *Nizhny Novgorod City Museum (Maxim Dmitriev Archive)*; Dr. Sergei Kudryashov; Artyom Zadikyan; Professor John Erickson; Alexander Ustinov.

Last, but by no means least, we wish to express our thanks to Lynne Jackson for her organisational abilities and Elisabeth Ingles for her editorial skills.

The following kindly supplied the photographs on the pages listed below:

Anipchenko, Sergei 300, 301
Baltermants, Dmitri, Archive 200, 209
Bodrov, Gennady (Title verso page) 4, 299
Borko, Dmitri 286, 304, 306, 307, 308, 309T, 310
Bulgakov, Boris 287
Burasovsky, Sergei 257
Donin, Sergei 266T
Gavrilov, Igor 252, 254B, 255, 267, 276, 277, 288
Gorshkov, Pavel 298T, 306
Grafov, Dmitry 183
Gubayev, Farit 295, 296, 316
Hulton Deutsch Collection, London 78, 96B, 97B, 98, 99, 246, 250T, 251BR
Ivleva, Victoria 292
Katamidze, Slava, Collection (Half title page) 1, (Title page) 2, 75, 87, 95, 106, 107, 110, 113, 115T,123T, 123B, 127, 131, 132, 133, 140, 143T, 147, 149, 155, 156, 157, 158, 159, 160, 166, 167, 169, 185, 194T, 198, 215, 221, 223B, 242R
KEA Publishing Services, London/CSAOR 26T
Khaldei, Yevgeny 190, 191, 219, 223T, 224, 225, 228, 229
Kotlyarov, Anatoly 234
Kuibyshev, Vladimir, Archive, Moscow 181
Lenin Museum, Moscow 53, 92, 93, 164, 165
Literature Museum, Moscow 32, 49, 128, 161, 251TR,
Lomakin, Alexander 290T
Magnum Photos, London 311, 313, 315
Mikhalyovkin, Boris 268,
Moukhin, Igor 274, 275
Musaelyan, Vladimir 259, 260T, 261, 265
National Library of Russia, St Petersburg 17B, 56, 57, 73BR, 81
Network Photographers, London 312
Nikitin, Vladimir, Collection, St Petersburg 16, 17T, 40, 68, 79, 195, 217, 251TL
Nizhny Novgorod City Museum (Dmitriev Photo Archive) 12, 30, 38, 135
Novosti, London 314T
October Revolution Museum, Moscow 55ML, 62, 84, 104
Pasternak Trust, Oxford 251BL
Petroukhin, Sergei 308R
Photochronika Tass, Moscow 125
Plotnikov, Valery 262, 263
Podgorkov, Sergei 272, 290B
Popperfoto, Northampton 305B
Raskopov, Yevgeny 176, 256
Rex Features, London 26B, 27, 55T, 55MR, 55B, 182B, 270
Rodchenko Lavrentyev Archive 177B
Rogozin, Mikhail 280, 284, 285
Russian State Archive of Film and Photographic Documents, Krasnogorsk 14, 15, 19, 20, 21, 24, 28, 34, 36, 37, 42, 48, 54, 66, 67, 72, 76, 86, 100, 102, 112, 116, 120T, 120B, 121, 122, 126, 129, 134, 137, 138, 139, 141, 142, 144, 145, 146, 148, 152, 162, 163, 168, 172, 174, 175, 177T, 178, 179, 180, 232, 244, 245TL
Savin, Michael 199, 208, 211, 214, 218
Shakhverdiev, Tofik 289
Shchekoldin, Valery 254T
Siomin, Vladimir 8, 279, 282, 283, 298B, 303
Sobolyev, Valentin 230, 302
Society for Cultural Relations with the USSR, London 188, 204, 205
State Archive of Film and Photographic Documents, St Petersburg 22, 23, 25, 29, 45, 46TL, 47B, 50, 51, 52, 58, 59, 61, 63, 64, 69, 71, 80, 83, 85, 88, 89,90, 94, 103, 108, 109, 170, 194B, 196, 236, 264
State Historical Museum, Moscow 73L, 96T, 97T, 114
State Museum of Theater and Music, St Petersburg 46TR, 46BR, 47T, 123M, 197
Tambulidis, Alexander 258
Titov, Felix 291
Ustinov, Alexander 189B, 192, 193, 222, 245TR, 249
Walston, Oliver 182T
Yegorov, Vasily 237, 240, 241, 243, 247, 260B
Zaitsev, Oleg 273
Zamakhin, Andrei 309B
Zelma, Georgi, Archive 198, 202, 207, 221

All other pictures were drawn from private collections within the former Soviet Union.